Connecting
the Dots

Connecting
the Dots

Government,
Community, and
Family

Peggy
Wireman

 Routledge
Taylor & Francis Group

LONDON AND NEW YORK

First published 2008 by Transaction Publishers

2 Park Square, Milton Park, Abingdon, Oxfordshire OX14 4RN
711 Third Avenue, New York, NY 10017

Routledge is an imprint of the Taylor & Francis Group, an informa business

First issued in paperback 2017

Copyright © 2008 Taylor & Francis

Library of Congress Catalog Number: 2008021799

Library of Congress Cataloging-in-Publication Data

Wireman, Peggy.
    Connecting the dots / Peggy Wireman.
        p. cm.
    Includes bibliographical references and index.
    ISBN 978-1-4128-0730-2 (alk. paper)
        1. Neighborhood--United States. 2. Community development--United States. 3. Community organization--United States. 4. Family--United States. I. Title.
HT123.W49 2008
307.3'3620973--dc22

                                                                        2008021799

ISBN 13: 978-1-4128-0730-2 (hbk)
ISBN 13: 978-1-138-50848-4 (pbk)

This book is dedicated to the millions of grassroots activists working to improve their communities, to the many politicians and government bureaucrats dedicated to making the American dream work for all families, and to my immensely supportive friends and family.

Contents

Acknowledgments

If "it takes a village to raise a child," it takes an international network to write a book. I am grateful to many people who contributed both directly and indirectly. The book draws upon the research and insights of many experts in academia, the government, and most importantly members of local communities where I have worked.

Because the book deals with a wide variety of substantive areas as well as treating both policy and grassroots practice issues, I am grateful to the following individuals who reviewed chapters for readability or to provide suggestions in their area of expertise: J. Simon Beck, Patricia Becker, Lynne C. Burkhart, Cephus Childs, Howard Czoschke, David Cook, Richard Davis, Edward R. Day, Luz Elena Solis Day, Lois Dobry, Alan Dobry, Judith Goren, Frances Griffiths, Mary Gulbrandsen, James Gullick, Ken Haynes, Bruce Hunt, Carole Hubbarth, Barbara Kellner, David Lasker, Richard A. Lehmann, Eleanor Roberts Lewis, Dode Lowe, Janet C. Marcotte, Janice Pasek, Carolyn Price, Holly Rogers, Hannah Rosenthal, Antoinette Sebastian, Arthur Thexton, Pat Turner, Barry Wellman, Victor Wilburn, Michael S. Wireman, and Tim Wise.

I am also indebted to the Madison Public Library, to David Null and the other reference librarians at the University of Wisconsin, and especially to numerous public interest groups and government agencies who maintain informative Web sites.

Several people read the entire manuscript or large sections more than once. They offered serious critical, many substantive, and editorial suggestions. The book was restructured in accordance with their concerns and chapters were rewritten, sometimes more than once. They helped forge a book from a wide range of ideas and information. As important, they believed in the book even during the many times when I didn't. Without their dedicated assistance the book would not have been completed. I am most grateful to Kathleen Bishop, Catherine Bloomer, Catherine R. Hill, Enis Ragland, Jac Smit, and Robert Van Hoesen.

Kristin Kronwall, Linsey Ray, and Sharon Nix provided typing assistance. Kent Palmer provided typing, assistance with formatting footnotes as well as valuable editorial and other suggestions. Milana Chernick Cox inserted changes, Web surfed extensively, formatted footnotes and made editorial suggestions. Stefanie Shull provided secretarial and editorial assistance. She played a major role in restructuring the entire book. Linda Wyeth assisted with typing, footnoting, and gave excellent editorial advice. Dave French provided clerical, editing, and footnoting assistance, and played a major role in obtaining and interpreting statistical and other data including the analysis about future job prospects for workers. Their assistance was invaluable. Sally Springett also provided helpful editing and advice. Marshall Cook gave publishing advice and encouragement. Extensive editing by Jimmy Wilkinson Meyer made the manuscript more coherent and readable. Without their assistance and personal support, this book could never have been completed.

It does, indeed, take a network to produce a book. I remain responsible for errors of fact and judgment.

Foreword

"What's your proposal? To build the just city?" asked W.H. Auden.
"I will," the poet answered. "I agree."
But it is not just for poets to make this agreement.
Nations must do the same, not once but constantly.

The evolution of the nation-state demands neither security nor prosperity but evolution – since security and prosperity are impossible in the absence of progress.

Most of the rest of the developed and developing world embraces the search for new ideas about how nations can change to make life better for their citizens. It is a natural and necessary impulse. Yet, in the United States, a country that once defined this progressive inclination, the last several decades – particularly as they have been defined by a uniquely dispiriting family from Texas – have seen a great nation searching for someone to blame for its malaise.

Peggy Wireman doesn't play the blame game.

A politically-savvy yet relentlessly optimistic public intellectual, she keeps imploring us to look beyond a failed status quo to the future that might yet be. In this sense, she carries forward an American tradition of faith in facts rather than fantasy as the solid grounding on which a great nation might be made.

No neo-conservatism or neo-liberalism for Wireman; in fact, there's not a "neo" bone in her body. She does not ask us to make a leap of faith. She asks us to look at the reality around us – a reality defined by deindustrialization that eliminates family-supporting blue-collar jobs at a staggering rate, outsourcing that will ultimately eliminate white-collar jobs at an even more staggering rate, and policies that perpetuate both these trends -- and she tells us this makes no sense. She looks at politicians who tell us we should worry more about some ill-defined conception of "morality" and tells us to start paying a whole lot more attention to the real immorality of poverty amidst plenty, families that lack the resources and time to care for one another and communities that are atomizing rather than coming together.

And then Wireman says, it's time to connect the dots.

Like the Wisconsin Progressives of the Robert M. La Follette era, like the New Dealers of Franklin Roosevelt's first 100 days, like the reformers of the 1960s who spoke of ending poverty in the foreseeable future, Wireman says the proper response to great challenges – and, make no mistake, America faces many great challenges today, as this book ably illustrates – is not despair.

The proper response is to get engaged, to get active, to recognize that the future will be as good as we make it. And with *Connecting the Dots*, Peggy Wireman has shows us that we can, indeed, make it good.

Or, to be more precise, we must make it good.

John Nichols
May, 2008

Preface

I wrote this book to counter the claims that local efforts of volunteers, community organizations, and religious institutions can handle the spillover effects of shifts in the American economy and family composition. Local efforts are crucial, but not sufficient.

As an academic, I know that good scholarship can provide the accurate data needed to counter decision-making by anecdote or by focusing on the exceptional case. From my grassroots and government experience, I know that those concerned with national statistics do not always comprehend what the facts underlying those statistics mean in terms of people's lives. So I have included illustrations showing how communities and individuals are affected as well as the information needed to present the larger picture.

The first part of the book attacks myths about family, institutions, community, and relationships in neighborhoods which too often underlie policy decisions. The second part of the book focuses on six specific tasks that are crucial to the well-being of families or single individuals. It points out both the importance and the limitations of efforts of local community groups in coping with the changes in the national economy and in our family structure. The concluding sections call for national commitments and actions by all stakeholders to support our families and communities.

When presenting data I considered the basis for the data and which numbers most accurately portray the realities affecting family and community life. Many commentators on current events, for example, report income statistics based on average incomes, failing to point out that by factoring in the huge salaries of executives the average implies that the salaries of most workers are higher than they actually are.

Since the information and issues relevant to this book change constantly, readers should be aware that a particular fact or statistic may be out-of-date or that some new research may seem to counter some of the points. Because of the scope of the book, it is impossible to claim definitive expertise in each area. I have, however, tried hard to obtain data from the most reliable sources and to update material whenever newer data seemed relevant. I was especially careful to look into newer data when it might counter previous studies. Where I lacked the ability or time to carefully analyze the original research, I went with the preponderance of evidence.

Even if a particular fact or statistic is out of date, the conclusions remain valid. Does it really matter whether 200,000 or only 150,000 children are sleeping on America's streets every night? From a policy stance, the numbers make no difference. Is it acceptable to have 150,000 children homeless but unacceptable to have 200,000 homeless? The numbers do not matter when deciding whether or not the nation considers action necessary. The numbers do matter when calculating budgets for programs designed to address the problem. As *Connecting the Dots* points out, historically most social programs have not been funded sufficiently to provide services to all those qualifying for the programs.

The examples used throughout the book were either directly told to me or come from my own experience. Although a few resulted from my consultant work, most stem from periods of employment in grassroots organizations or from my research. In some cases I have changed details such as sex, race, or geographic location in order to protect the identity of the individual or community. Although some of the events or conversations occurred years ago, they illustrate points that continue to be valid. For instance, the discussion about race includes examples that are decades old. Unfortunately, the issues described continue to be relevant today as evidenced by the furor recently raised by the racist and sexist comments by radio commentator Don Imus. The comments about the Allied Dunn's Marsh Neighborhood Center describe events that occurred in the 1990s. Despite continued difficulties in that neighborhood stemming from a complex set of city issues, the examples given still provide valid illustrations of the possibilities of neighborhood and community action.

Continued action at the local level by volunteers, nonprofit and religious institutions, and local governments remain important. The book provides a framework that such groups can use in determining how best to use their resources. Those interested in additional information on a specific issue or examples of successful programs should follow the leads provided in the footnotes and check the extensive material provided in the appendicies (see Author's Note, pp. xiii-xiv).

While I argue that local efforts are crucial, *Connecting the Dots* also calls for increased and more realistic action by national players. By examining the myths and realities about how our policies and programs affect families and community life, we can forge more appropriate and effective approaches.

Author's Note

The *Community Action Guide*

The *Community Action Guide* provides additional material to help readers of *Connecting the Dots: Government, Community, and Family* and other community activists decide how to focus the efforts of their communities in addressing the issues raised in the book. Seven short *Guides* cover how to build community and how to support families in accomplishing six basic family tasks: earning an income, providing their families food, housing and health care, maintaining their home and rearing their children.

The first *Guide* draws upon principles discussed in chapters four, five, six, and seven of the book on community, relationships in neighborhoods, racial and ethnic relationships, and community organizing. The others follow the organization of chapters eight through thirteen, dealing with each of the six tasks. The individual guide for each of the six tasks provides suggestions for identifying the most important issues and your community's assets for dealing with them, key questions to ask, examples of possible programs, and suggestions for lobbying to obtain needed changes in policies or program funding.

The *Guides* are meant both to supplement the book and to provide how-to-do it ideas for dealing with community issues affecting family life. They can be used as a framework for determining what to do. Each of these topics is vast. Many Americans and communities are acting daily to address these issues. The *Guides* provide an introduction to be used in mapping your own efforts.

Both the *Guides* and the book itself contain references to organizations that can provide more detailed information. Checking the authors and organizations cited in the footnotes will provide both good sources of data and leads to organizations and individuals active in researching the issues of concern to families or in operating successful programs.

The *Guides* are:

1. Building Community—How to Do It
2. Earning a Living—How Your Community Can Help Your Families.
3. Housing Your Neighborhoods' Families—Design Your Approach.
4. Healthy Living—Creating a Healthy Environment for Families.

5. Helping Families with Everyday Chores—What Can Your Neighborhood Do?
6. Healthy Eating–Healthy Families—What Can Your Neighborhood and Community Do?
7. A Good Place to Raise Children—What Can Your Neighborhood Do?

The *Community Action Guidebook* is available in electronic form only and may be purchased from www.transactionpub.com (ISBN: 978-1-4128-1143-9).

Introduction

Talk shows, politicians, religious leaders, and magazine writers constantly bemoan America's "loss of community" and exhort us to take more responsibility for our neighborhoods. They blame a myriad of perceived social problems, from teenage pregnancy to street crime, on the breakdown of the family, the loss of ties between neighbors and friends, and on the reduced effectiveness of local schools, churches, and volunteer organizations. Solutions range from new government initiatives to more grassroots involvement, from an increase in government funding to a return to religion and greater respect for family values.

Anthropological studies show that the composition of families and how they function varies widely among different societies. Historians prove that these change over time. In traditional societies, both historically and today, families have fulfilled numerous roles, bolstered by help from neighbors and friends living nearby.

Many Americans, however, no longer live in traditional families. To cut through the rhetoric and debate about the "failure" of America's families, this book identifies six tasks crucial for all families: obtaining food, shelter, and health care, earning an income, maintaining the home, and rearing children. Concentrating on family tasks can distinguish between supporting specific family forms and supporting all families in fulfilling their basic responsibilities. We examine aspects of these tasks that are influenced by people's immediate neighborhood environment and explore to what extent vital neighborhoods and local communities can help families and single individuals accomplish these tasks.

When we talk about "our neighborhood" or "the community," what do we mean? One researcher found ninety-four definitions of community in the scholarly literature alone.[1] He examined ten communities, concluding that although nineteen different traits occurred often, only three identical traits occurred in all ten. The common traits consisted of: the family unit, a territorial base, and some form of cooperative activity.[2]

Many now question the importance of the geographic community. People today often interact with one "community" near their homes, another at work, others through hobbies and professional groups, and additional ones through the Internet. People's homes, however, exist in a physical space. The surrounding

1

neighborhood or community affects the quality of their lives, especially those of their children. Vital communities provide residents with a sense of home and belonging, a place to earn a living, political power needed to shape their environment, and an opportunity to form organizational and social relationships.

People's concept of "neighborhood" varies. Some consider it to include only their immediate neighbors, while others expand their interest to encompass areas of several square miles housing more than 50,000 people. Given the complexity and variation in using the terms "neighborhood" and "community," this book uses them somewhat interchangeably. Readers must decide, in each instance, how the comments relate to their concept of neighborhood and whether the accomplishment of certain tasks would require involvement of a larger geographic "community."

Many today question whether today's communities have failed. Conversely, local, state, and national officials and politicians now emphasize their importance. Too often, however, beneath that rhetoric lies an unrealistic expectation that neighborhoods and local communities can compensate for all of the negative spillover effects of business and government policies and the societal trends emerging in the global economy.

I have attended hundreds of meetings where everyday citizens tackled improving their lives and communities. I remain deeply impressed by the common sense, vitality, and dedication displayed. Community efforts have produced marvelous results affecting individual lives, families, neighborhoods, and cities as well as state, national, and even international policies and programs.

Such efforts, however, do not operate in isolation from the economic and other realities of the larger society. Too often the lack of resources from the larger society results in unnecessary frustration, ineffective approaches, and limited results. I once directed a neighborhood center that housed programs for fifteen organizations and served 200 people each day, but lacked the funds to buy a copying machine. Conducting meetings without the ability to quickly reproduce a memo, a draft, or an agenda was inefficient.

Grassroots groups frequently attempt innovative solutions to problems. They often succeed where traditional programs have failed. Frequently, however, their success has resulted from Herculean efforts by a few leaders. Too often it depends upon a one-time grant for a "pilot project," leaving the organization no way to continue a program that has proven successful.

The problem is not only the continuation and replication of successful local programs, but also unrealistic expectations about the potential accomplishments of the myriad of contributors: family, friends, neighbors, volunteer organizations, schools, religious institutions, hospitals, businesses, local government, homeowner's associations, state government, federal government, and the media. This book examines the different roles of these stakeholders, evaluating their limitations as well as their potential.

Our discussion highlights the very real contributions that local communities and neighborhoods make toward supporting American families. It examines factors that contribute to healthy communities, enabling them to provide good settings for family life. It discusses ways to strengthen positive relationships among neighbors and provides examples of the achievements and potentials of the hundreds of community-based organizations. Much that occurs in neighborhoods, however, depends upon decisions by non-local businesses, governments, and the media. By including their roles in the analysis, the book provides clues for those responsible for decisions that affect neighborhoods. It also provides a basis for a realistic appraisal of the limitations neighborhood residents face, both in strengthening their own communities and in shouldering the responsibility for providing solutions for societal problems.

Today's neighborhoods and local communities exist in the context of a global economy, exponential technological change, and worldwide rapid communication for anyone with access to a cell phone, the Internet, television, or even a radio. Depending upon the orientation of the observer, this situation represents tremendous opportunities or dire threats. Many, often from opposite ends of the ideological spectrum, advocate a return to "community values." Many, from both the right and the left, advocate depending upon grassroots organizations for local economic growth and delivery of human services. Others urge the creation of sustainable communities through a regional approach with an integration of economical and environmental resources and production. Still others minimize the importance of local efforts, pointing to the growth of Internet chat rooms and other non-local "communities."

This book discusses family and community from the perspective that today's realities demand a "both-and" rather than an "either-or" approach.[3] Neither families nor local communities exist in isolation from the forces shaping the larger society. Fulfilling the most basic jobs of families requires the cooperative efforts of those living nearby. However, local efforts are not always sufficient. Neighbors cannot deliver round-the-clock skilled nursing care, and an individual's ability to obtain it may depend upon national policies regarding Medicare reimbursements. Neighborhood residents can educate themselves and their friends about how to prepare food safely, but must depend upon a national inspection system for the safety of the food purchased by local grocery stores and restaurants.

Today the national discussion too often rests on myths about the "ideal" family as well as myths about the nature of communities and the types of relationships that occur in them. Chapter 1 uses the example of Hurricane Katrina to illustrate the national impact of local events and, conversely, the effect of national policies on localities. Chapter 2 examines myths and realities about families. The next chapter discusses myths about our major institutions, including business and government, that often underlie our attitudes and policies. Chapters 4 examine myths and realities affecting our decisions about communities. Chapter 5 considers the range of relationships that can exist in neighborhoods and their potential for supporting families and building community. Chapter 6 addresses the reality of America's ethnic and racial diversity. Chapter 7 traces the history and contributions of community organizing and Community Development Corporations. Chapters 8 through 13 analyze how what happens at a neighborhood level affects key issues of families: their ability to earn a living, maintain their homes, and to provide food, child care, shelter, and health care for their loved ones.

The concluding chapter calls for national alignment on four propositions that could shift the national conversation about appropriate policies and actions. It outlines dismal scenarios illustrating the future if we simply continue current directions. Finally, the book suggests actions needed by business, government, the nonprofit sector, religious institutions, and the media. It includes specific suggestions for increasing their unique contributions.

For the most part the suggestions here and throughout the book do not require major changes in the basic composition or organizational structure of American families, communities, or society. Such changes may be desirable, ultimately even necessary, but this book focuses on approaches that could be achieved both in individual neighborhoods and throughout the society within a five- to ten-year period without major restructuring of the economy, political institutions, family composition, or even values. These actions will require thoughtful and realistic planning, dedication, cooperation, and partnerships. And they will require money. The funds needed are not beyond the capacity of the nation, although they are certainly beyond that of some of the individual communities. Taking these actions would dramatically change American families' prospects.

The nation, its families and its communities do face considerable challenges in adapting to a global economy and a world of conglomerates. Before despairing, however, the reader should remember that concern about the decline of America's "community" goes back at least to the laments of Boston's John Winthrop in 1650![4] This book will help readers determine how to tackle making communities vital places which support all Americans.

Notes

1. Hillery, G. A. (1955). Definitions of community: Areas of agreement. *Rural Sociology*, 111-123.
2. Hillery, G. A. (1968). *Communal organizations: A study of local societies*. Chicago: University of Chicago Press.
3. I am indebted to Julia Press for this distinction.
4. Bender, T. (1978). *Community and social change in America* (pp. 47-48). New Brunswick, NJ: Rutgers University Press.

Part 1

Families, Neighborhoods, and Communities:
Myths and Realities

1

America—One Nation Indivisible

"No man is an Island,
Entire of it self;...
Any man's death diminishes me,
because I am involved in Mankind;
And therefore never send to know
for whom the bell tolls;
It tolls for thee."
          –John Donne, Meditation XVII[1]

On August 29, 2005, Hurricane Katrina slammed into New Orleans. Within hours, the levees holding back the waters began to break, flooding the city, and debilitating most of its major infrastructures. In the days that followed, Americans watched with horror as thousands of residents fled, thousands more huddled in an overcrowded Superdome without enough food, water, or toilets, and hundreds drowned or died for lack of medical treatment. Throughout the nation people cried in disbelief, "But this is America!"

Many observers were startled to learn that many of those trapped in the city could not heed the warnings to leave because they had no cars, no money to buy bus or airplane tickets, and no credit cards. While some walked for miles to escape, others had physical limitations that made this impossible. As New Orleans residents continued to be stranded on rooftops for days without food or water, blank shock turned to angry questions: Why didn't the government do something to help the trapped families? Why hadn't officials taken better precautions?

The story of Hurricane Katrina serves as a metaphor for the themes in this book. We are one nation, and what happens in one city or neighborhood does ultimately affect us all. Individual and family self-reliance is important, but not always possible or sufficient. The efforts of neighbors, volunteers, and nonprofit organizations are vital, but not enough. Government actions matter. Money counts. How we define issues and responsibility shapes our decisions and our actions.

In the weeks following the hurricane, people protested the media categorization of those pouring into other cities as refugees. "These are not refugees," they argued, "they are Americans." Yet the images that filled the television screens looked very much like those of refugees in a third-world war zone. Suddenly, Americans became aware that many in our own country are vulnerable in ways that the better-off can't fully imagine, that questions of race still lie beneath the surface of American life, and that what government does, or does not do, matters. Officials had made decisions about budgets and priorities that affected the amount of money available to strengthen the levees. Seemingly oblivious to statistical data about the income levels in the city, they had created an evacuation plan that ignored the needs of those without cars. Hurricane Katrina, like other natural disasters, called forth the renowned generosity of America and its capacity for grassroots action. Individual volunteers opened their hearts, cleaned out their closets, showed up to help, and sent money. Relatives and friends threw blankets on their sofas, pulled out their sleeping bags, and stretched their family budgets to accommodate displaced relatives. Local churches and organizations pitched in.

The crucial nature of everyday needs became obvious during the days following Katrina. People had to find shelter, food, and health care. Those displaced needed money and a job. Although families, friends, neighborhoods, and strangers helped, the need for other resources quickly became clear. Families and neighborhoods could not handle the task alone.

This book is not about disasters. But millions of Americans face less drastic yet significant challenges in meeting six everyday responsibilities: (1) earning an income; (2) feeding their families; (3) maintaining their health; (4) finding housing; (5) handling everyday household chores; and (6) caring for their children. The storms that can debilitate families are figurative ones such as a medical emergency or a layoff. Even prosperous Americans often have less fortunate relatives or friends, and all Americans are affected by myriad conditions within their neighborhoods and communities.

This book addresses the complex relationships between family and community, and between community and other players affecting family and community life, including the private sector, government, nonprofit groups, and religious organizations. Although we show how local communities can operate in ways that create nourishing environments, we also point out the limitations of both local communities and individual families in dealing with the changes wrought by structural shifts in the economy. The experience of Katrina leads us to examine more carefully the condition of our family and community levees.

Contrary to much rhetoric, America doesn't suffer from a loss of family values, but from a shift in business practices and public commitments. The American dream of work hard, buy a home, and give your children a better life is no longer realistic for millions of workers, both white collar and blue collar. Families increasingly face two problems: (1) the loss of the implicit social contract between businesses and their employees and (2) the withdrawal of the national government from its role in ensuring that businesses meet their social obligations and from a governmental commitment to provide sufficient funding for programs necessary to support families and enhance community life.

Americans do not face a crisis in family values, but they increasingly face a workplace that does not value families. No longer can a man expect that working hard with one firm will ensure a permanent job, a rising salary sufficient to buy a home, health care benefits, and a comfortable retirement. Over the past several decades, the salaries of millions have either been reduced or stayed flat. Businesses are reducing pension plans and shifting more health care costs to their workers. Compared to other industrialized countries, Americans work longer hours per year, lack guaranteed access to health care, do not receive paid leave to care for a new baby, have less of a safety net if faced with unemployment or disability, and have the highest rates of poverty and least upward mobility.[2] Without government subsidies, millions of families, even those with one child, can no longer expect to enjoy even a modest standard of living.[3]

American families and communities also suffer from a change in attitudes toward government and its role in establishing the rules and the programs affecting workers and their families. Congress sets the minimum wage, but has not adjusted it to fully keep pace with inflation. Changes in regulations and policies have made it more difficult for unions to organize or be successful. Federal government funding has not kept up with the need for programs that provide a safety net for individuals and their families. Funds for community programs also have been cut.

Hurricane Katrina showed us homelessness. But every night in America approximately 200,000 children sleep on the streets or in shelters. Some three and a half million Americans experience homelessness each year, including workers with full-time jobs that do not pay enough to cover the rent for even a small apartment. Yet the nation spends more money providing tax relief to people buying homes and second homes than for programs providing housing for low-income workers.[4]

Katrina also illustrates the importance of proper planning and spending the necessary resources to prevent problems. In retrospect, how much money could have been saved by investing in levees that would have provided protection against a strong storm, rather than waiting and paying for the aftermath? The possibility of a powerful storm at some point was predictable, probably inevitable. In fact, it had been predicted. Yet in June 2004 the Army Corps of Engineers budget for levee construction in New Orleans was cut and in June 2005 additional cuts were made to funding for the Southeast Louisiana Urban Flood Control Project.[5] The collapse of the bridge on Interstate 35W in Minneapolis called national attention to decades of deferred maintenance to thousands of bridges.[6] We play the same kind of Russian roulette with our community infrastructure, our families, and our children.

I once saw kids in a neighborhood center in a low-income area flunking life in first grade. A thin, white boy believed he could not read, even though with proper urging he could identify words. A six-year-old black girl didn't want to hear stories about successful black women because, she said, "I don't like black people." Each suffered from image problems and needed individual attention. But the neighborhood center could not afford $8,500 for a second staff member for the forty-five children who streamed into the center after-school program.

This book addresses the need to take a fresh look at the national responsibility for all of our families and communities. It contends that the prosperity of individual families and communities rests not just on their own bootstrap efforts but also on an appropriate national response to the current economic and social realities.

We provide a framework for considering how the choices we make affect every American's ability to meet their basic needs. We argue that building strong families, strong communities, and terrific neighborhoods requires wise decisions and actions at both a national and local level. As illustrated by Hurricane Katrina, the efforts of individuals, volunteers and community organizations, however heroic, are necessary but not sufficient. People work, businesses function, and cities operate within the existing national and local community infrastructure and within a context of accepted values, beliefs, standards, practices, and laws. In some cases, this context no longer provides the best environment for creating healthy families and communities. Katrina showed us the need for not only a strong physical infrastructure, but also for a community infrastructure of public health workers, police, experts on environmental protection, and governments that function responsively and cooperatively at all levels.

This book does four things: (1) shows how the changed conditions in the economy affect the ability of families to meet their basic responsibilities; (2) shows the need for partnership between the private section, government, religious, and other institutions and community-based efforts; (3) examines the need for national as well as local approaches to enable families to meet six basic responsibilities; and (4) suggests actions neighborhoods and communities can take to provide family-friendly environments.

We argue that solutions are not local or national, public or private, not "either/or" but "both/and." We identify top-down structures, laws, and attitudes that create the context for family life that must be confronted. We provide bottom-up anecdotal examples to ground the policy-oriented discussion and the statistical data needed to develop realistic solutions. The analysis provides a framework for policymakers, local community leaders, and neighborhood activists to use in analyzing their situation and for selecting the most appropriate actions.

Building strong families, strong communities, and terrific neighborhoods requires acting on the basis of reality, not myths. The next three chapters consider myths about families, about community, and about the institutions that shape or supplement families' abilities to meet their basic responsibilities: the private sector, government, religious institutions, nonprofit organizations, and volunteers. Chapter 6 examines diversity, since how we handle racial and ethnic differences remains crucial to our future.

Chapter 7 discusses ways in which communities have created social capital, community cohesion and local organizational ability. Chapters 8 through 13 examine income, housing, health care, food, household maintenance and rearing children. Each chapter shows how both national and local actions affect family life. Each provides examples of actions local communities can take to provide a supportive environment for family life, but also points out how those actions will be most effective within a context of national support for both families and communities.

The final section of the book details what various players can and must do to uphold the American dream. Otherwise, if current national trends continue, we will be faced with four undesirable scenarios.

Scenario One: The economy increasingly will rely upon workers who cannot support or ever expect to support a family. The gap between rich and poor will increase. The numbers of individuals, including parents, working several jobs will increase. The economy will continue to depend upon a continual stream of new immigrants, including millions of illegal ones.

Scenario Two: Despite the effects on families of scenario one, the government will not use tax funds to supplement low wages adequately through the Earned Income Tax Credit or other means. Individuals lacking food, housing, or health care will need to turn to charity. Many find accepting charity demeaning, an unspoken acknowledgment that neither they nor the work they perform are valuable. This may ultimately affect their morale, self-esteem, and work ethic. They will place the same value on their work as granted by their employers and the larger society.

Scenario Three: Those with full-time jobs at certain large companies will have excellent health care. Millions of others will not be able to afford medical care. Older people who worked for a large organization that continues to provide health care benefits for their retirees will be well covered. Others may be unable to afford procedures or drugs recommended by their doctors.

Scenario Four: Millions of children will raise themselves or be placed in child care and after-school facilities that lack proper staff and safety provisions. Children will arrive at school unprepared to learn. Teenage suicide, crime, irresponsible sexual behavior, alcohol and drug abuse rates may well rise.

The unwillingness to face the ugly truths represented by these scenarios reflects the tendency of policymaking by myth. Given our faith in individualism and belief in the Horatio Alger myth, the nation has ignored the realities of the recent structural changes in both the family and the economy. Our policies must acknowledge these realities of our current family structure: (1) one-half of the American children alive today will live in a single-parent household sometime during their childhood; (2) one-third of America's children will be poor at some point in their childhood; (3) almost one-fifth of all American families are single-parent families, mostly headed by a female; and (4) most female-headed households will remain poor.[7] No amount of rhetoric, nostalgic longing, or even changes in societal attitudes or individual behavior will alter the fact that for the foreseeable future most of the demographic structure of society has already been set. Millions of older women are already widowed, and very few will find a new husband. Millions of children now alive will grow up without the benefit of living with both their biological parents because they were born out of wedlock or because their parents have already divorced. Unless drastic changes occur in the economy, most women will continue to hold jobs outside the home. Their massive withdrawal from the workplace would have far reaching effects not only on the standards of living of their own families but also on the overall gross national product and the resulting tax income available to the local, state and national government. Insuring a decent life for all becomes a question of how to address the needs of each family regardless of its form while enhancing its strengths.

Katrina showed that family, community, and government resources and the efforts of nonprofit organizations and religious groups are all necessary in an emergency. The following chapters show the same need for these support systems in everyday life.

Notes

1. John Donne. "Meditation XVII," in *The Oxford Dictionary of Quotations*, 3rd ed. (1979). p. 190.
2. Economic Policy Institute. (2004). *Facts and Figures from The State of Working America 2004/2005*. U.S. & the World. Retrieved November 29, 2006 from http://www.epinet.org/books/swa2004/news/swafacts_international.pdf. Economic Policy Institute. (2006). *Facts and Figures from The State of Working America 2006/2007*. Chapter 8: U.S. & the World. Retrieved November 29, 2006 from http://www.stateofworkingamerica.org/news/SWA06Facts-International.pdf.
3. Wider Opportunities for Women. (2001). *Six strategies for family economic self-sufficiency*. The self-sufficiency standard. Retrieved November 29, 2006 from http://www.sixstrategies.org/sixstrategies/selfsufficiencystandard.cfm.
4. Joint Committee on Taxation. (2005, January). *Estimates of federal tax expenditures for fiscal years 2005-2009 (JCS-1-05)*. Table 1: Tax expenditure estimates by budget function, fiscal years 2005-2009, p. 30. Retrieved April 12, 2005, from http://www.house.gov/jct/pubs05.html.Joint Committee on Taxation. (2005, January). *Estimates of federal tax expenditures for fiscal years 2005-2009 (JCS-1-05)*. Table 3: Distribution by income class of selected individual tax expenditure items, at 2004 rates and 2004 income levels, p. 42. Retrieved April 12, 2005, from http://www.house.gov/jct/pubs05.html. Burt. M. R. (2001, September). *What Will It Take To End Homelessness?* Washington, DC: The Urban Institute. Retrieved March 26, 2007, from http://www.urban.org/uploadedPDF/end_homelessness.pdf .
5. Roberts, D. (2005, June 6). US Army Corps of Engineers Braces for Record Cuts. New Orleans City Business. Retrieved August 30, 2007, from http://zfacts.com/p/93print.html and http://www.findarticles.com/p/articles/mi_qn4200/is_20050606/ai_n14657367.
6. Scherer, R. (2007, August 3). Bridge collapse spotlights America's deferred maintenance. About one-quarter of America's 577,000 bridges were rated deficient in 2004. Retrieved August 30, 2007, from http://www.csmonitor.com/2007/0803/p01s05-usgn.htm.
7. Children's Defense Fund. (2000). *The state of America's children*. Washington, DC: Author. Retrieved from http://www.childrensdefense.org/release010407.htm.

2

What Family Lives in America's Neighborhoods?

"It all depends upon what you mean by home...
Home is the place where, when you have to go
there, They have to take you in."– Robert Frost,
"The Death of the Hired Man" (1930)[1]

Frost's poem relates a discussion between a husband, reluctant to house a dying former farm hand, and his more compassionate wife. The husband questions why any responsibility rests with him; the man has a brother. His wife argues that the dying man cannot turn without shame to a brother from whom he became alienated years before. She pleads with her husband, claiming that the man has come to their farm to die at the only place he feels at home.

As the poem poignantly illustrates, people can consider their "home" to be with people other than relatives. The words "home" and "family" are not synonymous. Frost's words raise the issue of people's need for a place of acceptance, a place where they feel "at home," as well as questions about who has responsibility for caring for someone without a family-based "home." In the case of a neighborhood, what responsibility do neighbors have for neighbors and for neighborhood children?

Many people argue that society should depend upon local communities, churches, volunteers, and families to correct what they perceive to be the ills of today's society. They frequently call for a return to the "traditional" family and its values. The discussion of the media and policymakers about the American family too frequently rests upon (a) unexamined underlying assumptions; (b) a lack of historical knowledge and perspective; (c) inaccurate data about current family composition; (d) ignorance about the prospects for short run changes; and (e) a lack of analysis of the full implications or spillover effects of recommended actions.

Historians and anthropologists have documented extensive differences in the form and functions of families in different societies and across time. The formal and informal rules governing sexual behavior have varied, at times sanctioning second wives, concubines and mistresses. Laws establishing the economic obligations and privileges of families have differed in determining rules for inheritance and control of children. Many immigrants to America during its initial period, for example, were second sons from England whose prospects there were limited by laws that required that the family's property could not be divided but was to be left to the first son. The point here is not to examine the vast literature on families, but to point out that family forms and their tasks change.

To best design policies and programs that suit today's American families, we must relinquish myths about families that cloud our thinking about reality. This chapter examines four prevailing myths that frequently drive policy decisions and program designs affecting both families and neighborhoods. The myths' underlying assumptions fuel much of our political debate and considerable academic research.

Myths about the American Family

Myth One: The typical American family consists of a white man, married to a white wife not employed outside the home, and several children, all living in a single family house with a green grass lawn. For almost fifty years Norman Rockwell's portraits of the American family celebrating this myth regularly graced the cover of the *Saturday Evening Post*.

Myth Two: The typical American family of our forefathers consisted of an extended family with parents, children, and grandchildren living and working together as a happy, self-reliant unit.

Myth Three: The typical American family today consists of a working Mom, happily balancing a successful career with a meaningful relationship with her husband or "significant other," along with devotion to her children's growth and well-being.

Myth Four: Poor families don't measure up and consist of a Welfare Mom watching soap operas while collecting government checks, entertaining male friends, and ignoring her children.

Different versions of these myths exist and have dominated the media at various times. Like all-powerful myths and symbols, each reflects some reality along with distortion of that reality. Separating the two will help Americans design realistic approaches for supporting all families.

Myth One: The Norman Rockwell Family

From the end of World War II until the mid-1980s, the media generally considered Norman Rockwell's pictures to represent the typical American family. Many older Americans grew up in that type of household. Many remember those times with nostalgia, based on happy memories of a nourishing, comfortable childhood.

In a book aptly titled *The Way We Never Were*, Stephanie Coontz notes that this portrayal of the "happy" family of the 1950s perpetuates a myth.[2] Many such "ideal" families contained bored and/or alcoholic women filled with despair, self-doubt, and resentment, emotions that helped fuel their daughters' search for a more fulfilling life. During the women's movement of the 1960s and 1970s, millions questioned both this myth and its underlying assumptions and values. Men were also shortchanged by this romanticized division of labor. Many 1950s breadwinner husbands complained in later life that they did not know their own children. They had spent their time commuting from suburb to downtown job, relying upon their wives to handle the home and children.

This idyllic picture also applied to only a fraction of the population. Millions of others struggled in grueling poverty. Approximately one-fourth of the population remained poor throughout the 1950s. One-third of the children grew up in poverty. The majority of the elderly existed on low incomes without health insurance.[3]

Television rarely portrayed a minority in a role other than a servant. Good parenting for Jews and African Americans included telling their children that they could not go to the beach or swimming pool because it was "restricted." In *Families on the Fault Line,* Lillian Rubin provides a poignant memory of a black mother's difficulty. An adult black woman reflecting on her childhood during that period recounts, "...I used to watch the Mickey Mouse Club and all I wanted to be was a mouseketeer. I'd tell my mother that I was going to be a mouseketeer, and she'd always say that's silly, but she never said why. Now I know it's because she didn't know how to tell me that I wasn't good enough because I was black."[4]

In addition, the family of the 1950s represented what Coontz called "a historical fluke." Americans enjoyed an unusual prosperity created partly by an extraordinary level of personal savings accumulated during World War II that enabled people to purchase the goods not affordable during the Depression and not obtainable during the war. America enjoyed a unique competitive advantage due to the destruction of other nations' industrial strength. The federal GI Bill for veterans financed widespread education, leading to better jobs and increased productivity.[5] Federal highway and mortgage loan programs fostered the creation of major new suburban developments.

Ideology regarding the "ideal" family changed following World War II. Women who had built tanks during the war were urged, if not coerced, to remain at home. Companies that had established day care centers when mobilizing workers for the war effort dismantled them. Movies and publicity about movie stars shifted from glorifying the strong independent female to upholding the importance of domesticity. The suburban nuclear family came to epitomize American values.[6]

Focusing on the desirability of stay-at-home wives conveniently sidesteps two crucial questions: What is it about paid employment that makes parenting difficult for both men and women? What must be done to provide care for a growing number of frail older persons? Serious debate about issues such as child care, time off for emergency care of a parent or flexible hours makes no sense if the basic unspoken assumption is that the working woman should not have had a family or should not have taken the employment. Even those few fathers with a stay-at-home wife may find that long hours, frequent out-of-town travel, required overtime, and compulsory moves to another city to retain employment or as a prerequisite for promotion limit their ability to fulfill their parenting or elder care responsibilities. Thus, helping families and communities flourish depends upon actions of business as well as individuals and neighborhoods.

Although most of us realize intellectually that the Norman Rockwell myth no longer accurately describes the American family, if it ever did, Rockwell's paintings enjoy continued popularity and the myth they represent continues to influence attitudes and policy. The image retains its power as an unacknowledged ideal underpinning much of the rhetoric about family, community, and American values, even though millions of American families do not match the picture.

Myth Two: Our Happy Forefathers

Another American view of the family glorifies "the good old days," with an extended family of parents, children, and grandparents living and working as a happy, self-reliant team. This picture of "Our Happy Forefathers" also portrays a myth. Indeed, historically, the greatest proportion of households living in extended families, 20 percent, occurred between 1850 and 1885.[7] But extended family households then, as now, often arose out of dire necessity rather than preference, and did not necessarily guarantee family stability or welfare. Child labor on the farm, in the factory, or producing piecework at home harmed children's health and hampered their education, restricting social mobility. Stress often resulted from cramped living conditions and conflicts over authority between generations. Marriages often continued for solely economic reasons despite emotional distance and unhappiness.

Other variations of the "Our Happy Forefathers" myth exist: Southern families in the large manor house of their plantations sipping cool drinks while gazing at cotton fields; Northern merchants' wives providing lavish meals and entertainment for relatives and guests. Movies and literature picturing these nostalgic scenes generally overlook the families of the slaves and indentured servants whose work supported the lifestyles of the patrician families.

Close families provide many benefits but can limit personal growth and independence. American historical migration patterns often reflect the desire of second-generation immigrants to strike out on their own, escaping the traditions of "the old country" valued by their parents. A classical sociological study of a New England city traced the economic and social progress of different groups of migrants over several generations. It vividly depicted the struggles of couples and children torn between the values and habits of their parents and those of native-born Americans.[8] Although much of the popular media portrays pioneer families in covered wagons settling the West, it fails to note the desire for independence, far from their extended families, that helped fuel those migrations. So while historically a small minority of families did live together, it was usually for reasons of economic necessity, sometimes at great costs in personal independence and fulfillment.

Myth Three: The Successful Career Woman "Having it All"

In the "Having it All" myth, magazines and television ads portray glamorous young women happily balancing work and children. Numerous articles assure them that if they become experts at time management, use their lunch hours for errands and spend "quality time" with their children, their lives will be fulfilled, leaving plenty of time for romantic dinners with their spouses or dates. Several versions of this myth have flourished during the past twenty-five years. All invite easy solutions that ignore the complex realities.

As will be discussed in more detail in the chapter on income, employment remains the only means for most women to ensure that they and their families can exist at even a modest standard of living. While many, if not most, women enjoy their jobs and want to work, few enjoy the glamor and financial rewards portrayed by the Having it All myth. For the most part they work at non-glamorous jobs with limited privacy. They lack control over their work schedule, the pace or flow of work, choice of tasks or priorities. Control over each of these provides more flexibility for juggling family and work responsibilities. Lack of control creates stress. In fact, despite the myths of the over-stressed hard-working male executive, his female secretary probably experiences a higher rate of stress-related illness due to her constrained ability to exert control over her time. And keep in mind that this situation is the rule, not the exception. Four of the six top occupations generally held by women provide little job flexibility: secretaries, cashiers, registered nurses, and an occupational category that include nursing aides, orderlies, and attendants. The other two occupations, manager/administrator and sales supervisor/proprietor, may or may not provide job control and flexibility.[9]

Many employees experience considerable stress fulfilling job requirements while meeting family needs. Women, especially, struggle with a "dual role and double burden." Several studies have shown that while some men now contribute more to household and child rearing tasks than formerly, their contribution remains limited. They spend less time than their wives on household chores and child care. Their help more often consists of taking the kids to the zoo occasionally rather than making sure they do their daily chores or homework.

Researchers also note that the fatigue and tension of squeezing constant multiple tasks into limited time affects many marriages. Friction between spouses about the appropriate division of chores—and about who has the right to say what that division should be—can eat away at marriages.[10] One teacher at a technical college in Madison, Wisconsin, commented in 1998 that her mostly white students could handle readings and discussions about race with no problem, but almost came to blows when discussing who should do the dishes!

Men who take responsibility for household chores, or those who have sole custody of their children, suffer the same types of time crunches. Their bosses and colleagues may be even less sympathetic to their problems. As changing gender roles began to be widely discussed in the 1970s, pop culture began to reflect these tensions: the 1979 movie *Kramer vs. Kramer* includes such hilarious scenes as Dustin Hoffman walking into a corporate meeting with an armload of groceries.

The trend toward part-time work further complicates the problem. Part-time jobs rarely include sick leave or time off to take a child to the dentist. Many parents hold two, and in some cases three, part-time jobs. In 2004, more than three and a half million women held more than one job.[11] Juggling several jobs adds transportation time to the daily schedule as the worker dashes from one location to another.

Thus, the structure of the modern workplace clearly does not match the myth of Having It All. The reality tarnishes the image of the mythical "super mom."

Myth Four: The Welfare Mom

Many Americans believe that women receiving welfare choose it as a way of life because they are unwilling to work. They believe that welfare recipients are lazy, irresponsible, unmarried women who give birth to additional illegitimate children in order to remain on welfare. Unfortunately, today the phrases "single mom" and "single parent household" seem to carry some of the same negative connotations of irresponsibility despite the fact that although some women may choose single parenthood, millions of "single moms" are widowed, abandoned, separated from an abusive husband, or divorced through no fault of their own. Most single mothers are not on welfare.

Although Congress replaced the traditional welfare program in 1996 with a program that places strict limits on the length of time a recipient can receive benefits, the "Welfare Mom" myth bears examination. The underlying assumptions continue to drive much of our rhetoric and social policy. The cliché was never true, but negative public attitudes have persisted over time. Three surveys taken between 1969 and 1990 showed that over 90 percent of Americans believed that lack of effort causes poverty.[12] Welfare recipients themselves have shared the Welfare Mom myth. In a detailed study of Wisconsin's welfare system in the 1990s, Mark Rank quotes women on welfare who carefully pointed out the difference between their own situation and those of other recipients. The women condemned the others, citing the typical stereotypes.[13]

The stigma attached to welfare affects not only recipients' self-perception but also their treatment by landlords, medical providers, and others. Even receiving food stamps and free school lunches, needed by millions of full-time working parents, evokes criticism and shame. A simple personal example from a grocery store illustrates why: a thin boy of about eight shyly asked a checkout clerk for the location of the ice cream. The clerk replied curtly that he couldn't use food stamps for ice cream. The child looked upset. When I inquired, he told me that his mother had sent him to the store to get ice cream, and he didn't know what to do next. My request to the clerk to actually check whether ice cream could be purchased with food stamps elicited only another short and unpleasant response. Finally, I bought the ice cream, complimented the boy on being a help to his mother and sent him home. One can only imagine the psychological impact of such experiences on a small child's psyche, each conveying a derogatory message about families who receive assistance.

The facts about welfare recipients never supported the myth. Most people living in poverty are the working poor, and even people receiving welfare do not fit the myth. The greatest number of welfare recipients have been white. The majority of recipients used the benefits for less than two years. Many women entered welfare after a divorce or separation. One-half left within the first year, and three-quarters left within the first two years. Women sometimes quit jobs and returned to welfare to obtain needed health benefits for their children. Even before the elimination of traditional welfare, only 15 percent of recipients remained on welfare continually over a five-year period.[14] Many who left, however, returned due to loss of jobs during economic downturns, ill health or other reasons such as caring for an injured child. Indeed, some people use welfare cyclically to bridge gaps in year-round income. A television documentary described how the families in one California county depended upon seasonal farm work, followed by unemployment benefits, followed by welfare payments, followed by re-employment when the crops ripened. By combining these various sources the women managed to sustain their families in an area with only seasonal employment.

Families on welfare actually had *fewer* children than other families. Researcher Mark Rank found that the fertility rate of women on welfare in Wisconsin turned out to be considerably less than for other women in Wisconsin or the nation. The overall birth rate for women aged eighteen through forty-four nationally was 71.1 children per 1,000 women. Wisconsin women not on welfare bore 75.3 children per 1,000 women while Wisconsin women on welfare bore only 45.8 per 1,000. Furthermore, the longer a woman remained on welfare, the more her fertility rate decreased. Rank found that the stereotypes regarding the birth rates of African American recipients were also misleading.[15]

At its most blatant, the Welfare Mom myth is not only inaccurate but also racist. Although most welfare recipients have actually been Caucasians, "welfare" became a code word for immoral, lazy, African American women with many children. In the early 1990s, Wisconsin's Governor Tommy Thompson declared that the state's high rates of welfare payments served as a magnet attracting women from other states to Wisconsin. For weeks the front pages of the leading Madison newspaper contained statements that implied that Madison was being plagued by undesirables, presumably black, from Chicago. Eventually a short article buried on an inside page reported that, in fact, the average woman moving to Madison and obtaining welfare was a young white woman with one or two children from a nearby rural town.

The legacy of welfare reform is hard to evaluate. After the federal Temporary Assistance for Needy Families program replaced traditional welfare in 1996, the welfare rolls across the nation dropped drastically. In a number of states, no one knows what happened to many of the women. Although some may have found employment that provided respect, satisfaction, and a decent income, most worked at a poverty wage. Furthermore, their initial success in finding jobs depended to a large extent on the extraordinary economic boom at the end of the twentieth century. Many lost those jobs when the economy turned sour. The number of unemployed single mothers, including former welfare recipients, rose 25 percent between late 2000 and late 2001.[16] Moreover, the success of removing women from the welfare rolls at the end of the 1990s depended partly upon changed rules and additional funding that provided the recipients with child care, transportation, and help with overcoming barriers to work. In Wisconsin, for example, the welfare rolls were reduced dramatically, but the cost of the program actually increased.[17]

The myth also distracts us from careful examination of the underlying causes of the behavior of those women who do remain on welfare for extended periods or who use welfare on more than one occasion. Recipients often suffer from depression or problems of alcohol and drug dependency. Recently those working to help women leave welfare have realized that many also suffer from domestic violence and have histories of childhood physical and/or sexual abuse. Studies indicate that some one-quarter to one-third of welfare recipients suffered childhood sexual abuse.[18] Abuse can cause physical and mental problems and interfere with training and job performance. In many cases, obtaining welfare provided an abused woman an alternative to remaining in a homeless shelter or returning to an unsafe situation.[19]

Although personal and family benefits often occurred when women left welfare for paid employment, in some cases their employment also stripped neighborhoods of the very people who had been providing a range of volunteer programs as well as informal support and supervision of children. In the late 1990s, the director of Wisconsin's effort to end welfare suggested that the child care problem could be solved if parents left their children with neighbors. This option ignored the fact that women who live in "troubled" neighborhoods are extremely careful when deciding whom to entrust with their children. The booming economy plus the pressure to leave welfare meant that those women most likely to be considered positive role models by other parents were also those most likely to leave the neighborhood for paid employment. The remaining neighbors were more likely to have physical limitations, mental health problems, or a history of drug or alcohol addiction, making them incapable of providing adequate child care. The history of welfare and welfare reform shows us that reality is much more varied and complex than the myth of the Welfare Mom.

Today's Reality

Myths perform certain valuable functions for society. They express values, provide models, and simplify complexity. Unfortunately, they can vilify and demonize as well as glorify. Both extremes prevent realistic examination of reality. The myths about families act in consort to obscure the reality of what today's families actually look like and how best to support them. If an undeclared assumption is that all families should resemble the Norman Rockwell myth, then families that don't match that ideal either suffer from the inadequacies related to the Welfare Mom myth, or contain selfish Having It All women who pursue their own career goals to the detriment of their children. This mixture of myths and half-truths provides a poor basis for policy decisions at either the national or community level.

The assumption that the Norman Rockwell nuclear family represents the norm ignores both historical and current data. This view often includes the implication that other family arrangements harm children. Although some Norman Rockwell families continue to exist, Americans today live in slightly more than 111 million highly varied households. Over 27 percent of American households in 2005 consisted of persons living alone, while less than 22 percent contained couples with children.[20]

We use family and household synonymously, but readers should remember that the terms differ. Household refers to a physical space that can be occupied by an individual, unrelated individuals, a nuclear family, an extended family, a family and unrelated individuals, or two or more families. Families, consisting of those related by blood or marriage, do not necessarily live in the same household. In the discussion that follows, when we refer to family tasks, keep in mind that people living alone or with non-family members must also accomplish the same tasks.

Even if starting today the stork delivered every newborn to a stable nuclear family and into a community where divorce, parental deaths and desertions miraculously disappeared, millions of children whose parents already have separated will spend part of their childhood in a single parent family. In 2003, almost 20 million, 27 percent of all children, lived with one parent. Although 70 percent of children lived in two-parent families, approximately 25 percent of those lived with a stepparent.[21]

Furthermore, in most households with children, both adults are employed. Less than one-third of two-parent families with children have a stay-at-home mom.[22] The disparity between today's reality and the myth becomes even greater when the myth's components include being white and living in a single family home. Thus, any approach to family and neighborhood support today must include the reality that few of today's families resemble the Rockwell myth.

Extended families in America today take several forms. Almost 4 percent of all households consist of a multigenerational family including parents, children, grandparents, and in some cases even great-grandparents or great-grandchildren.[23] As throughout American history, many recent immigrants live in extended families. A small, but recently increasing, number of households consist of parents along with adult children who have returned home after college, divorce, or illness or because the young people lack the funds or initiative to set up their own homes. Other households now consist of "blended" families, a married couple with children from a previous marriage, often along with children from their new union. An estimated one-third of Americans are now a part of a family that includes step-children or parents.

While families in each of these circumstances may be enriched by each other's presence, the potential for stress exists, especially for employed women who continue to carry most of the responsibilities for both the practical and the emotional care of the family. The children in blended families can welcome their new siblings, but may resent sharing their parent's affection and attention. One father who married the mother of his teenage son's best friend discovered with dismay and shock that David, who had loved spending time with Bob as a friend, did not welcome him into his home as a brother.

Unlike the extended households of the Our Happy Forefathers myth, today's families often do not live in large houses surrounded by ample yards or fields with numerous opportunities for members to retreat for moments of privacy. After my father retired, my mother laughingly complained that "I married him for better or worse, but not for lunch!" In a more serious vein, she remarked that "any two adult women who have both had their own households cannot live together peacefully." While some manage, many people do not like living with their mother or mother-in-law, with whom they may never have enjoyed the best relationship. Most older persons do not want to live with their children. They love their grandchildren, but often find their energy exhausting and their modern manners and music choices appalling. Moreover, the great increases in life span combined with the rapid changes in technology and American attitudes create greater generational differences today than would have been experienced by Our Happy Forefathers.

The availability of the time and effort needed to maintain close ties among extended family members relates to another myth, that of the working woman Having It All. Employed women have less time to arrange or prepare for family celebrations. When care for an extended family member requires considerable time, this often harms the woman performing the tasks by reducing her time for leisure and sleep. Working women may find their ability to obtain promotions reduced. Many even quit work or shift to part-time employment, hurting their future work opportunities including their ability to retain health care benefits and save for their own retirement.

The structure of cities and suburban sprawl adds to the stress on families. Recreational activities, medical appointments, and other business usually require that someone provide chauffeuring services. Given the complexity of today's life with multiple schedules for children's school and other activities and the increased life span of people with severe health problems, the physical and emotional strains on extended families can be huge. This burden exists even if the family member needing support lives nearby rather than in the same household.

The Welfare Mom myth ignores the fact that the real problem is not the atypical woman abusing the system, but the low wages that do not permit single parents to support themselves and a child or two. Most welfare recipients did not have eight children, were not minorities, and did not stay on welfare for extended periods of time, although some returned to it during periods of economic downturn or an emergency such as a seriously ill child.

Recently some scholars, religious leaders, and politicians have begun rearticulating the Norman Rockwell myth. They bemoan the high rates of divorce and unmarried motherhood and believe that today's social problems result from the fact that most mothers work. Although such statistics may be a cause for concern, those voicing the myth rarely examine the factors contributing to the rise in the number of working mothers, including those who are married. The majority of women who hold paid employment are either the family's sole support or provide over one-third of the family income.[24] The critics of working women also ignore the extent to which both the national economy and most families' livelihoods depend upon women's paid employment.

The proponents of this resuscitated myth fail to seriously examine another underlying issue: how to support employed parents, both fathers and mothers, in their child rearing responsibilities. A study by the National Institute of Mental Health found that most men took no more than five days off from work to care for a new baby, even after the passage of a law protecting parents from losing their jobs if they took such unpaid leave. Their decisions were partly financial, but were also driven by concerns that their workplace culture would stigmatize them as uncommitted workers.[25]

Moving Beyond the Myths

If America wants to provide nourishing environments for all families and the millions of people living alone, we must base policies and programs upon reality, not myths. The Norman Rockwell myth, that often implies a middle income lifestyle, leads us to ignore the real difficulties of millions of American families struggling on a modest income as well as the problems of single parents and those living alone. The Our Happy Forefathers myth leads us to assume that extended families will take care of the growing elderly population, despite evidence that many families lack the necessary time, money or, in some cases, inclination. The Having It All myth leads us to ignore the need for widespread subsidized quality child care, paid family leave, flexible work schedules, living wages, equal pay for women, and the policies and programs necessary to care for the growing elderly population. The Welfare Mom myth leads us to ignore the difficulties of all people who work for low wages, especially single mothers.

Myths hamper sensible discussion about what we really want for ourselves, our families and our communities and a clearheaded examination of the best ways to achieve our goals. We must question simplistic judgments about today's family that are based on glorification of a fantasized past or an idealized present. Concentration must shift from idealizing or vilifying particular family forms, whether real or mythical, to concentrating on how to help all American families, whatever their composition.

We must base policies and actions on existing family structures. The national discussion needs to shift from lamenting changes in the American family to examining ways to help people accomplish specific tasks that must be performed by all families, including people sharing a household and those living alone. Furthermore, we must acknowledge that the basic situation will not change significantly for at least a generation.

Attention and policies must focus on such reality-based questions as how to best help a two-income family rear their children or care for their elderly parents, how to assist a suburban widow to remain in the home she shared with her husband for forty years, and how to ensure that children of parents working for low wages receive adequate food and health care. Each neighborhood and community can and must ask these questions in terms of its own population. And the nation must address them for the entire country.

Current discussion about families often ignores the fact that many people do not live with or even near their families. Addressing the needs of Americans for companionship, support, and community must consider not only households with several family members but also the millions of Americans living alone. Although this book refers to family throughout, over one-fourth of American households consist of an individual living alone, who must also perform basic everyday tasks.[26]

If today's family will face difficulties handling all of its tasks as a self-reliant unit, can its members rely upon neighbors to help out? Katrina showed us the importance of neighbors, friends and extended family. But it also showed us the crucial need for appropriate outside help, and the interconnectedness of the various institutions of our society. To critically explore how families can accomplish everyday tasks in their neighborhoods, we first need to examine the specific role of the private sector, the government and other major institutions in establishing the context within which families operate. The next chapter considers the extent to which these players can be depended upon as supports for families.

Notes

1.   Frost, R. (1930). The death of the hired man. In *Selected Poems of Robert Frost* (pp. 49-55). New York: Halcyon House.

2. Coontz, S. (1992). *The way we never were: American families and the nostalgia trap* (chapter 2). New York: Basic Books.
3. Coontz, S. (1992). *The way we never were: American families and the nostalgia trap* (pp. 29-30). New York: Basic Books.
4. Rubin, L. B. (1994). *Families on the fault line: America's working class speaks about the family, the economy, race, and ethnicity* (p. 155) [quotation]. New York: HarperCollins.
5. Coontz, S. (1992). *The way we never were: American families and the nostalgia trap* (p. 28). New York: Basic Books.
6. Goodwin, D. K. (1994). *No ordinary time: Franklin and Eleanor Roosevelt: The home front in World War II.* New York: Simon & Schuster.
7. Coontz, S. (1962). *The way we never were: American families and the nostalgia trap* (p. 12). New York: Basic Books.
8. Warner, W. L., & Srole, L. (1945). *Social systems of American ethnic groups.* Hartford, CT: Yale University Press.
9. Rose, S. J. (2000). *Social stratification in the United States.* New York: The New Press.
10. Hochschild, A., & Machung, A. (1989). *The second shift* (pp. 1-32). New York: Avon Books. Rubin, L. B. (1994). *Families on the fault line: America's working class speaks about the family, the economy, race, and ethnicity* (chapters 4 and 5). New York: HarperCollins.
11. U.S. Department of Labor. (2005, May). *Women in the labor force: A databook.* (Table 35. Multiple jobholders and multiple jobholding rates by sex and race, May of selected years, 1970-2004, not seasonally adjusted). Retrieved December 11, 2005 from http://www.bls.gov/cps/wlf-table35-2005.pdf.
12. Wilson, W. J. (1996). *When work disappears: The world of the new urban poor* (p.160). New York: Vintage Books.
13. Rank, M. R. (1994). *Living on the edge: The realities of welfare in America* (pp. 142-143). New York: Columbia University Press.
14. Wilson, W. J. (1996). *When work disappears: The world of the new urban poor* (p. 167). New York: Vintage Books.
15. Rank, M. R. (1994). *Living on the edge: The realities of welfare in America* (pp. 72, 73, 76 and 151). New York: Columbia University Press.
16. Children's Defense Fund. (2002, April 11). *The recession hits children: 2001 undoes much of the '90s employment gains for parents.* Washington, DC: Author. Retrieved June 17, 2002, from http://www.childrensdefense.org/fs_recession01_1.htm.
17. The author has been a member of the Dane County oversight committee for the program.
18. DeParle, J. (1999, November 28). Early sex abuse hinders many women on welfare. *New York Times National Sunday*, Section 1, page 1.
19. National Coalition for the Homeless. (2002, September). *Why are people homeless? NCH Fact Sheet #1.* Washington, DC: Author. Retrieved March 2, 2004, from http://www.nationalhomeless.org/causes.html.
20. U.S. Census Bureau. (2006, August 15). *2005 American Community Survey. United States: General demographic characteristics: 2005.* Retrieved November 9, 2006 from http://factfinder.census.gov/servlet/ADPTable?_bm=y&-geo_id=01000US&-ds_name=ACS_2005_EST_G00_.
21. Bernstein, R. (2003, June 12). *Two married parents the norm: About 7-in-10 children live with their parents, according to Census Bureau pre-Father's Day release.* Washington DC: United States Department of Commerce News. Retrieved April 25, 2005, from http://www.census.gov/Press-Release/www/2003/cb03-97.html.

Stepfamily Association of America. (n.d.). *Stepfamily facts.* Retrieved April 26, 2005, from http://www.saafamilies.org/faqs/index.htm.

22. Children's Defense Fund. (2001, April). *Early childhood development: Child care basics.* Retrieved December 31, 2004, from http://www.childrensdefense.org/earlychildhood/childcare/basics.asp.

23. U.S. Census Bureau. (2001, September 7). *Multigenerational households number 4 million according to census 2000.* Retrieved June 10, 2002, from http://www.census.gov/Press-Release/www/2001/cb01cn182.html.

24. Bureau of Labor Statistics, U.S. Department of Labor. (2005, May). *Women in the labor force: A databook.* Report 985. Retrieved December 5, 2006, from http://stats.bls.gov/cps/wlf-table24-2005.pdf.

25. McMahon, A. (1999). *Taking care of men: Sexual politics in the public mind* (p. 171). Cambridge: Cambridge University Press.

26. U.S. Census Bureau. (2005). *United States: General demographic characteristics: 2005.* Retrieved November 9, 2006 from http://factfinder.census.gov/servlet/ADPTable?_bm=y&-geo_id=01000US&-qr_name=ACS_2005_EST_G00_DP1.

3

Crucial Partners

Creating vibrant communities and neighborhoods that support families requires actions from and multiple partnerships among many individuals and organizations at all levels of American society. It calls both for grassroots action and for supportive national policies. Creating thoughtful discussion about policies and programs dealing with complex issues requires separating reality from myth, facts from wishful nostalgia. Because all neighborhoods and local communities are affected by the actions of outsiders, any determination about how to meet the needs of families in those neighborhoods must examine the myths about those outside influences. When these institutions fail to play their role in supporting America's families, local communities and neighborhoods find themselves scrambling to react to crises created by external forces. Analyzing those myths will provide a more realistic basis for sorting out appropriate roles and identifying needed public policies.

America's varied families live and work within a framework of rules, standards, and assistance largely established by national institutions. When these institutions fail to support American families, local communities and neighborhoods must scramble to react to crises created by external forces. This chapter examines common myths and assumptions that often cloud thinking about the roles and responsibilities of business, government, nonprofits, religious institutions, and the media.

The Private Sector: Myths and Realities

Several myths about the private sector affect Americans' approach to family and community issues. Myth one assumes that what is good for business is necessarily good for American families and communities. During much of the twentieth century, the need to make profits was balanced by an implicit social contract with workers. Companies shared increases in productivity with their employees. Often businesses were small, owned and managed by persons who had grown up in the local community. They were an integral part of the local social fabric. Today even local firms are likely to be part of an international conglomerate whose managers often move and will be judged by the most recent quarterly earnings report.

Businesses must make profits. Responsible businesses provide decent employee benefits, treat workers with respect and fairness, and operate both legally and ethically. But in the twenty-first century a manager who concerns himself with the effect of his decisions upon the community to the detriment of a possible increase in the bottom line profits is likely to soon lose his job. Corporate officers who increase profits by laying off workers receive promotions. Managers receive bonuses for calculating that their international company can save money by closing a branch office of the bank or the only plant in a small town. Managers are not paid to worry about the spillover effects of their decisions on American families, neighborhoods, or communities. They do not have to find jobs for displaced workers or help an elderly lady who, since her local bank closed, has to take the bus to the other side of town to cash her checks.

The present crisis in the subprime housing market resulted from businesses operating in an unregulated market, encouraging people to sign mortgage contracts that were not appropriate for their financial situation. The individual broker had an incentive to steer borrowers into mortgages with low interest rates that would later rise significantly. The broker would not suffer if borrowers lost their homes.

Many firms do practice appropriate environmental controls, donate to the United Way, encourage their executives to serve on the boards of nonprofits and their employees to volunteer in soup kitchens. Frequently, however, those contributions of time and money relate directly or indirectly to producing a profit. They are often undertaken to establish a positive image and relationship to the community, which in turn generates more business. For example, companies lend executives to serve on committees and boards with high visibility and good press. Those memberships provide contacts with important players in local politics and business. Sponsoring a prestigious museum exhibit heightens a company's visibility, providing excellent public relations. Business foundations donate to a variety of good causes, but rarely to organizations that promote social change or deal with controversial issues.

These good deeds on behalf of the community can be viewed as either genuine philanthropy or a calculated public relations attempt to enhance the bottom line. Whatever the motivation, these contributions are actually paid for indirectly by consumers, stockholders, and taxpayers. Business charitable contributions usually are tax deductible, reducing the amount of taxes paid by business and increasing the amount to be raised through other taxes. Business executives are likely to contribute to organizations that match their own tastes, such as the opera, or provide public recognition by listing their name on the wall of a new building. Their contributions to health causes may be based upon the health issues of a family member rather than a realistic assessment of the greatest health needs in a community. In effect, business philanthropy shifts decisions about expenditures of potential tax money from elected officials to the CEOs of major corporations.

A second myth claims that the private sector, assisted by individual families, volunteers, churches, and neighborhoods, can resolve current problems if "the government would just get out of the way." Several difficulties exist with this approach. First, many of the problems we face are created by the business sector itself. Second, business attention to solutions too often occurs only under pressure from government. Reductions in air pollution, safety devices in automobiles, restrictions on selling tobacco to minors, bank investments in housing in lower income and minority neighborhoods, increases in the minimum wage—all occurred only after the enactment of laws and implementation of government regulations that were vigorously opposed by business. In addition, when pressed to clean up the environmental spillover effects of their operations, businesses lobby for tax breaks or special incentives. Many seem to calculate that it is cheaper to pay inspection fines and lawsuit settlements than to install appropriate environmental safeguards. Furthermore, unless the government passes laws and monitors compliance for all firms, individual businesses can claim, with some justification, that socially responsible actions on their part might provide an advantage to their competition.

Another problem with the "just get the government out of the way" approach relates to scope. Quick solutions often are appealing until one examines the scope of the problem. Few would argue against the idea of adult children providing ongoing assistance to their aging parents. But many factors make this ideal potentially untenable: the geographic mobility of Americans, the increase in women's employment outside the home, shorter hospital stays, and longer life spans. The scope of this problem lies beyond easy solution by individuals or by individual firms trying to be responsive to the needs of their employees. An effective solution must involve numerous actors from different societal institutions and requires a national approach.

Ensuring that no family goes hungry illustrates another problem with the "just get the government out of the way" approach—that of scale. The private sector can contribute to local food programs, provide land, tools, and volunteers for community gardens, contribute to the community's United Way, and encourage employees to volunteer at soup kitchens. But private sector contributions cannot match the financial commitment of federal assistance. For example, one year the Food Stamp Program served 19 million individuals throughout the nation. Fewer than 400,000 ate a meal at a soup kitchen that year. At holiday time the media regularly display pictures of volunteers and politicians serving meals to the hungry. Viewers could easily conclude that soup kitchens are a viable solution to the problem of hunger. Although such efforts provide needed supplemental resources, the undue media emphasis implies that volunteer solutions are preferable to government programs, even though the latter feed far more people, and provide the help in a more dignified manner. Furthermore, soup kitchens and food pantries rely heavily on food provided by government programs or tax-deducible contributions from businesses donating surplus food supplies.[1] Moreover, neighborhoods and communities most likely to house families needing food assistance are those least likely to include thriving businesses able to make substantial contributions.

The widespread belief that private charity will compensate for declining public services provides a false hope. For example, in the early 1990s, at a time of increasing prosperity, two-thirds of public charities suffered a decrease in income. While the wealth of many individuals and corporations soared, philanthropic giving remained constant, at less than two percent of income.[2] Although private contributions rose during the first years of the twenty-first century, private giving does not necessarily replace the need for government funding. For example, the total private contributions for human services in 2003 was three billion dollars *less* than the benefits people received from the Food Stamp Program alone.[3]

The third myth about the private sector assumes that its actions are more effective and efficient and less bureaucratic than those of the public sector. Politicians and the press constantly bemoan the ills of government programs and the ineptitude of government bureaucrats. Beginning with Richard Nixon in 1972, every successful late twentieth-century presidential candidate campaigned promising to make the government more efficient. Yet studies show that government workers compare favorably with those in private industry in terms of qualifications and performance.[4] Moreover, many private firms also suffer from bureaucratic ills.

Frequently, complaints about government inefficiency actually reflect disagreement with a government policy. Government officials are blamed for being inappropriate or ineffective because they are trying to implement laws and regulations that an individual or company would prefer to ignore. Yet elected officials and government bureaucrats have the mandate to adopt policies for the larger public good, while the concerns of an individual business are geared toward a narrower objective, its own welfare.

Myth four asserts that the free market is sacrosanct, a value-free mechanism dependent only upon individual choices and neutral laws. In fact, the free market itself depends upon collective decisions that create a framework within which it can operate, such as a system of laws and courts to enforce contracts. Also, the free market does not create the physical or human infrastructure needed for the economy to function, such as airports and a literate workforce. Furthermore, government intervention often provides considerable assistance to individual economic sectors or firms. In the early part of the nineteenth century, the national government used tariffs to protect America's emerging industries from competition from cheaper European goods. The government offered credit and land to assist in the development of canals and railroads. The 1862 Morrill Act provided land to establish agricultural and mechanical colleges, aiding both agriculture and industry.[5] During the twentieth century, much of the research and development that led to products such as the Internet resulted from work conducted for the military or in federal government laboratories. America's economy has always been governed partly by a relatively free market and partly by collective decisions. The ground rules under which any economy operates are established by society and reflect political decisions.

The fifth myth follows from the fourth, asserting that market decisions can and should be relied upon to determine societal values. If people are willing to pay for something it is valuable and presumed good for society. Conversely, if people aren't willing to pay for something, then it is not valuable. According to this measure, an executive's elective cosmetic surgery costing $4,500 is more socially valuable than a $100 pair of eyeglasses for a ten-year-old who cannot see the blackboard.

This approach denies that some decisions should be made collectively on the basis of something other than economic values. Economic arguments delayed the abolition of slavery, justified child labor, and are marshaled against environmental laws and regulations. Relying solely upon economic approaches also ignores the difference between private goods and public goods. The marketplace does not provide for a clear and convenient way to select a public good. One can buy a book at a bookstore, but one can only buy a book for the public library very indirectly by paying taxes. When paying taxes, few people think, "I am buying books for my public library."

Businesses tout the public good in terms of consumer choice and low prices for consumer goods but ignore the public good created by decent wages and sound environmental practices. Someone who buys a product because of its low price is not consciously deciding to transfer American jobs overseas or to deny workers their health benefits. But that may well be the collective result of many individual purchasing decisions. Only through the government can citizens choose to require businesses to act responsibly towards their employees and their communities.

The myths about the private sector that underlie much of Americans' ambivalence about the role of government can actually hinder the public sector's effectiveness. Cutbacks in government staff can result in work not being performed thoroughly. Such reductions encourage contracting work to private firms that may not have any dedication to serving the public interest. After Hurricane Katrina devastated New Orleans, former government officials told Congress that government cutbacks had reduced staff at the Federal Emergency Management Agency. Unfortunately, some of the departed employees had possessed the most expertise and experience.[6]

Both cuts in government staff and a distrust of government workers negatively impact the monitoring of contractors and compliance with national laws and regulations. Indeed, government employees who raise questions about private sector performance often suffer retribution. Off and on for some fifteen years a

Washington, DC., newspaper ran articles about one employee who had constant difficulties because he wanted defense contractors to account for what he saw as wasting millions of taxpayer dollars.[7] Only strong Congressional threats potentially affecting the Defense Department's budget kept him from losing his job on several occasions. The message was conveyed clearly to any informed government employee, few of whom had Congressional contacts to protect them.

Government: Myths and Realities

Myths abound about the U.S. government. Some people attack the validity of almost any government action. Since the time of Thomas Jefferson, one prominent strain of American thought has assumed that government is bad, claiming that the best government is that which governs least. Yet when Jefferson became president, he used the power of that office to double the size of the nation through the Louisiana Purchase, then commissioned Lewis and Clark to explore the West.

Like Jefferson, proponents of small government theory often ignore those government actions that benefit them. Throughout American history the federal government has provided substantial benefits to individuals and their families, often indirectly. Suburban residents hardly consider their homes the result of federal expenditures, yet those homes could not have been built without federal highway programs. Third-generation farmers proudly recount the struggles of their homesteading grandparents. Rarely do they mention the fact that the land often became available for nineteenth-century homeowners only after federal troops had removed the original inhabitants, Native Americans. And where would businesses be today without highly skilled employees who were educated in the public schools and public universities?

A second version of the evil government myth stresses the preference for local or state government over national government. While in some cases this approach makes sense, often the rhetoric obscures issues, forgets people's long-term interests, and ignores the spillover effects of the practices of one jurisdiction upon others. The boundaries of states and local jurisdictions are based on historical accidents and political considerations. They do not necessarily represent the most effective or fairest way of organizing community life or allocating resources. Given the geographic mobility of Americans, do the residents of one state or locality not have a vested interest in the employability of the high school graduates of another jurisdiction? Should only wealthy suburbs and prosperous states produce computer-literate high school graduates? As Katrina showed, people migrate from poor locations to wealthier ones because of personal disaster or in search of a better life, bringing with them any unresolved problems or educational deficiencies.

Often policies and programs desired at the local level cannot be achieved without national clout and resources. No community-based organization can by itself affect the policies of a nationwide bank without relying upon the provisions Congress mandated in the Community Reinvestment Act of 1977. For decades women could not collect court-awarded child support payments once their former spouses moved to another state. Tough new federal legislation, including a national hiring and wage reporting system, increased child support collections to mothers by 65 percent in four years. Seventeen million parents received an additional 18 *billion* dollars in fiscal year 2000,[8] twice as much as the corporate charitable contributions to *all* causes the following year.[9]

Individuals, politicians and the media rarely distinguish between different levels of government. Most federal tax funds for non-defense programs actually are sent directly to individuals or support services in state or local government or a wide variety of nonprofit organizations. Neither the neighborhood police officer nor the public health nurse providing immunization shots is a faceless Washington bureaucrat, but their efforts often depend directly or indirectly on federal funds. States also frequently send large parts of their own budgets to local governments and school districts to hire employees or to contract for services. Rarely do people realize that the benefits they are enjoying from state or local groups were indirectly paid for by federal tax dollars.

Local actions often affect communities in other states. Air pollution blows and water pollution flows across state boundaries. Contaminated meat produced in one state is shipped to others. The adequacy of local facilities and services everywhere affects visitors to those locales. John F. Kennedy could afford the best medical care in the country. Yet when he was shot in Dallas, he, as any person in any emergency, was rushed to the nearest hospital. In 2006 about 38 million Americans traveled by car more than fifty miles from their homes over the Thanksgiving holiday.[10] Some had accidents and suffered serious injuries, receiving treatment at whatever facilities were available.

Another myth proclaims the failure of government programs, especially as a solution for social problems. Many such programs have actually achieved remarkable success. Social Security radically reduced poverty among the elderly. In 1960, over one-third of senior citizens lived in poverty, despite the fact that half of the men were still employed. By the turn of the century, only 20 percent of the senior men were still employed, yet only 11 percent of the elderly lived in poverty. Nearly one-half of those Americans who receive Social Security would be classified as poor without it.[11]

The Supplemental Food Program for Women, Infants, and Children (WIC) saves the government money and alleviates human misery. A study of WIC results in five states showed that prenatal WIC participation increased birth weight and reduced premature births. In each state the program paid for itself, saving between almost two and over three times the program cost in the first sixty days of the child's life alone.[12] Such savings are compounded when one adds the medical costs and special education expenditures that may be necessary to treat conditions that could have been prevented by proper prenatal care.

In other examples of governmental accomplishment, the Office of the Surgeon General led the effort to educate the public about the dangers of smoking, and the GI Bill enabled millions of Americans to attend college who could never have managed it otherwise. The Job Corps, created as part of the Great Society programs of the 1960s, successfully prepared many inner-city youths for productive adulthood. In the dozen years after national laws banned lead from paint and plumbing supplies and phased out lead in gasoline, lead levels in children's blood dropped over 80 percent.[13]

Despite such successes, several problems get in the way of a realistic assessment of the effect and desirability of government programs. It is extremely difficult to calculate the return on such investments. Profit and loss statements may be inadequate or nonexistent. Evaluative research requires complicated and expensive long-range studies. Successful programs often reach a limited proportion of the appropriate target group. They, therefore, do not create a visible impact on the overall problem, leading critics to contend that the program failed. A particular program might be successful, but societal conditions may change, worsening the original situation and obscuring any good results. Social programs often face rapid expansion or cuts in funding, which lead to modifications that damage the original successful design. Social programs also suffer in comparison to more traditional government responsibilities. Evaluation of social efforts often differs from that of military programs. When a military test rocket explodes, the scientists concentrate on the technical malfunction and how to prepare for the next endeavor. When a social program runs into problems, critics attack its basic validity, and the program faces a high likelihood of being shut down.

Furthermore, governments often take responsibility for policies and actions that, while desirable for the nation as a whole, adversely affect some businesses, states, communities or individuals. Tobacco companies do not want people to stop smoking. Some town managers prefer giving contracts only to "the good old boys," resenting any government requirements to seriously consider minority or female candidates or firms. Businesses tout the need for price increases because of government regulation, ignoring their own problems of mismanagement, poor judgments and soaring executive salaries and bonuses. Oddly enough, local people sometimes welcome the "intrusive" laws and regulations that provide them cover for taking needed or ethical actions. They can always blame shutting down a polluting industrial plant on "those Feds."

The issue here is not that government policies or workers cannot and should not be subject to criticism, performance evaluations or attention to improvement. The problem lies in holding the government responsible for inconsistencies in our national desires and conflicting goals among localities and groups. The government receives the blame both for interfering with the operation of private industry and for not protecting the public from harmful actions by industry. For example, both the public and the drug industry want the federal Food and

Drug Administration to approve new drugs more rapidly, but both blame the government if an inadequately tested drug hurts someone. We want our waste disposed of cheaply and safely, but not in our backyard. We want good schools but not the high property taxes needed to provide small class sizes.

Before September 11, who would have supported the federal government in hiring additional Federal Aviation Administration staff to monitor the security performance of the airlines? What would have been the airlines' response if the federal government had required them to spend more money to ensure that the private security firms paid, screened and supervised their workers more effectively? Anti-government sentiment obscures the issues and makes finding solutions more difficult. Given our complex society, government actions necessarily will be controversial, and any action will be disliked by many. No one wants children to lack dental care or be hungry, but many object to raising the minimum wage or increasing funds for school lunches. In a climate of distrust of government effectiveness, providing money for programs can seem pointless. Yet private industry cannot provide the same services. While corporations, for instance, may occasionally give a tax-deductible contribution of a few books or computers to a special program, they do not have an ongoing mission to make sure that every child in the country has access to the best learning tools. Private firms can, and are, contributing to solving specific family and community problems. But to expect them to resolve complex and often controversial issues on a massive scale, and to the possible detriment of their profits, remains wishful thinking.

Volunteers and the Nonprofit Sector: Myths and Realities

If private industry will not and government should not provide substantial assistance to families and communities, can volunteers, religious institutions, community-based organizations, and the nonprofit sector provide solutions to problems faced today by many families and communities? Yes and no. Volunteers contribute immense resources, knowledge, skills, creativity, and vision. Dedicated individuals and groups have created many successful social programs. Their efforts build community networks and pride.

According to political scientist Robert Putnam, however, volunteers have been switching from community projects to one-on-one service.[14] Such volunteering helps individuals but it will not build widespread community bonds, increase community capacity, or lead to institutional change or substantial amounts of additional funding. Moreover, volunteers cannot provide the level of assistance needed when, for example, the frail mother of an employed woman needs twenty-four-hour-a-day attention.

If individual volunteer efforts are necessary but not sufficient, are non-profit organizations the answer? Nonprofits create and operate many excellent programs. They monitor the activities and policies of business and all levels of government. They serve as an important balance, an independent voice, a place for average citizens to contribute and help create community pride and networks. But here again, myths prevail. Most such organizations are small, with little or no staff. Although they might be considered to reflect true grassroots activism, their contributions, while valuable, remain limited. Often nonprofits spend inordinate amounts of time scrambling for enough money and volunteers to keep their doors open.

Many nonprofits, especially the larger ones, do not fit the idealized model of indigenous grassroots organizations with volunteers stepping forth to meet locally identified concerns. Often they consist of local branches of national or international organizations with offices and lobbyists in Washington, D.C., and New York, considerable staff, and large budgets. A quick glance at the social service organizations listed in the telephone book's Yellow Pages shows a number of such groups including the American Cancer Society, Catholic Charities, Boys & Girls Club, Special Olympics, March of Dimes, the YWCA, the NAACP, and the Urban League.

These organizations may provide excellent services, but their own self-serving or parochial agendas might not be the best fit for a community. Like business and government agencies, nonprofit and charitable organizations can also make mistakes, continue programs that are no longer successful, and follow misguided priorities. Many Americans, for example, expressed concern about the way the American Red Cross initially handled the donations that poured in for the September 11 victims and their families. As sociologist Xavier de Souza Briggs aptly points out, "'nonprofit' is an indicator of tax status, not of sainthood."[15]

Some community organizations and Community Development Corporations (CDCs) have successfully undertaken difficult projects, especially in providing low- and moderate-income housing. To a large extent, however, the efforts of community development organizations have depended directly or indirectly on government funding and continue to do so.[16] CDCs cannot rely on the private market to finance such projects, since serving distressed neighborhoods or lower income people is not sufficiently profitable to attract the private housing market.

Many of the most successful CDCs grew out of the programs and philosophy of the Great Society of the 1960s and have relied heavily on federal funding, training and technical assistance. To cite only one example, during one two-year period in the mid-1980s, the Economic Development Administration (EDA) of the U.S. Department of Commerce granted approximately one million dollars to national organizations that provided technical assistance and training to local and state neighborhood groups.[17] One national recipient organization, later a major player in community-based efforts, probably would have gone under in the mid-1980s without the EDA's support.

Another problem with depending only on volunteers and nonprofit organizations consists of scale. Lisbeth Schorr's *Common Purpose: Strengthening*

Families and Neighborhoods to Rebuild America provides a brilliant analysis of the difficulties of adopting a successful grassroots program as a national solution. Successful local efforts too often rely upon a dedicated, charismatic individual or unique local circumstances. Efforts to expand or duplicate such programs frequently try to cut costs and fail to consider carefully the specific ingredients that made the original effort a good one.[18]

Religious Institutions: Myths and Realities

Another approach to social problems proclaimed by politicians and on media talk shows advocates a return to religion and a reliance upon religious institutions for solutions. Careful consideration of this approach reveals complex issues not easily resolved. Concerns about the appropriate role of religion in America range from advocates for ironclad separation of religion and state to those who blame all of society's problems on the reduced role of religious institutions, lack of prayer in school, or government indifference or hostility to religion.

Given the diversity of religions as well as these differing views, those advocating a greater dependence upon religious institutions for transforming American families and community life need to consider carefully how our diverse religious institutions can support the various types of families that exist today. How can religion unify rather than divide neighborhoods and communities? While searching for a neutral place to bring together fractious people and institutions in a Midwestern town of 30,000, the author heard with dismay, "Don't hold the meeting at any of the churches. People from one congregation won't come to a meeting at another church." Thus, emphasis on religion may divide communities rather than offer a way to bring people together to solve problems.

To a large extent membership in religious institutions reflects other forms of local and national separation, since people of different racial and ethnic backgrounds and levels of wealth tend to worship with others like themselves. Religious institutions played major roles in the Civil Rights movement, yet it has been said that the most segregated hour in the week occurs during Sunday morning church services. Churches and other religious institutions may, therefore, not be the best vehicle for building community or providing social services. Recently megachurches have arisen with congregations numbering in the thousands. While they provide a variety of activities and social services for their members, they may not serve families outside of their own congregations or contribute to greater community coherence.

Some religious institutions, however, do undertake projects for the wider community. They have built elderly and low-income housing and operated soup kitchens. Some religious institutions, realizing that they were attacking symptoms and not the problem, have lobbied for basic social change. In Baltimore, Maryland, the living wage movement was sparked by religious leaders who noticed an increase in employed persons using their soup kitchens. A prominent rabbi and the bishops of the Episcopal and Methodist churches wrote a newspaper article urging that "employees are paid enough to support themselves and their families in basic dignity."[19]

On the other hand, certain religious institutions and their spokesmen have blamed the problems of society on women who do not accept the moral authority of their husbands. Several days after the September 11 terrorist attacks, Rev. Jerry Falwell blamed the feminists, homosexuals, pagans, and others for creating the ungodly atmosphere that led to God's retribution.[20]

Many religions actively strive for converts and do not consider religious tolerance a virtue. Many nations have exhorted their soldiers to kill others in the name of God or to fight a Holy War.[21] Throughout history religious intolerance has resulted in vicious discrimination, mass murder, and wars. America has not been exempt from religious intolerance. At one point during the twentieth-century Catholics could not teach school in Iowa.[22] In the 1950s, Jews could not move into certain neighborhoods in suburban Washington, D.C.[23] American Muslims have suffered hostility and even physical attacks since September 11.

How can neighborhoods best tap into the values and teachings that underlie most major religions without further dividing their communities? Three different versions exist for the Ten Commandments: Jewish, Catholic, and Protestant. The wording of the Catholic and Protestant versions of the Lord's Prayer used to differ. A 2007 report estimates that there are 2.35 million Muslims nationwide.[24] How can we acknowledge and respect the beliefs of the followers of each religion? Simply recognizing the complexity of the question, the dangers of religious intolerance, the perils of forcing religious views on others, and the diversity of religious affiliations throughout the nation represents the first step. Each community must consider how each of its religious institutions can best contribute to all of the families in the area.

Each of these sectors, business, the government, nonprofit groups, and religious institutions, have important roles to play in supporting American families. Each affects the major tasks that families face in conducting their everyday tasks within their communities. Yet we cannot rely solely upon any of them to compensate for societal changes that have adversely affected our families and communities.

This chapter has focused on the complex issues involved in deciphering how our major national and local institutions contribute or detract from family well-being. Their actions impact what occurs in every community. In considering how communities respond to the challenges and opportunities presented by changing national conditions, we must understand how communities actually function. The next chapter addresses myths and realities about community.

Notes

1.   Food & Nutrition Service. (2004, October 26). *Food Stamp Program participation and costs: Data as of October 21, 2004).* U.S. Department of Agriculture. Retrieved

November 19, 2004, from http://www.fns.usda.gov/pd/fssummar.htm. Nord, M., Andrews, M., & Carlson, S. (2003, October). *Household food security in the United States, 2002.* Section 3, *Use of food pantries and emergency kitchens.* United States Department of Agriculture, Economic Research Service. Retrieved November 9, 2004, from http://www.ers.usda.gov/Publicationsfanrr35/

2.   Boris, E. T. (1998, July). Myths about the nonprofit sector. *The Urban Institute: Charting civil society* (No. 4). Washington, DC: The Urban Institute.

3.   American Association of Fund-raising Counsel. (n.d.). *Giving USA 2004.* Table: 2003 contributions: $240.72 billion by type of recipient organization. Retrieved April 9, 2005, from http://www.givingusa.org/about/aafrc/index.cfm?pg=bytypeof67.html.

4.   Dresang, D (2002). *Public personnel management and public policy* (4th ed.). New York: Addison Wesley Longman. Goodsell, C. T. (1994). *The case for bureaucracy* (3rd ed.). Chatham, NJ: Chatham House. Freund, W. C., & Epstein, E. (1984). *People and Productivity.* Homewood, IL: Dow Jones-Irwin.

5.   United States Congress (1862). *Congressional Globe, Senate, 37th Congress, 2nd session, no. 165,* Wednesday, June 11, 1862, and *Congressional Globe, House of Representatives, 37th Congress, 2nd session, no. 170,* Thursday, June 19, 1862. Retrieved November 10, 2006, from http://memory.loc.gov/ammem/amlaw/lwcg.html.

6.   Graham, S. (2005, September 12). *Cities Under Siege: Katrina and the Politics of Metropolitan America.* An essay commissioned by the Social Science Research Council, in Understanding Katrina: Perspectives from the Social Sciences. Retrieved November 29, 2006 from http://understandingkatrina.ssrc.org/Graham/

7.   Personal recollection of author.

8.   United States Department of Health & Human Services. (2002, July 31). *HHS role in child support enforcement.* Retrieved from http://www.hhs.gov/news/press/2002/pres/cse.html.

9.   Charitable giving reaches $212 billion: Giving USA annual report for 2001 shows mixed results in year of recession and crisis. (2002, June 20). *American Association of Fund Raising Counsel Press Release.* Retrieved December 25, 2002, from http://www.aafrc.org/press3.html.

10. *2006 Thanksgiving weekend travel projections.* About.com: Chicago. Retrieved January 23, 2007, from http://chicago.about.com. Retrieved January 23, 2007, from http://chicago.about.com/od/thanksgiving/a/111806_thanks.htm

11. Rose, S. J. (2000). *Social stratification in the United States: The new American profile poster* (Rev. and updated ed. New York: The New Press.

12. Devaney, B., Bilheimer, L., & Schore, J. (1991, April). The savings in Medicaid costs for newborns and their mothers from prenatal participation in the WIC program (Vol. 2). *United States Department of Agriculture, Food and Nutrition Service, Office of Analysis and Evaluation.* Retrieved from www.fns.usda.gov/oane/MENU/Published/WIC/FILES/SavVol2-pt7.pdf.

13. HHS helps in efforts to eliminate childhood lead poisoning. (2002, March 4). *United States Department of Health & Human Services.* Retrieved February 12, 2003, from http://www.hhs.gov/news/press/2002pres/lead.html.

14. Putnam, R. B. (2001). *Bowling alone: The collapse and revival of American community* (p. 128). New York: Simon & Schuster.

15. Briggs, X. de S. (2000, September 27). *Community building: The new (and old) politics of urban problem-solving in the new century.* Public address at the Second Annual Robert C. Wood Visiting Professorship in Public and Urban Affairs, University of Massachusetts/Boston.

16. Stoutland, S. E. (1999). *Community Development Corporations: Mission, strategy and accomplishments.* In R. F. Ferguson & W. T. Dickens (Eds.). *Urban problems*

and community development (pp.193-240, especially p.206). Washington DC: Brookings Institution Press.

17. At the time the author was directing EDA's Technical Assistance Program.
18. Schorr, L. B. (1997). *Common purpose: Strengthening families and neighborhoods to rebuild America* (especially Chapter Two, Spreading what works beyond the hothouse). New York: Anchor Books, Doubleday.
19. Pollin, R., & Luce, S. (1998). *The living wage: Building a fair economy* (p. 9). New York: The New Press.
20. Kahn, C. (2001, September 15). Falwell blames gays, feminists for attacks. *Wisconsin State Journal.*
21. This section was written months before September 11.
22. Family history of author.
23. Personal recollection of author.
24. Pew Research Center. (2007, May 22). Muslim *Americans: Middle class and mostly mainstream.* pp.9-10. Washington, DC: Pew Research Center. Retrieved September 25, 2007 from http://pewresearch.org/assets/pdf/muslim-americans.pdf

4

Communities and Neighborhoods:
Myths and Realities

Despite changes in American society, place-based communities and neighborhoods continue to exist, most even thrive. But myths hinder our ability to address problems and foster more family-friendly communities. After a brief comment on why place-based communities matter, we will examine the global changes that have affected our communities and myths about the nature of communities. We then describe crucial tasks that successful communities must accomplish.

Continued Relevance of the Place-Based Community

Neighborhoods still remain important for children, regardless of what tasks have been taken over by other institutions or have moved to other geographic locations. Do gangs control a child's ability to walk to the store safely? Do older residents comment on the figures of young girls who are waiting for the bus? Do adults condone, use, or encourage racial slurs? Are there places where children of different ages can meet their friends for varied activities or are meeting places limited to tot lots for preschoolers? Do children have an opportunity to become acquainted with adults of a variety of ages, occupations, interests, and racial and ethnic backgrounds, preparing them to live in a diverse country where everyone they meet will not be carbon copies of their parents? Can adults establish common standards of community behavior? Do they feel comfortable taking responsibility for helping neighborhood children who are in trouble or correcting those who clearly are misbehaving? Do persons working in the neighborhood take similar responsibility? Do the norms of the neighborhood support such interventions or will they likely result in arguments and hostility?

Whatever their interactions with neighbors, all individuals are affected by the environment, institutions, and services of the area where they live. Pollution, the quality of the stores, and police responsiveness impact all residents. The physical space, including such aspects as heavy traffic or beautiful old elm trees, can affect people's psychological identification with an area. Lovely outdoor space, sidewalks, and nearby stores encourage people to walk, to smile and say hello, to chat with their neighbors. The places people love, and in some cases have loved for centuries, display attractive notable physical features: the wide, tree-lined streets and monuments of Washington, D.C.; the sweeping skyline and lakefront parks of Chicago; the outdoor cafés in Paris; the temple gardens in Kyoto. By contrast, people's first thoughts about places such as Los Angeles may be smog and bumper-to-bumper traffic.

All neighborhoods perform several basic tasks. They provide residents with housing, a place to rear children, a setting for social relations. They serve as a delivery point for a variety of social, economic, and political services. While some of these services can be performed elsewhere, the neighborhood often offers the most logical and convenient place.

Rarely do people mean exactly the same thing when they say "neighborhood" or "community." When asked to describe their neighborhood, people's answers vary from talking about their block to mentioning an area as large as some towns. The Hyde Park-Kenwood neighborhood in Chicago, for example, has a population of over 50,000, above the national standard for classification as a metropolitan area. Yet it has maintained its identity as a community for over forty years despite significant challenges. This chapter uses the terms neighborhood and community interchangeably. Readers should consider carefully how the ideas apply to the geographic area of their concern. Some aspects of community life, such as whether people treat neighbors in a friendly fashion, affect residents regardless of whether they live in rural small towns, older suburbs, newly planned developments, small cities, large cities, areas of rapid development around small towns or what has been called an "edge city." The latter term describes large new developments which have sprung up rapidly around concentrations of office and retail space, often in areas with little or no previous development.[1] Some comments will be more relevant for large city neighborhoods than for new developments, although older suburbs, small towns and outlying areas now face many issues formerly thought to affect only central cities. Every American community, however, has been and continues to be affected by certain national trends, leading many to bemoan the decline of community.

Is Community Dead?

Local community autonomy and cohesion has been declining for over a hundred years with: (1) a greater division of labor; (2) closer ties between local institutions and the larger society; (3) bureaucratization; (4) urbanization and suburbanization; (5) changing values; and (6) the transfer of tasks formerly provided by families and neighbors to profit enterprises, government, or the nonprofit sector.[2] The end of the twentieth century saw the growth of the global economy, the Internet, and an accelerating rate of change and speed of information flow, all exacerbating these trends.

Roland Warren distinguished between the community's vertical and horizontal patterns. Vertical patterns consist of the relationships between a community or individuals and non-local institutions or influences. The horizontal patterns consist of the relationships among locally based individuals, organizations and institutions.[3] A neighborhood police officer and the director of a recreation program in a neighborhood might have a relationship with each other (horizontal), but each probably has stronger (vertical) ties to the city or private organization that hired them and to the state and national organizations that set the standards for their professions. Neighborhood stores, for example, now increasingly operate as subunits of national, even international, corporations.

Social capital describes the advantages gained by individuals and communities through sharing a feeling of belonging and through enjoying the emotional and practical support often provided by people who interact regularly. Such capital includes the relationships among individuals and within groups. It creates a glue enhancing individual and community life, and it preserves the social cohesiveness and the trust that enable communities to function well. In his book, *Bowling Alone*, Robert Putnam cites numerous statistics in support of his claim that social capital has declined sharply since the 1950s.[4]

According to Putnam, Americans today are less likely to participate in almost all forms of organizational and informal social interaction that create social capital. They visit neighbors less, belong to fewer bridge clubs or bowling leagues, attend church less frequently and drive to work alone rather than in car pools. They see friends less often, talk less frequently to their children, and are less likely to take a family vacation.[5]

Putnam analyzes a range of possible causes for this decline. He eliminates changes in the family composition since while getting married and having children often increases participation in youth-related and church activities, it decreases membership in other organizations and informal socializing with friends and neighbors.[6]

Capitalism per se cannot be blamed for the decline in social capital. America has epitomized market capitalism for over two centuries, during which time marked swings in social capital and civic activity have occurred. Since local business leaders often played major roles in community life, could the recent trend toward global corporations have affected local involvement? Putnam cites this example: "'Where are the power elite when you need them?'" one Boston developer asked, complaining, "'They're all off at corporate headquarters in some other state.'"[7] While this statement may reflect an increase in the intensity of the movement of businesses from local to national orientation and control, the trend is not new and was well underway before the middle of the twentieth century.[8] Furthermore, as Putnam asks, how could changes in business ownership explain either the reduction in voting at the local level or the amount of casual socializing such as having friends over to play poker? [9]

The downward trend of social capital cannot be attributed to big government or the growth of the welfare state either. The amount of federal domestic spending as a percentage of Gross National Product has not varied substantially since the late 1940s, and the size of federal domestic spending in relation to state and local spending has remained constant for the past twenty-five years. Furthermore, variations in social capital among political jurisdictions do not correspond to differences in either government size or welfare spending. Putnam also dismisses crime, fear of crime, and the decline in church attendance as causes since some states with high social capital have low church attendance and vice versa.[10]

What then does account for the loss? According to Putnam, approximately one-half of the decreased participation represents a generational shift. People born after 1940 are substantially less likely to participate in civic and social activities than their parents and grandparents.[11] Twenty-five percent of the decline results from people staying at home to watch television. Putnam attributes 20 percent of the loss to time pressures and increased commuting. He calculates that each additional ten minutes spent commuting reduces civic involvement by 10 percent. The reduction affects not only the commuters but also other area residents.[12]

Putnam notes some exceptions. Volunteering has increased among the generation over sixty, reflecting an increase in free time among retirees. Another exception, involvement in the evangelical churches shows an increase in bonding among its own members. Putnam found, however, that these churches, as well as their individual members, are the least likely to reach out to people outside of their own congregations.[13]

Other analysts have found only minor shifts in informal socializing with friends and neighbors. They point out that Putnam ignores new forms of social organization such as soccer clubs, environmental groups, professional associations, exercising regularly with the same people, social activism, or a wide variety of support groups such as those for widows or people facing specific health crises.[14] A recent study, however, found that Americans are significantly more socially isolated than twenty years ago.[15] The issue here is not to debate the extent of social capital loss, but to note that a loss or increase in such capital can affect a neighborhood's ability to support its families.

A danger exists in assuming that all of today's ills result from a loss of social capital or could be resolved by increasing informal social networks. The decline of labor unions, for example, may be important in terms of loss of camaraderie among union members, but it is far more significant in terms of lower wage rates. Our ability to address changes in social capital or other aspects of community requires dispelling myths about the nature of a good community. Simply attributing today's problems on a loss of community social capital can reflect a reliance on myths about the nature of our communities.

Myth One: *It's a Wonderful Life*

Millions of Americans view the movie *It's a Wonderful Life* every Christmas, enthralled when the community mobilizes to repay years of kindness by a small town banker who gets into trouble from bending the rules on their behalf. The hero, played by Jimmy Stewart, portrays admirable traits of loyalty, self-sacrifice, and modesty. The town responds by looking after its own.

Many Americans long nostalgically for such a community, just as many savor the image of an ideal family holiday dinner, forgetting the tension that often accompanies large family gatherings. The reality of small-town life includes problems and conflicts, as well as desirable aspects, but the alluring myths remain. In 1929, planner Clarence Perry incorporated this ideal into his neighborhood unit plan, describing an ideal neighborhood where people could walk to school and shops over pleasant paths. Despite Americans' love of the automobile, this image has been extolled by many planners since then. Developers of the new towns of Columbia, Maryland, and Reston, Virginia, used the concept. Recently it reemerged as part of the recommendations of the New Urbanism, Neo-traditionalism, and Smart Growth advocates.[16]

Myth Two: Home as Haven

Stephanie Coontz's label for post-World War II suburbs, "Home as Haven," reflects her analysis of the unique situation of the American family during the 1950s with the development of suburbs focused on family living. Such areas reflected a glorification of the husband as provider, the wife as homemaker, the friendliness of neighbors, and the importance of children.[17] Suburbs, however, generally differ significantly from rural small towns. They tend to separate homes from places of employment and to house together people of similar incomes, race, ethnicity, and stage of family formation. Children can grow up without ever seeing a child of another race or ethnic group in their neighborhood or school. Indeed, one suburban child visiting a city during World War II asked, "Mother, when the war is over, will all the colored people go back to their own country?"

Myth Three: The Urban Villager

In his 1962 book, *The Urban Villager*, Herbert Gans documented the existence of an enclave of Italians within Boston whose life style reflected that of a European village.[18] The residents' lives focused on relationships among an extended group of siblings, aunts, uncles, and cousins. Most members of the community knew each other well, attended the same church, and frequented the same bars, corner grocery store and other local institutions. They liked the area in which they lived and their way of life. They treated the streets and local institutions as extensions of their homes: places to meet friends, gossip, and keep in touch with each other. Today, neighborhoods housing new immigrants may reflect similar characteristics.

Barry Wellman referred to such areas as "Community Saved." Living in a "saved" community can provide many advantages, but it also can stifle ambition of young people determined to obtain more education than desired by their classmates.[19] Daily contact can highlight the differences in child rearing practices between an immigrant parent and American-born daughter or daughter-in-law causing friction and tension. For example, Amy Tan's *The Joy Luck Club* poignantly portrays the joys but also the frictions among immigrant Chinese and their American-born children.[20]

Identification with saved communities may not reflect a positive attachment but an adoption of the insidious label given to the neighborhood by the press, government officials, or realtors. Often such communities continue not because their residents feel reluctant to leave friends and family, but because discrimination and lack of low and moderate income housing elsewhere make leaving impossible.

Myth Four: Love that Internet

Some scholars define community in terms of "networks of interpersonal ties that provide sociability, support, information, a sense of belonging, and social identity."[21] People form such communities of like-minded people regardless of where they live. They participate in far-flung academic research collaborations, serve on boards of national organizations, visit remote Pacific islands with fellow scuba divers, and maintain multiple friendships via telephone, facsimile and the Internet.

Internet contacts can consume more time and grow more meaningful than relationships with neighbors or even family. Howard Rheingold described important relationships he formed through on-line discussion groups. "During the past fourteen years I have attended three weddings of people who met in virtual communities...sat by the deathbeds of two people I never would have known if we had not connected through words on the screen...helped pass the hat when members of my virtual community fell on hard times."[22]

The ability of Internet networks to regulate behavior is likely to be limited. While computer exchanges among a group may enhance the intellectual understanding of a certain situation, the lack of social clues can make developing trust and consensus more difficult. The relative anonymity can invite frankness but also can increase rudeness and invective. The new technology may enhance existing community connections, but it may be less effective in building trust, commitment, reciprocity, or creating larger community bonds.

Steven Brint suggests that the often praised egalitarianism of Internet communities exists primarily because people can easily withdraw without significant penalty. Participants do not have to see each other on a frequent basis and can more easily ignore personality traits or behaviors that they may not like.[23]

Members of these virtual communities do not necessarily have any relationship to others who do not share their specialized interests. The "Love that Internet" approach, therefore, has limitations in providing a comprehensive understanding of community. Virtual communities lack the three traits that historically have been considered crucial for community: they do not necessarily involve families; they do not necessarily involve cooperative projects; and they do not involve a specific geographic area.

This does not imply that communities of interest lack importance in today's society. With the growth of the Internet and the use of cell phones, such connections will become more common and reach around the world. Such communities, however, may not represent a community at all but an interest group. They might more accurately be called subcultures.[24]

The rapid use of the Internet still does not involve all members of a geographic area or the overall society. The digital divide exists with lower Internet use by older persons, those living in rural areas and those with lower incomes or less education. In 2000, only 40 percent of American households had someone using the Internet at home, and 80 percent of the households with incomes below $25,000 lacked Internet access.[25] Those with lower education are less likely to hold jobs that provide computer access or knowledgeable colleagues to help them learn computer skills. Moreover, the content of Internet documents generally is written for English speakers with an average or advanced literacy level. Forty-four million adult Americans do not have this level of reading skill, and 32 million do not use English as their primary language.[26]

The full impact of the Internet remains to be seen. Some research suggests that heavy users of computers may isolate themselves from their families and friends, that people depending upon Internet friendships can actually experience increased rates of loneliness. However, Wellman and others have found that the Internet increases the contact among family and friends, and that Internet contacts supplement rather than supplant existing relationships.[27]

A number of neighborhoods currently are exploring ways to connect their residents through e-mail and listservs using the new technology to enhance more traditional types of relationships. Keith Hampton and Wellman found that in a wired community the contacts among neighbors increased.[28]

Space—Social and Psychological Involvement

Virtual connections have their limits. Certain tasks must be performed by someone physically present. Only neighbors can snatch a child from the path of a speeding car or provide a safe place for a child to go if a parent is late getting home from work. Neighbors watch over houses when people are on vacation. The willingness of neighbors to report crime affects the area's crime rate. Neighbors often become aware of and report child abuse or domestic violence. Successful neighborhoods manage their physical environment, creating a sense of place and a psychological identification with their geographic area. They promote positive social contacts among residents, maintain economic viability, build strong organizations and exercise political clout.

Psychological identification—a sense of belonging to this particular space—can be enhanced by clear boundaries, by actions of residents and by the rhetoric and actions of politicians and administrators. A community organization can undertake activities that promote such identification and develop an area's social capital. Many communities have created a positive identification with the neighborhood by working together on specific tasks.

Even casual interactions with neighbors and people passing by on the street affect feelings of safety, belonging, and whether a person is likely to "have a happy day" or arrive at work angry from an unpleasant encounter. The author recalls reading a newspaper article reporting on the "retirement" of a man who for decades had stood on his lawn each morning waving and saying "good morning" to everyone who passed. When he announced that he intended to stop this daily ritual, hundreds of people reported how important his daily greetings had been to them, especially during their childhood. His simple act had an astonishing impact on the neighborhood environment.

Managing the local physical environment ranges from picking up papers in the park to lobbying to prevent a highway from bisecting the neighborhood. It requires everyday actions by all, or at least most, residents. Walking in the winter on sidewalks in northern neighborhoods remains safe only if everyone shovels the snow. Beauty prevails only if everyone throws their trash into trash baskets rather than tossing it on the sidewalk, if all homeowners and landlords maintain their buildings, and if flowers bloom in numerous yards or balconies. Residents in a lower income area when asked about its assets noted its attractiveness and beauty, responding, "That woman over there, she always has beautiful flowers." Over forty years later, the author recalls with fondness the houses on her route to school that had the weeping cherry tree, the crocuses, and the forsythia in their yards.

Having services nearby can help reduce the stress of household maintenance. A grocery store, a park, a place to jog, a facility to rent for a wedding, anniversary party, or a support group meeting can enhance employed adults' abilities to balance work, child rearing, exercise, and social life. For those without cars, neighborhood-based services may be the only ones available. Even when public transportation exists, expense may make frequent trips costly. Transferring from one bus to another makes trips difficult, especially if travel involves managing young children while waiting for a bus in zero degree weather in Iowa or sweltering in the summer heat of Texas.

Neighborhood location of services may be the best way to insure that people actually use them. If people have limited mobility, funds, or speak English poorly, tapping into the resources of the larger community often proves overwhelming. Community centers throughout the nation provide services ranging from teen drop-in centers to alcohol and drug treatment programs. They often house offices of neighborhood organizations.

In the mid-1990s the Allied-Dunn's Marsh Neighborhood Center in Madison, Wisconsin, for example, provided space for two neighborhood associations and some fifteen other organizations, serving approximately one out of every six neighborhood residents. At one point an outreach team included a white middle-aged woman, an older black man, a college-aged Hmong male youth, an older black woman, a middle-aged white male, and an older Cambodian man. Activities varied from blood pressure checks by the public health nurse to a Cambodian dance group. Although in traditional Hmong society women socialize only within their households, husbands in this neighborhood permitted their wives to take English classes at the center, providing some exposure to American life. When a local hospital wanted to reduce the number of people being treated in their emergency room, they asked the center to help them develop neighborhood-based preventive services.

Economic Tasks

Even though local communities and neighborhoods have become a part of the global economy, they still must rely on local economic strength to maintain an adequate quality of community and family life. Any neighborhood needs: (1) an economic base sufficient to support local services, organizations and institutions; (2) access to credit for building or maintaining housing; (3) sufficient economic clout to obtain appropriate services from city and county officials and other external organizations; (4) jobs within the neighborhood and adequate transportation to those jobs or to jobs elsewhere; and (5) the ability to capture the economic benefits of neighborhood assets and spending.

Fewer employees now live near their workplace, increasing commuting time and lessening the opportunities to socialize outside of work or to know each other's families. Local business people are less likely to know or befriend neighborhood children. Without an economic base, businesses needed by residents will not flourish. The neighborhood loses jobs, convenient services and sources of financial and leadership contributions for neighborhood programs.

Too often the economic benefits of local firms revert to absentee owners or stockholders rather than being reinvested in the neighborhood. With suburbanization, the tax base for many older cities disappeared, a problem now being faced by the older suburbs as firms move still further out.

In addition to having funds to buy desired services, economic power can also mean having extensive influential networks that provide access to business and political officials. Large political contributions from people in a neighborhood may not buy a politician's vote, but they probably ensure access to the politician or his staff.

Political Tasks

Neighborhoods and local communities have four political tasks: (1) creating psychological identification; (2) establishing internal control; (3) exerting external clout; and (4) creating and maintaining structures for building cohesion, settling disputes, making decisions, and mobilizing action. Some neighborhoods have individuals and organizations skilled at mediating community disagreements and conflicts. They can create an atmosphere of trust and support for those interested in improving community life and organize forums where disagreements can be aired and community consensus developed. Other communities squabble over every decision, gossip about and back-bite whomever steps forward to attempt leadership. Neighborhoods need the ability to set and enforce norms for behavior for residents and for outsiders who come for business, pleasure or merely pass through. Effective communities can set, or at least influence and monitor, standards of behavior for police officers, school teachers and others delivering services or working for neighborhood institutions.

Creating psychological identification both creates and results from residents' willingness to pay attention to the physical maintenance of their area and to engage in positive social relationships and community activities. The ability to control local behavior varies. In urban village neighborhoods, behavior is controlled through scrutiny by family, friends and neighbors. Sociologist Gerald Suttles discusses "Defended Space," the ability of some inner-city gangs to restrict access to their neighborhood by members of different gangs or those of a different racial or ethnic group.[29] Analysts from Jane Jacobs and Oscar Newman to proponents of the New Urbanism have stressed the importance of the physical arrangements of buildings, streets and other spaces in a manner that provides "eyes on the street" as people walk by or observe others from their porches or windows.[30]

Another approach to behavior control has been the creation of homogeneous communities. During the first half of the twentieth century, until stopped by a Supreme Court decision, builders used restrictive covenants attached to land sales to insure that no Jews or African Americans would move into certain neighborhoods. Suburban tracts often sell houses in the same price range with the same number of bedrooms, resulting in purchase by families with similar incomes and family compositions. The assumption is that they will exhibit similar behavior characteristics.

The end of the century saw a marked increase in planned unit developments, cooperatives, condominiums, and gated communities. Their sales deeds establish rules to insure conformity with certain community standards and create associations that manage the common property, such as the swimming pools and the elevators. The associations can issue rules governing such aspects of design as the type and color of window shades and even for such private behaviors as the ownership of cats. Some communities are designed to house and provide services for seniors and can prohibit children from living there. In certain developments, anyone entering must stop at a gate for clearance by a guard. Interestingly, some of these protective restrictions apply to populations at opposite ends of the economic scale: residents of public housing as well as those in affluent areas.

As will be discussed later, many neighborhoods have turned to an alternative approach, community organization. Such organizations can take action to eliminate destructive street behavior, to create desirable community assets and to foster cohesion.

The population base needed for a community to adequately handle its various tasks depends upon the size of the area, the ages and family composition of the residents, the available business and institutional resources, and the area's organizational structure and abilities. A small suburban residential tract may be a good place to raise children but does not provide its residents with varied job opportunities. An area performing all the neighborhood roles described above might require a population between 50,000 and 100,000, the same population as a moderate-sized city.

New Trends in Thinking about Community

Some of those concerned with the interrelationships of environment, poverty, and the quality of life have articulated a vision for a sustainable community. Various versions exist, developed by international bodies as well as government agencies and local communities. Basically, the sustainable community approach rests on the assumptions that: the resources of the earth remain finite and must be preserved; present policies and actions of individuals, businesses and governments cannot be sustained indefinitely; economic development can and must be coordinated with environmental preservation; the problems of the poor must be addressed; economic growth can be sustained in a manner that does not harm the environment and distributes resources more equitably; and people should be involved in the decision-making about their communities.[31]

One of the key tenets of this movement focuses attention on long-term rather than immediate results. The American Planning Association's *A Planners Guide to Sustainable Development* includes a quotation from the law of the Iroquois, "In our every deliberation, we must consider the impact of our decisions on the next seven generations."[32] The author remembers being awed by the several-hundred-year-old moss in an exquisite garden in Japan. At another garden with beautiful vistas, a guide explained that gardeners had based the location of the trees according to what they would look like in 300 years.

Confusion about priorities can result partly from different time perspectives. During the Depression of the 1930s when President Franklin D. Roosevelt was developing programs to help unemployed workers, one aide commented that an alternative program would be more effective in the long run. Another aide snapped, "'People don't eat in the long run. They eat every day.'"[33]

Activists at the Allied-Dunn's Marsh Neighborhood Center displayed similar differences in their concerns. Mary focused on families who needed food that afternoon, Joan stressed programs that would produce results in three months to three years, and Bob looked farther ahead, at the three generations he felt would be needed before the last effects of the trauma suffered by the Cambodian immigrants from the Vietnam War would be eliminated.

Although this book shares the assumptions and philosophical orientation of the sustainable community efforts, it takes a narrower focus and considers a shorter time frame. Both short- and long-run approaches are needed.

Conclusions

Strong local communities and neighborhoods continue to remain vital as the settings for family life. Considering national trends which have affected local life and the various concepts about community can help to focus attention on the different meanings of community. Regardless of the type of community, successful ones manage their physical and social environments. In part 2 we examine the role local communities and neighborhoods play in helping families meet their six basic responsibilities: earning an income, providing food, housing, and health care for their members, maintaining a home and caring for children. Chapter 7 discusses community-building activities. Additional specific examples of how local areas have assisted families with each of the six tasks are contained in the *Community Action Guide* (see Author's Note, pp. xv-xvi).

The ability to provide an effective environment and support families in accomplishing their own responsibilities also depends upon how a neighborhood addresses issues of diversity, how it addresses the varied social relationships in the area, and whether it can create and maintain effective organizations. The next three chapters address these issues.

Notes

1. Garreau, J. (1991). *Edge city: Life on the new frontier.* New York: Doubleday. Lewis, J. (2002, May). *Exploring edge cities: Report of a national survey of senior planners.* Chicago: Roosevelt University Institute for Metropolitan Affairs. Retrieved October 2, 2007, from http://roosevelt.edu/ima/pdfs/edge-city.pdf.
2. Warren, R. (1978). *The community in America* (3rd ed.). Chicago: Rand McNally.
3. Ibid.
4. Putnam, R. D. (2000). *Bowling alone: The collapse and revival of American community.* New York: Simon & Schuster.
5. Ibid., pp. 62-63, 72, 93-115, 212.
6. Ibid., p 278.
7. Heying, C. (1997). Civic elites and corporate delocalization: An alternative explanation for declining civic engagement. In R. D. Putnam. (2000). *Bowling alone*, p. 283.
8. Stein, M. R. (1972). *The eclipse of community: An interpretation of American studies.* New Jersey: Princeton University Press.

9. Putnam, R. D. (2000). *Bowling alone*, p. 283.
10. Ibid., pp. 280-281, 309-312.
11. Ibid., pp.247-276.
12. Ibid., pp. 212-215, 283-284.
13. Ibid., pp. 77-78.
14. Fischer, C. S. (2001, August). *Bowling alone: What's the score?* Paper presented at the American Sociological Association, Anaheim, CA. Putnam, R., & Resnick, P. (2000, June 25). Closing the divide: Turning virtual communities into real ones. *Seattle Post-Intelligence.* Talbot, M. (2000, June 25).Who wants to be a legionnaire? *New York Times Book Review.* Wills, G. (2000, July 17). Putnam's America. *The American Prospect, 11*(16). Retrieved August 14, 2003, from http:/www.prospect. org/print/V11/16/wills-g.html.
15. McPherson, M., Smith-Lovin, L., & Brashers, M. E. (2006, June). Social Isolation in America: Changes in Core Discussion Networks over Two Decades. *American Sociological Review* 71: 353-375.
16. Perry, C. A. (1920).*Neighborhood and community planning.* New York:. Regional plan of New York and its environs. Wireman, P. (1976). *Meanings of community in modern America: Some implications from new towns.* Doctoral dissertation. American University. Wireman, P. (1984). *Urban neighborhoods, networks, and families: New forms for old values.* Lexington, MA: D.C. Heath and Company. Krizek, P., & Power, J. (1996). *A planner's guide to sustainable development.* Chicago: American Planning Association. Leccese, M., & McCormick, K. (Eds.).(1999). *Charter of new urbanism.* New York: McGraw-Hill. National Association of Home Builders. (1999). *Smart Growth: Building better places to live, work and play.* Washington, DC: Author. Retrieved from http://www.nahb.org/generic.aspx?genericContentID=384.
17. Coontz, S. (1992). *The way we never were: American families and the nostalgia trap.* New York: Basic Books.
18. Gans. H. J. (1962). *The urban villagers: Group and class in the life of Italian-Americans.* New York: Free Press.
19. Wellman, B. (1979). The community question: The intimate networks of East Yonkers. *American Journal of Sociology, 84,* 1201-1231.
20. Tan, A. (1989). *The joy luck club.* New York: Ivy Books.
21. Wellman, B. (2000, May). *Physical place and cyberspace: The rise of networked individualism.* Toronto: University of Toronto, Department of Sociology. Retrieved November 4, 2000, *from http://www.chass.utoronto.ca/~wellman/publications/individualism/article.html.*
22. Rheingold, H. (1998). Virtual communities. In F. Hesselbein, M. Goldsmith, R. Beckhard, & R. Schubert (Eds.). *The community of the future* (chapter 11) [Quotation on p. 117]. San Francisco, CA: Jossey-Bass Publishers.
23. Brint, S. (2001). Gemeinschaft revisited: A critique and reconstruction of the community concept. *Sociological Theory, 19*(1), 1-23.
24. I am indebted to Dr. Michael S. Wireman for this suggestion.
25. Newburger, E.C. (2001, September). Current Population Reports: *Home computers and Internet use in the United States.* Retrieved August 14, 2003, from http//www. census.gov/prod/2001pubs/p23-207.pdf.
26. Fong, E., Wellman, B., Kew, M., & Wilkes, R. (2001). *Correlates of the digital divide* (pp. 3, 4, 9). Toronto: University of Toronto, Department of Sociology. Retrieved August 14, 2003, from http://www.chass.utoronto.ca/~wellman/publications/digitaldivide/digital.report2d.pdf.
27. Wellman, B., Haase, A. Q. Witte, J., & Hampton, K. (2001, November). Does the Internet increase, decrease, or supplement social capital? Social networks, participa-

tion, and community commitment. *American Behavioral Scientist, 45*(3), 457-56. Wellman, B., & Haythornthwaite, C. (Eds.). (2002). *The Internet in everyday life.* Oxford: Blackwell Publishing.

28. Hampton, K. and Wellman, B. (2003, December). Neighboring in Netville: How the Internet supports community and social capital in a wired suburb. In *City & Community, 2*(4), 277-311.

29. Suttles, G. D. (1973). *The social construction of communities.* Chicago: The University of Chicago Press.

30. Jacobs, J. (1961). *The death and life of great American cities.* New York: Random House. Newman, O. (1996). *Creating defensible space.* Washington, DC: U.S. Department of Housing and Urban Development. Leccese, M., & McCormick, K. (Eds.). (1999). *Charter of new urbanism.* New York: McGraw-Hill.

31. Krizek, K. J., & Power, J. (1996). *A planning guide to sustainable development* (Planning Advisory Service Report No. 467). Chicago: American Planning Association.

32. Krizek, K. J., & Power, J. (1996). *A planning guide to sustainable development* (Planning Advisory Service Report No. 467). Chicago: American Planning Association.

33. Burns, J. M. (1956). *Roosevelt: The lion and the fox*, p. 196. New York: A Harvest Book, Harcourt, Brace, & World, Inc.

5

Neighborhood Relationships

"Good Fences Make Good Neighbors"
—Robert Frost, "Mending Wall"[1]

Myths about Neighborhood Relationships

What is a good neighbor? Is Robert Frost's poem *Mending Wall* correct? For some people living in a good neighborhood implies living near people who will become their close friends. But other possibilities exist. Most Americans probably assume that a good neighbor would provide a variety of small helpful services, such as taking in packages, watching over a child in an emergency, dropping off a pot of soup after a death in the family, calling the police if they see someone suspicious lurking nearby.

People both want and actually have many types of relationships with their neighbors. Some seek close friendships; others prefer privacy and strive to avoid intimacy. A variety of complicated personal factors influences people's desires. Neighborhoods often contain people representing both ends of a continuum of desired or actual neighborly relations.

Good neighbors do not have to be good friends. Years ago the author read a magazine article on the concept of good neighbors that described a woman's recollections of a former neighbor who regularly had helped her maneuver an awkward baby carriage up and down the apartment stairs. That kindness had been the two neighbors' only contact but remained a memorable one. Whether people perform such roles adequately depends upon a number of factors. These include personality, available time, and degree of comfort with neighbors of a different race or ethnicity. Interior and exterior design of buildings and the general atmosphere and expectations created in the community also can affect neighbors' relationships.

The myths about family and community addressed earlier embody assumptions about the type of relationships that exist in neighborhoods and communities. These assumptions range from fond memories of neighborhood childhood playmates to visions of indifference and alienation. One example of the latter occurred in 1964 when thirty-eight people in Queens, New York, heard Kitty

Genovese scream for help during the half hour it took her assailant to stab her to death, yet not one of them called the police until after she had died.[2] Separating myth from reality about the types of neighborly relationships that exist or are desired in a particular situation can open up creative thinking about how to strengthen relationships that can support families.

This chapter presents some insights into the range of relationships possible and the potential of each to contribute to neighborhood health and family support. Six possibilities are: stranger, friendly recognition, casual acquaintance, casual friend, friend, and kin. We then present two other types of relationships that can help bind communities together: close-knit relationships and intimate secondary relationships.

Types of Neighborhood Relationships

The Stranger

Strangers, by definition, are unknown to us. A variety of factors determine whether people in the neighborhood greet a stranger with a welcoming smile or fearfully avoid eye contact. Is the person wearing a uniform or driving a vehicle identifying him as providing a service such as a UPS delivery? Is the person walking a dog, or holding a child's hand? Is she working in a neighborhood store? How is he dressed? What gender, age, or race is the person?

In larger communities, strangers often pass by without notice. In some communities, residents eye every stranger with suspicion. Increasingly, developers build gated communities, often with full-time guards who prevent strangers from entering unless identified by a resident. Some public housing buildings in Milwaukee, Wisconsin, among other places, issue cards to residents, similar to those used in hotels, to restrict building entry to residents and their guests.

Friendly Recognition

Friendly recognition describes the type of relationship that develops among neighbors who ride the same bus to work every morning or people who regularly find themselves on the same elevator in an apartment building. People nod, smile, or perhaps engage in small talk. Sometimes, of course, they develop closer relationships. Friendly recognition plays an important role in community life, whether or not the participants become friends. Friendly recognition means, "I have seen you before. You are not a stranger. You belong here." More importantly, it usually means, "You will not harm me." In communities with significant amounts of racial or income diversity, such relationships spread comfort and confidence—the neighborhood provides safety and a friendly, comfortable atmosphere for daily living. This does not deny that in some cases or communities people respond with appropriate fear to some neighbors. Generally, however, friendly recognition relationships can reduce tension and help build positive community spirit. People more often ask questions of people they recognize, making such relationships a factor in spreading neighborhood news.

Friendly recognition relationships can develop in numerous ways. Any neighborhood project that promotes people coming together, especially on a regular basis, will do. The East Madison Community Center, in Madison, Wisconsin, hosted a monthly Sunday supper, attended regularly by approximately seventy people. Many communities sponsor urban gardening programs. The coordinator of a program in Cleveland some years ago remarked that in "a lot of areas people are afraid...[The garden] gives them an excuse [to talk to their neighbors]." A leader in another city commented that the community garden created a friendly atmosphere. "Even people just passing felt like stopping and talking to the gardeners." Such contacts help people to recognize that the person walking down the street is a neighbor, not an outsider.[3]

These relationships can play an especially important role in neighborhoods with race or class differences. In Chicago's Hyde Park-Kenwood neighborhood, residents of a middle-class, racially integrated, cooperative housing apartment complex shared a common back fence with lower income African American apartment dwellers, some of whom received welfare. One summer, residents of both groups met outdoors weekly to discuss painting the fence and other block issues. The group dispersed when winter came—there was no indoor place for public meetings, and the social distance between the residents gaped too widely for them to feel comfortable in each others' homes. Nevertheless, a year later residents still felt differently about their neighbors and more comfortable about living on their block because of the joint experience. When they met at the bus stop, they no longer met fearfully as strangers.

Casual Acquaintances

When people refer to a "casual acquaintance," they imply more involvement than merely recognizing someone from passing them frequently on the street or seeing them at a community meeting. The author, for example, sings in a large choir. While I recognize many of the choir members if I pass them on the street, I would only classify the few that I regularly stand next to and talk to at breaks as casual acquaintances. Obviously, individuals' definitions of "casual acquaintance" vary.

Casual acquaintances can contribute to healthy dynamics in a neighborhood. They aid the flow of neighborhood information. Someone active in neighborhood affairs may tap casual acquaintances for funds for a community project or ask them to volunteer. Such relationships can directly support individuals or families, especially as a source of information. One sociologist dubbed relationships between people who do not maintain regular contact or even know each other very well as "weak ties." In his study of middle-management men, Mark

Granovetter found weak ties to be more useful for finding jobs than the more intimate ties with family and friends.[4] Generally the men already were aware of the opportunities known by their family and friends; therefore, relationships with people they did not know produced more helpful new job leads. Weak ties can exist between once close friends who have lost touch, such as former classmates who meet at a reunion. Weak ties may include friends of friends with whom the individual has had no previous relationship. Granovetter cites the example of a man who obtained a job he had heard about through someone he met at a picnic, a friend of the person who had invited him.[5]

Even casual acquaintances can provide role models for children. A number of studies have shown that children often have negative images of the elderly.[6] Many children live far from grandparents and pick up negative messages about older persons from the media and adults. Children who have actual experience with older persons, whether their own grandparents or others, have more positive attitudes. Children also pick up negative messages from society about those of a different race or people who dress differently. From meeting only their parents' friends, children may conclude that the adult world consists only of people with lifestyles, attitudes and jobs similar to those of their parents. Through casual acquaintances, they may glimpse a larger world, peopled by a wide variety of individuals, families, and work possibilities.

Casual Friends

Casual acquaintances can grow into casual friends, people with whom to share occasional outings or activities. One large study of networks found that the number of companions a person had to share activities was more highly correlated with better moods than having someone with whom to discuss problems or from whom to obtain practical support.[7] Claude Fischer found that while people in cities do make friends within their neighborhoods, for the most part, the friendships lacked much intimacy. Fischer considered these friendships of convenience rather than commitment, suggesting that if one of the individuals moved, they would not maintain contact. They would be more likely to form another such limited friendship in their new neighborhood.[8]

Still, such relationships can be a vital part of social life. They offer single people friendly contact without necessarily leading to involvement. They provide parents an opportunity for adult conversation and recognition of adult status, apart from that of parent. Even if these friendships of convenience continue only until one party moves, they may provide important support for individuals and families.

Friends

Friends vary from those who border on casual acquaintances to those intimate enough to be considered family. Indeed, people often bestow fictitious family status on close family friends, calling them "Auntie" even though no blood or marital relation exists. Some people formalize such relations by inviting special friends to be godparents to their children.

Friends provide both childhood and adult intimacy, shared experiences, shared confidences. Friends celebrate triumphs, mourn losses. Long-term friends provide a benchmark for acknowledgment of growth, a sense of continuity. The author remembers visiting a friend shortly after her husband died. While we had been fairly close when working in the same town in Missouri, we had seen each other only occasionally after we all moved to Washington, D.C. I had known the couple during a period of difficulties in their relationship, witnessed their success in adopting a child, and one evening chatted with them during the husband's home dialysis. Since I had not seen them for some time and had learned about his sudden death several weeks after the funeral, I felt awkward visiting. Yet when I walked in, the new widow hugged me, exclaiming, "You knew us!" My presence provided a continuity and a history not available from her new friends.

Adult friends provide a means of sharing interests, intimacy and an identity that may never become fully expressed with family due to different tastes, lifestyles and values. How many people avoid "touchy" subjects at family gatherings, subjects that they would freely debate for hours with friends? Robert Putnam claims that informal socializing has declined significantly since the 1970s, with a 45 percent drop nationally in entertaining at home. These social contacts did not shift to restaurants or local bars, since the numbers of those establishments also dropped (with the telling exception of fast food places). Other scholars have suggested that changes have been far less drastic. Even according to Putnam, Americans continue to visit friends often, with one-third meeting friends during the previous week at their home for dinner, to play cards or enjoy some other activity.[9]

Friends often develop as a result of neighborhood contacts, particularly among children, parents with children of the same age, or those involved in neighborhood politics or programs. According to Putnam, however, socializing in neighborhoods has also declined. Spending a social evening within the neighborhood fell about one-third between 1974 and 1998. Nevertheless, according to his data, single people still spend an evening socializing with someone in their neighborhood nearly three times a month and married couples do so nearly twice a month.[10]

Kin

Many Americans live in the same neighborhood as their relatives. Even those who do not often live within easy visiting distance. Putnam notes that during the last quarter century Americans visited with relatives nearly every other week. In addition, people maintain contact with both relatives and friends through e-mail and the telephone. In 1998 two-thirds of American adults called a relative or friend the previous day simply to chat.[11]

Relatives, of course, may or may not be considered friends. Some relatives actually drain their family members in negative ways, ranging from interfering with their marital relationships or asking them for money to engaging in inappropriate sexual contact with a niece or cousin. For the most part, however, relatives, even those not counted as friends, provide three kinds of support. First, they offer a sense of the continuity of life, a connection with the past and with the future. They remember. They want to share reminiscences about your childhood, even those you would prefer to forget. They recognize your grandmother's china and the ornaments on your Christmas tree. They show up for holidays, weddings, and funerals, providing comfort and a sense of belonging.

Second, relatives provide help in a crisis. Eugene Litwak analyzed under what circumstances people relied upon friends, neighbors, and kin for support, and when they turned to formal institutions such as hospitals or social agencies. He found that despite twentieth-century changes in family composition and geographic distance between family members, people continue to rely on kin for tasks that require a long-term commitment or a permanent trust relationship. Thus, the elderly depend upon kin to handle finances, and people turn to kin, rather than even very close friends, to rear their children in case of death.[12] While friends might pitch in during a health problem lasting several weeks, such as an inability to drive due to a broken leg, Litwak found that for long-term health problems, people turned to their kin. They substitute modern means of communication and transportation for living nearby. They call; they send money; and they come.[13]

Finally, relatives provide alternative contacts for children. Extended kin, aunts, grandfathers, cousins, cousins-in-law, all provide children a different view of the world. Extended family can prove to children that many people care for them, and offer a chance to relate to various types of people. A book entitled *Aunties: Our Older, Cooler, Wiser Friends* (given to me for Christmas by my nephew and his family) outlines a number of roles that aunts can and do play. "You can cry on an aunt's shoulder or ask for advice (even if you don't take it) and get some support...these...aunties provide us with something else--a tolerance for differences, a realization that all kinds of people live in the world..."[14]

Since most kin do not have the main responsibility for child rearing, they can share skills and talents that parents may not have or that become lost in the hassle of everyday routines. Extended family members often have the money for special gifts, the time to take a niece to a museum or a nephew to a rock concert. Distant relatives often send thought-provoking cards from far away places or take their grandchildren on trips. Relatives living nearby can play the largest role. One grandmother in Madison, for example, conscientiously attends all of the athletic events and school plays of each of her twelve grandchildren, providing praise or consolation.

Each of the types of relationships discussed can benefit communities. Even the existence of strangers can acquaint children with knowledge of the larger world. Those concerned with enhancing the vitality of neighborhoods and the lives of their residents should consider the range of actual and potential types of relationships that exist or might be encouraged and the potential contribution of each. Some help to build what Putnam calls "bonding" social capital; others create what he distinguishes as "bridging" social capital.[15]

Bonding social capital refers to that which develops within families, country clubs, members of the same religious congregation, and urban village neighborhoods. Such bonding involves mutual obligations, the exchange of small and large favors and emotional support over a long period of time. This may not be mutually beneficial in the short-term. People may provide different material or emotional benefits. The exchanges may not be reciprocal on a direct one-to-one basis but circulate within a network, depending upon who can provide the benefit needed. While such bonding may be positive for the individuals connected, it can have negative effects on the larger community. Bonded groups may not be aware of or concerned with other community members or other neighborhoods. Such groups have included racially and gender restricted clubs, juvenile cliques or gangs, the Ku Klux Klan, the Mob, and al Qaeda.[16]

Bridging capital refers to contacts that connect disparate groups or types of people. Bridging capital enables people to relate comfortably and cooperatively with those of a different religious, ethnic or racial background, style of life, or point of view. Such capital develops in heterogeneous neighborhoods or work situations and in organizations or movements that attract people from different backgrounds.[17] The civil rights movement and many interest-based civic groups and organizations such as community choirs, political organizations, and city-wide councils of religious institutions all create bridging capital. Both kinds of interpersonal social capital are important for neighborhoods. The next section illustrates the different contributions possible from two types of networks with almost opposite characteristics, one exemplifying bonding, the other bridging social capital.

Networks of Neighborhood Relationships

Close-Knit Networks

Close-knit relationships are bonding relationships, the kind that occur in a small town or a city's ethnic enclaves. The networks in such areas can create positive or negative energy. In one town of 30,000 the author asked, "Who in this town does everyone trust, that is, trust in the sense that if they tell you something it's straight information?" I asked five people before I got one name. People would not work with each other because of incidents that had happened years before. They did not trust outsiders, including people who worked in the community every day or had lived there for over ten years. There was no place in town where I could hold a meeting that everyone would attend. Some would not come to a meeting in "that church," while others would not step foot in another church or in the community center. People did not share their true thoughts about problems publicly, inhibiting chances of resolving them. During a forty-five-minute public presentation about community problems, the audience sat grim faced. People smiled only once, when I reported an earlier conversation with a woman who, when asked the week before if she would repeat her private comments publicly at the upcoming community meeting, had replied, "Oh, no; I live here."

In another town of 15,000 that shared a boundary with a major city, several individuals commented that they had a hundred relatives living there. Members of this same town reported that people there did not consider smoking pot to be very serious. In fact, children got pot from their families who justified their actions with, "I'd rather have them do it at home than on the street corner." Clearly any efforts by social workers or teachers to reduce pot smoking would have been undermined by someone within the family network. On the other hand, during a time when many well-to-do communities regularly defeated school bond issues, this same community mobilized to build a magnificent high school. They voted to tax themselves, despite a 38 percent poverty rate, extremely low adult education levels, and at least one-third of voters over age sixty-five.

Neighborhoods with close-knit relationships continue to exist in some small towns, ethnic enclaves and in many public housing complexes. Unfortunately, such relationships often may exist not because of strong positive bonds but because people lack alternatives due to limited income, limited knowledge of English or discrimination. People who live close together may not have or want a close-knit relationship with their neighbors. One resident of Columbia, Maryland, extremely active in community affairs, carefully avoided getting close to families in his cul-de-sac. "Once you let someone into your personal life," he claimed, "it is difficult to get them out if you turn out to have different tastes or values."[18] A resident of a public housing project in Madison, Wisconsin, pointed out that she had moved into the project from a farm. She was used to space and privacy. She now lived in a cul-de-sac of two-story buildings housing several hundred people, with six families using the same entrance. She maintained some sense of privacy by avoiding most contact with her neighbors.

Intimate Secondary Relationships

People participating in leadership roles in neighborhood organizations can develop another type of relationship, what I call an intimate secondary relationship. These relationships combine some characteristics of a secondary relationship, such as those experienced with a cashier in a store, with some characteristics of primary relationships, such as those with family and friends. The concept grew out of observations of a community board in Columbia, Maryland, in the mid-1970s. It also has been observed firsthand in Madison, Wisconsin; Hyde Park-Kenwood, Chicago; and Reston, Virginia, and has been substantiated by anecdotal reports from elsewhere.[19]

The term "intimate secondary relationships" conveys the paradoxical nature of such relationships. The characteristics similar to those found in primary relations include: intense involvement, warmth, a sense of intimacy, a sense of belonging, knowledge of each other's characters, and rapport. The characteristics similar to those of secondary relations include: involvement of the individual rather than the family; a commitment limited in both time and space with a relatively low cost of withdrawal; a focus on specific rather than diffuse purposes; a consideration of public rather than private matters; and the use of public meeting places rather than private homes. Individuals may question one or more aspects of the description as it applies to their community. Yet the idea may help community members recognize and value a type of relationship that contributes to community vitality.

Intimate secondary relationships often develop among members of a board of directors of a community organization. As participants work together, they experience the warmth, sense of intimacy and rapport (or intense arguments and hostility) often associated with families or groups of friends. Members of intimate secondary groups, however, do not concern themselves with the details of each others' personal lives. Often they do not know other members' personal backgrounds, family relationships or even their tastes. Although the personal information shared varies among individuals and groups, generally it is limited and not necessary for group effectiveness. For example, the chairwoman for a neighborhood council in Toronto, Canada, suffered from epilepsy. This might never have been known except that she suffered a seizure and could not chair the annual meeting. Fellow board members were shocked to realize that they had known her for several years yet been unaware of a serious chronic physical disorder.

This illustrates how intimate secondary relationships can have the intensity of involvement normally associated with primary groups but lack the sharing of personal information or socializing usually found in such groups. They differ from secondary relationships in that participants know each others' characters in sufficient depth to be able to develop trust or to determine whether or not trust is warranted. One member of a village association board in Columbia, Maryland, commented that he was not asked where he came from or about previous activities and jobs. The board members, however, did know his character and understood how he would act on matters that concerned them all.

Another dimension of intimate secondary relations that has more in common with secondary relations is they tend to involve individuals rather than families. In the midst of the women's movement in the 1970s, a former chairman of a community group in Falls Church, Virginia, commented that husbands and wives never became active in the same group simultaneously. The chairman attributed this to a desire to avoid competition between spouses and to permit each a separate opportunity for growth. In Columbia, Maryland, residents noted that participation in the community association provided women not employed outside their homes an opportunity to develop skills, confidence, and an identity separate from their roles as wives and mothers.

An intimate secondary relationship differs from both primary and secondary relationships in terms of commitment. In most primary group settings, such as friendships or families, the activities and time commitments tend to be open-ended and diffuse. Attempts to establish stricter limits or to end a relationship involve considerable costs, and sometimes arouse personal hostility. Withdrawing from a close work group can be accomplished peacefully by changing jobs, but this may be difficult and costly. Even withdrawing one's children from a neighborhood play group or one's self from a circle of friends may not be easy. Joining a community board and developing intimate secondary relationships with members, however, does not imply a long-term commitment. The scope of the commitment is confined to the actions necessary to fulfill the limited role of board member.

The commitment observed among members of the Oakland Mills Village Board in Columbia, Maryland, illustrates the concept. Board members estimated that they spent from ten to twenty hours per week on business, representing a substantial time commitment and many contacts with other board members. The individuals became intensely involved in the group's activities. They did not necessarily, however, become close friends. One community activist in Columbia reported being very careful about socializing with people he met through community association activities. If the relationship revolves only around community business, people who become tired of the other board members can resign or not run for a second term, easier to accomplish than withdrawing from a friendship.

Intimate secondary relationships develop when people work together to perform specific public tasks. People come together for public business, rather than private friendship or personal business. Members have clear roles and obligations determined by the secondary setting rather than by the personal tastes of the individuals. They generally see themselves in a public role, carrying out a public responsibility. For example, one block group in Hyde Park-Kenwood met for years without engaging in personal social relations. The leader explained that in his area people did not necessarily become friends but did fulfill their role obligations as neighbors. Traditionally, "once a month you come out and meet your neighbors."

These relationships not only form around public business, but also generally develop in public places such as a community center. During a debate about whether the community centers in Columbia were necessary, one person explained that although many of the meetings were small enough to be held in residents' homes, holding them in the community center made it clear that everyone had a right to attend. If the meeting was held in the community center, people could just wander in and sit down. But if the same meeting was scheduled in a home, they would "have to go up and knock on the door and say, 'May I come in to your meeting?' With meetings at the center, 'You don't have to ask someone's permission.'" People also feel freer to leave a public place without apology. One woman explained, "You could get up and walk out of boring meetings, but I would feel terribly rude walking out of a private home." The use of public space avoids the establishment of a host-guest relationship, including the nuances of deference owed to a guest or a host. It also avoids problems of expectations of reciprocity, especially important where great economic or social distances exist.

A block group in Hyde Park-Kenwood had flourished for many years. While racially homogeneous, the block contained single-family homes and apartments inhabited by African Americans of various ages, family compositions, and incomes. The group held their regular meetings in public places. This enabled the leader to include all of the diverse residents of the block in their public roles as neighbors, yet still permitted them freedom in selecting their friends. Neighbors provided each other with mutual support through maintaining surveillance over potential criminal activities and sending cards to hospitalized residents of the block. By coming together in a public place, residents were able to overcome social distances to meet as equals, temporarily setting aside any differences in status, tastes, incomes, or values. The group had created neighborhood solidarity sufficient to encourage owners to rehabilitate their homes and to prevent the city of Chicago from demolishing their block during a neighborhood revitalization effort. Yet despite a ten-year track record of accomplishing community actions, they had never hosted a successful social event.

For further clarity, compare intimate secondary relations with the type of relationships found in support groups for those with specific health problems, such as cancer, or other circumstances, such as a recent divorce. In each group the commitment remains voluntary and limited in time and scope; individuals rather than families often participate; intense personal relationships form rapidly and in sufficient depth to reveal important aspects of peoples' characters and for them to develop mutual trust or distrust; and an emphasis exists on equality within the group. Such groups do not emphasize status based on outside job roles, personal wealth, race, age or gender. Putnam notes that at any one time, some two to five percent of adults are active in a self-help or support group.[20] He found, however, that in most cases, membership in such groups did not promote any other form of community involvement.[21]

The relationships in self-help or support groups differ from intimate secondary relationships in the amount of personal information shared, particularly about family matters, and in the focus on private rather than public issues. A subtle difference also exists that is crucial to understanding the essential public and community basis of intimate secondary groups. In the case of elderly persons attending a support group, the relevant topics would likely involve personal concerns such as declining health, relationships with adult children, or loss of status due to retirement. The discussion likely would focus on individuals' feelings and the reactions of other group members to similar problems. In the case of a neighborhood-based organization with intimate secondary relationships, the focus more likely would be on the public response necessary to accommodate needs faced by many elderly in the community, such as constructing ramps to buildings or improving public transportation.

The basis for intimate secondary relationships, thus, is mutual involvement around public community tasks. Group members have defined roles and obligations, including regular attendance at meetings at specific times. Intimate secondary relationships are more similar to those relationships formed in a work situation than to those formed in an Internet chat room. For the purposes of this book, the question is how intimate secondary relationships can be facilitated at the local level and how they can contribute to creating community bonds and strength.

Intimate Secondary Relationships and Family

Women can find that joining a volunteer group and forming intimate secondary relationships provides a first step in obtaining a job and entering the world of more formal secondary relationships. This result has been observed both in communities such as Reston, Virginia, and Columbia, Maryland, where families typically have higher than average incomes and education, and at the Allied-Dunn's Marsh Neighborhood Center in Madison, Wisconsin, among women on welfare with limited educational backgrounds. A minister in Reston reported that intimate secondary relationships helped women in unhappy marriages obtain the support needed to face dissolving their marriages. The relationships presumably provided the women with validation of their own individual worth. On the other hand, by taking on new roles outside the home, some women improved the dynamics of their marriages. The intimate secondary relationships provided an opportunity for growth, a chance to experience close relationships with men without having an affair, and a way to develop new interests and skills.

Although intimate secondary relationships can provide support to people undergoing marital stress, the support offered reflects the secondary nature of these relationships more than their primary aspects. One Columbia resident explained that members of several different village boards had undergone marital conflict or separation during their terms of office. The group supported them by providing sympathy and, more importantly, by continuing the existing warm contacts on a businesslike but intimate basis. Members told their fellow board members about their marital situation as a matter of status change that fellow board members needed to know to avoid embarrassing comments or incidents. They did not share the feelings that might have been conveyed to a personal friend. Board members might sympathetically inquire, "How's it going?" leaving the individual free to accept the sympathy without discussing details.

The importance of the continuation of an intimate secondary relationship on a business-as-usual basis can be better understood by considering that marital difficulties frequently cause severe strain on primary relationships. Friends may ally with one partner or feel awkward about inviting a single person to a gathering of married friends, especially ones who also know the former spouse. Relatives may express concern, but also may express anger or criticism, and their inquiries may infringe on private matters.

Communities with Population Mobility

Americans move frequently. Approximately 15 percent of Americans change residence each year. In 2003, over 40 million Americans relocated.[22] Even in stable neighborhoods, people die, move away, or move in. Intimate secondary relationships can permit newcomers to experience warm relationships quickly but make their commitments to friendships slowly. Irwin Altman has called privacy the "selective control of access to the self or to one's group," emphasizing the importance of achieving the desired balance between feelings of crowding or intrusion and feelings of loneliness or isolation.[23] Newcomers' fears of unwanted obligations may be especially great in neighborhoods with apartments or other high-density housing that provide limited physical privacy.

Intimate secondary relationships can encourage a feeling of belonging, adding to community integration as well as personal satisfaction. One of Columbia's board members commented that he felt as if he had lived in Columbia a long time, although he had been there only a year. Many of the board members had become active in community affairs within six months of arriving. Such relationships allow new residents to experience some warmth and intimacy without commitment to personal friendships or loss of privacy, to learn about community resources and norms, to identify with the community, and to join with others on projects of mutual interest and neighborhood improvement.

Heterogeneous Neighborhoods

Intimate secondary relationships in heterogeneous neighborhoods can help people accept all residents as legitimate members of the community regardless of race, ethnicity, age, income, lifestyle, tenancy (whether homeowner or renter) and type of residence (apartment or house). In intimate secondary groups, neighbors can interact with others on a neutral, limited basis. Such relationships encourage an understanding of the needs of persons with different characteristics. They help define a community's responsibility for meeting the needs of all of its members and create a network of trust relationships that supports the conduct of community business.

Even the limited contact in intimate secondary relationships may be sufficient to increase understanding and empathy among different groups, or at least create public recognition of each group's needs. One study during the early days of Columbia found that African Americans in the community tended to socialize among themselves and participated only minimally in village board activities. Their limited participation, nevertheless, created some sensitivity to issues that might otherwise have been overlooked.[24] In both Hyde Park-Kenwood and Columbia, serving on local boards enabled residents of different backgrounds to feel comfortable with each other and to tackle community problems together.

Many people remain active on the same community board or neighborhood organization for a number of years. Another common pattern involves intensive activity for several years followed by a period of withdrawal into personal and family affairs or membership in a different organization, frequently one covering a larger geographic area. Former members occasionally may be asked to perform specific tasks. They often demonstrate continued loyalty and contact through participation in fund-raising events or attending the group's annual meetings.

The trust and understanding established in intimate secondary relationships networks may help when someone wants to sound out an opinion on a sensitive issue or test a position on a potentially controversial subject. In Hyde Park-Kenwood, Columbia, and Madison such networks played an important role in the intricate dynamics of public attitudes toward race and toward low-income residents. In Columbia several former village board members later worked in county agencies or became members of the county council. They continued to maintain their networks of intimate secondary relationships as a means of staying in touch with neighborhood sentiments.

Intimate secondary relationships can facilitate building coalitions among diverse interest groups. The manager of a subsidized housing project in Columbia gradually became active in several community organizations, each of which gave him increased contacts and credibility as a spokesman for the low-income residents.[25] A woman who had known him through her work on a village board later urged him to run for the governing board of Columbia's community association and actively supported his campaign. Thus, networks of intimate secondary relationships can provide access to political and social centers of power, resources, and institutions beyond those of the immediate neighborhood.

Madison regularly receives high rankings in magazine lists of desirable places to live despite its legendary Wisconsin winters. The author, a newcomer, has noted an extensive network of intimate secondary relationships, as well as those of kin and close friends, which crisscross the city. I suspect that these have enabled the city to successfully meet a number of challenges and undertake its numerous civic improvement projects.

Effects of Various Types of Relationships on Neighborhood Vitality

Except for the role of stranger, each of the relationships discussed potentially contributes support for families and individuals and for overall community vitality and health. Friendly recognition provides a sense of security and belonging. Casual acquaintances and casual friends provide companionship and people to pitch in for community events or problem-solving. They help promote harmony, especially in neighborhoods with heterogeneous populations. Any relationship that helps people feel at home promotes neighborhood vitality. Feeling comfortable with neighbors increases the likelihood that people will be willing to become involved with improvement efforts. Friends satisfy deeper needs and provide short-term assistance in troubled times. Kin offer a sense of continuity and long-term help during times of crisis.

Friends, kin, and close-knit relationships fall into Putnam's category of bonding relationships. Friendly recognition, casual acquaintances, and intimate secondary relationships illustrate his concept of bridging relationships. Bridging relationships, both within a community and with outsiders, may be especially important in an increasingly diverse America. The complicated dynamics of diversity will be addressed in the next chapter.

Notes

1. Frost, R. Mending wall. In E. C. Lathem (Ed.). (1967). *The poetry of Robert Frost* (p. 33). New York: Holt, Rinehart and Winston, Inc. (Original work published 1914).
2. Sternfeld, J. (1996). *On this site: Landscape in memoriam* (see the description next to the sixth photograph). San Francisco, CA: Chronicle Books.
3. Wireman, P. (1984). *Urban neighborhoods, networks, and families: New forms for old values* (p. 79). Lexington, MA: D.C. Heath and Company.
4. Granovetter, M. (1974). *Getting a job*. Cambridge, MA: Harvard University Press.
5. Granovetter, M. (1973). The strength of weak ties. *American Journal of Sociology*, 78, 1360-1380.
6. Kupetz, B. N. (n.d.). Overcoming ageism through children's literature (reprinted from newsletter). *Texas Child Care*. Austin, TX: Texas Wordforce Commission. Retrieved February 9, 2002, from http://www.parentinginformation.org/ageism.htm.
7. Fischer, C. S. (1982). *To dwell among friends: Personal networks in town and city* (pp. 135-137). Chicago: University of Chicago Press.
8. Fischer, C. S., Jackson, R. M., Stueve, C. A., Gerson, K., Jones, L. M., & Balclassare, M. (1977). *Networks and places* (p. 53). New York: Free Press.
9. Putnam, R. D. (2000). *Bowling alone: The collapse and revival of American community* (pp. 96-108). New York: Simon & Schuster. Monti, D. J. Jr., Butler, C., Curley, A., Tilney, K., & Weiner, M. F. (2003). Private lives and public worlds: Changes in Americans' social ties and civic attachments in the late–20th century. *City & Community*, 2(2), 143.
10. Putnam, R. D. (2000). *Bowling alone: The collapse and revival of American community* (p. 105). New York: Simon & Schuster.

11. Ibid., pp. 97, 166.
12. Litwak, E., & Szelenyi, I. (1969). Primary group structures and their functions: Kin, neighbors and friends. *American Sociological Review, 34*, 465-481.
13. Ibid.
14. Tradeder, T., & Bennett. J. (1998). *Aunties: Our older, cooler, wiser friends* (pp. 16 & 35). Berkeley, CA: Wildcat Canyon Press.
15. Putnam, R. D. (2000). *Bowling alone*, pp. 22-23.
16. Ibid.
17. Ibid.
18. Wireman, P. (1984). *Urban neighborhoods, networks and families: New forms for old values* (p. 4). Lexington, MA: D.C. Heath and Company.
19. Ibid., pp. 1-14. Wireman, P. (1976). *Meanings of community in modern America: Some implications from new towns.* Dissertation Abstracts International, 38 (03), 1672A. (UMI No. 7718716), 113-150.
20. Putmam, R.D. (2000). Bowling alone, pp. 149, 150.
21. Ibid., p. 151.
22. Schacter, J. P. (2004, March). *Current population reports: Geographic mobility: 2002 to 2003.* Washington, DC: U.S. Census Bureau. Retrieved April 19, 2005, from http://www.census.gov/prod/2004pubs/p20-549.pdf.
23. Altman, I. (1975). *The environment and social behavior* (p. 18). Monterey, CA: Brooks/Cole Publishing Company.
24. Wireman, P. (1977). *Meanings of community in modern America*, pp.,113-150.
25. Burkhart, L. (1981). *Old values in a new town: The politics of race and class in Columbia, Maryland.* New York: Praeger.

6

How Can We All Get Along?
Race, Class, and Ethnicity

Exploring Myths, Realities, and Possibilities[1]

Introduction

"People,...can we all get along?" pleaded Rodney King in the midst of the 1992 Los Angeles rioting sparked by the acquittal of the white policemen who had beaten King while arresting him.[2] The Los Angeles riots protesting police brutality and the jury's decision included their own visions of racial hatred, with blacks pulling a white driver from his truck to beat him and selectively targeting stores owned by Koreans. This chapter cannot resolve the problem of racial and ethnic hatred or the milder forms expressed in prejudice, discrimination, or even feelings of discomfort or perplexity that may arise between people of a different race, ethnicity, or place of birth. It will, however, explore issues that affect American society and discuss how local communities and neighborhoods can help families and individuals who differ to get along.

The author, who is white, has lived in racially integrated neighborhoods most of her adult life. She has worked in racially integrated situations, has both supervised and been supervised by members of different races, has traveled extensively and has worked in Asia and in Central and South America. This does not make me "the expert" or even "an expert." But it has provided extensive experience.

The issues around difference, whether racial, ethnic, religious, class, or age, are extremely complex. An immense body of scholarly literature exists on these subjects. This chapter does not attempt to summarize or interpret that literature. Nor does it deal in depth with a number of politically charged issues about diversity. Rather, it provides a reminder, as did Katrina, that race continues to affect our policies, our attitudes, and our lives. It provides a framework that may be useful to policymakers, neighborhood residents and community organizations dealing with diverse residents and to those in homogeneous situations trying to rear children who will live in an increasingly heterogeneous society.

For the most part, this chapter deals with black-white situations, since the author has the most experience with those. Hispanics now outnumber African Americans in the U.S., and many areas of the country have been experiencing a major influx of immigrants from numerous countries. The reader should ask whether the issues raised here apply to any groups in their community, including senior citizens and those with health limitations, or different sexual orientations.

The play, *Spinning into Butter*, by Rebecca Gilman, focuses on the complexity of black and white relationships.[3] The Madison Repertory Theatre hosted an after-performance discussion led by a multiracial and multiethnic panel. An Asian man, when asked whether the black-white dynamics portrayed in the play would differ in a white-Asian situation, said they would not, but noted that the specifics would differ. That is, the nature and content of the prejudice would depend upon the stereotypes held about each specific ethnic group. Sometime later I heard a Native American woman on television discussing her objection to the use of certain school team names. She said the names seemed to glorify only the warrior aspects of Indian history and culture. Why, she asked, would you want to use a term that historically has been used to demean someone?

Sticks and Stones

First, a note about words. "Sticks and stones can break my bones, but words can never hurt me." This response shouted by children to insults protects the shouter from acknowledging the truth: words do hurt. Words label people as good or bad, as having desirable or undesirable characteristics, as being members of a valued or a disliked group. People care what words others use to refer to them. Flinging an insulting label can ignite schoolyard fist fights as well as adult violence.

Realizing the potential importance of group descriptors will help any community promote better intergroup relations. This can be tricky. Sometimes an individual uses an offensive word deliberately or from indifference. But often people do not know the appropriate word, especially if the preferred word has shifted or if a group, such as those speaking Spanish as a native language, contains people from various nations or cultural backgrounds. When trying to decide whether to use Hispanic or Latino in this book, the author received conflicting advice. The words groups prefer vary over time, and there are distinct regional preferences. A word used in one neighborhood may be considered rude in another area. Members of a group may use a derogatory term among themselves in a joking manner but be highly offended if an outsider uses the same term.

Individual members of a group may not like the currently popular term. A black friend declared, "I hate the concept of African American. I'm a Kentuckian or an American. I was raised in the U.S. and on military bases overseas. I'm an Army brat. The closest connection to Africa I have is when I change planes in Abidjan or visit the continent."

How can a neighborhood navigate these stormy linguistic waters? The Texas Association of Museums developed a remarkable short book, *An Action Plan: Multicultural Initiatives in Texas Museums,* to guide its members in developing programs and materials for a diverse audience. The appendix lists names of various groups with a discussion about how the descriptive terms have been used historically along with suggestions about current preferences. The length and diversity of the list startle the reader into recalling the number of groups who have faced negative stereotypes during the nation's immigrant history: Irish, Italians, Polish, Jews, Russians, Mexicans, African Americans, Hispanics, Chinese, Japanese, Native Americans—almost every group in America. People from the Middle East have experienced an increase in prejudice, outright hostility, and even physical attacks, since 9/11. The derogatory terms are not only used by the white majority against people of a specific racial or ethnic group but often are also used by these same groups against each other.[4]

How does a neighbor know what to call someone from a different group? The *Action Plan* reaches a remarkably simple solution: ask them. When conducting a workshop with some twenty African American teenagers, the author started by discussing the need to listen to each other with respect, for value in what each person said regardless of their appearance or the way they expressed themselves. I asked, "How many of you want to be called black?" Then, "How many of you want to be called African American?" We went around the room with each youth indicating which term they preferred. Half wanted to be called black; half preferred African American. I pointed out that unless they listened with open minds, one-half of them would not hear anything I said to them during the workshop. Regardless of which term I used, half of the group would be insulted. Addressing the issue openly established good rapport for our time together.

Asking may not always work, but most people will respond honestly to a straightforward sincere request for information. People of color may assume that a white person does not respect them because they have not been treated well by white people in the past and because of the historical experience of their racial or ethnic group. "Respect, if you can just get people to respect each other." Edward R. Day, a lawyer in San Antonio with years of community organizing experience, claims that creating a respectful environment where people can disagree without feeling put down is crucial. "Usually the disagreements over the issues are not all that great and can be settled fairly easily if people feel that they had an opportunity to speak and were heard." Using the wrong word unknowingly may insult someone who then quietly withdraws from neighborhood participation.

When the new towns of Columbia, Maryland, and Reston, Virginia, were started in the 1970s, their developers were pioneers in pursuing racial integration.

Both communities achieved a higher level of integration and greater community support for integration than did nearby counties. But residents still continued to face difficulties. Their children attended county schools outside of Columbia. One black woman in Columbia complained that a white teacher called her teenage son "boy." The teacher either didn't know, or forgot, or didn't care that whites historically used the term to deny a black male the dignity and status of adulthood. At about the same time, black residents in Reston protested when a community group's fund raiser planned to auction a "slave for a day." They felt that those who planned the event showed insensitivity about a tragic part of black history.[5] Unfortunately, the problem persists. More than twenty years later, in 1998, a similar situation arose in Madison, Wisconsin, over a fraternity float featuring a slave block.

In 2007 students at a number of colleges engaged in activities stereotyping blacks. The popular radio commentator Don Imus created a national uproar when he called the Rutgers basketball team "nappy-headed hos." The term ho means whore and the term nappy-headed has been used to denigrate the hair texture of Africans since the days of slavery. Although Imus was fired from his $40 million dollar contract by CBS over the specific comment, he had used racist comments before, and is likely to be reinstated in a well-paid radio job quickly.

Making light of blacks' history that caused so much pain dishonors those whose ancestors may have been affected. Ignorance and insensitivity may reflect an individual's lack of knowledge or carelessness or it may result from conscious or unconscious prejudice. In either case, the appearance and the effects may be the same.

On Being a Minority

Whites reading these examples might easily say, "What's the big deal? These are minor issues or even slips of the tongue. Why are blacks so sensitive?" An explanation can be found in the many examples in Lena Williams' book, *It's the Little Things: The Everyday Interactions that Get under the Skin of Blacks and Whites.*[6]

Most whites have no idea of the importance that being black plays in the lives of blacks or the high personal cost in their daily lives. This ignorance, even more than any lack of information about a particular term or aspect of black culture, leads to miscommunication and misunderstandings.

Being white is almost never an issue for whites. Except occasionally, as in a discussion about affirmative action, whites do not consider their race an issue. They unconsciously take it as the norm. Many whites seldom see anyone of another race. Others see them only briefly in a public place. Very few whites see people of color in a situation where they, as a white person, are the minority. Few have the experience of having a person of another race, who may or may not be prejudiced, be in a position of authority over them.

The reverse situation confronts blacks. A black mother in Madison, Wisconsin, a city that prides itself on its tolerance and liberal attitudes, refused to let her teenage daughter go to the shopping mall with more than one friend. She feared that a group of five or six black girls would be suspected of shoplifting. A highly effective black official in Madison's city government said that every black man he knows has been stopped by police for questioning, for no reason other than being on the street and being black. He said that when he walks through a neighborhood and sees another black person, he nods or says hello even if they are not acquainted, as a means of acknowledging unity in a sometimes hostile world. In some cases, black teenagers have found that when they hang around a shopping area, white shoppers fear them, even though they live in the neighborhood, their parents hold similar jobs to those of the shoppers, and white teenagers hang around the stores in similar clothes.[7]

Blacks often experience a significant amount of uncertainty about acceptance and safety in all-white settings. In 1998, a black woman attending a conference on museums and community said that if she walks into a museum and "there is nobody that looks like me at the ticket counter, no signs or posters that have anything to do with my culture, I don't know whether or not I'm welcome." A highly educated professional black man was invited to speak about race to a religious group attended mostly by whites. The discussion and questioning that followed his presentation seemed to me like an open and honest exploration of this complicated issue. I was astonished to find later that he felt that we had ganged up on him, that he had opened up only to be confronted with what he experienced as a "lynch mob."

People of color continually face the challenge of determining when an action or comment reflects racism, and when it does not. One man who had served as the only black member of a community board said that for a year he was not sure whether his comments were being ignored because he was the new board member or whether he was a victim of subtle racism.[8]

Many people of color grew up in largely minority neighborhoods, often in large cities, and attended mostly segregated schools. People of color may experience uneasiness with neighbors whom they suspect grew up in a predominantly white suburb. A white neighbor may find his initial overtures of friendship treated with suspicion or hostility and draw his own negative conclusions.

Some blacks harbor suspicion or outright hostility toward whites. One black woman who grew up in the 1950s told me about her mother's insistence that she carefully polish her black and white saddle shoes every morning when she started attending an integrated high school, lest she provide the white students an excuse for negative impressions about black people. After four years of daily polishing while thinking "the white kids don't have to polish their shoes," she graduated from high school with high grades and applied for a job on the Atlantic City, New Jersey boardwalk selling cotton candy. The manager told her that he never hired blacks. Recalling her mother's pressure to dress well, study hard, and prove her worth by "being better than" her white classmates, she reacted with shock and resentment when rejected for such a low-level summer job. "For years," she confided, "I hated all white people." This woman resolved her feelings, moving on to living in and contributing to building an interracial neighborhood in the 1960s. Such stories, however, remain a part of the legacy told to black children. Painful incidents, both real or suspected, can stir up remembrances of past grievances and lead to a rage that might seem like overreaction to an outsider.

White people generally are unaware of the extent to which their words and actions convey their assumption that white is the normal standard for human beings. This assumption may insult people of color. In one case, a white teacher wanted her class to write about their experiences, both favorable and unfavorable, with people of different races. In copying the assignment on the board, she suddenly realized that her notes read African American, Asian, people of Spanish heritage, and American Indian. She had not included Caucasian and probably would never have noticed except for the fact that the class contained one African American. She quickly added Caucasian to the list, sighing with relief that she had not ignored the experiences of the African American student. The inclusion drew forth unexpected answers from some Caucasian students who wrote about both positive and negative experiences with members of their own race as well as the others.

For the purposes of this discussion, prejudice can be considered as negative assumptions about a person or group based on their race or ethnicity. Some reactions of white people result from prejudices passed down from their parents or misinformation conveyed by the media. For example, a recent study of residents in Chicago, Baltimore, and Seattle found that people in neighborhoods with low crime felt that crime was a big problem if young black men were present in the area. Their fear was not related to the amount of actual crime or the characteristics of the neighborhood.[9]

Millions of white girls have been taught to fear black men. An adult white woman may automatically cross the street at night to avoid walking by a black man, without ever considering whether this is a realistic reaction to a threat. A more realistic action would be to cross the street to avoid a white man since most criminals victimize people of their own race.[10] If questioned, the woman probably would deny being prejudiced. Yet would she take the same action upon seeing a white man in the same scenario? This unconscious habit, perhaps formed in childhood, might be her only prejudiced action. Yet the man in question, who certainly knows about whites' fears, experiences one more case of rejection based on color.

Minorities absorb the negative messages at very young ages, as the following example illustrates. A white staff member at a neighborhood center came to the after-school program several Mondays in a row to read from the book, *I Dream a World: Portraits of Black Women Who Changed America.*[11] One African American first grader startled her by asking, "Why are we reading about black women? I don't like black women." The astonished teacher looked at the child and responded, "What? You don't like black women? You don't like Mary, who's the color of dark chocolate, or Tashia, who's the color of milk chocolate like you?" Looking at her own hands, and truly noticing their actual color for the first time, the teacher said, "I'm pink. We're all different colors."

The following week for some reason the woman did not read to the class. The next day the girl confronted her. "Yesterday was Monday and you didn't read that book." The teacher read the book again that afternoon. The girl and her sister later participated in a trip to the Milwaukee Art Institute to see an exhibit of the photographs that formed the basis for the book. This incident helps explain why blacks insist on the importance of teaching their history and including their contributions in textbooks and celebrations. Or why a woman might be irate at not being able to purchase a certain kind of hair products in the neighborhood, ones designed for the texture of her hair, not the "standard white hair."

Whites' ignorance of both black history and the continuing presence of discrimination can reflect a lack of interest in and respect for members of that race. Many blacks are hurt and angered by this ignorance. Such treatment fails to acknowledge the considerable contributions that blacks have made to our country, their strengths in struggling with the complicated effects of past discrimination, and the reality that they must face discrimination and prejudice as part of their daily lives.

Continued Discrimination and Institutional Racism

While prejudice is a mental prejudgement based on race, discrimination is an action based on prejudice. Although many, if not most, whites assume that the civil rights laws have resolved the problems of past unfairness, research shows that discrimination continues to exist, adversely affecting people of color in many ways. It affects their ability to obtain employment, housing, and, in some instances, to walk down the street without harassment.

People may not even be conscious that they are practicing discrimination by treating whites more favorably. One study traced the experiences of job candidates who had been carefully matched according to relevant character- istics and trained to give similar responses to interview questions. The study found a series of barriers to success faced by candidates of color. The potential employers offered the minorities fewer opportunities to interview, fewer jobs or referrals to other opportunities, less pay, and less access to higher level posi- tions. Persons conducting the interviews, for example, would tell a candidate who was a person of color to start at a different and lower level job than the position advertised. They told the white candidates about higher-level positions for which they could apply but did not volunteer this information to the black candidates. Studies indicate that such discrimination also affects Hispanics, Asians, and Native Americans.[12]

Since the actions by employers often are both subtle and not under outside scrutiny, complaints by minorities who fail to be hired can easily be dismissed by non-minorities as unreasonable griping. Yet a review of several careful studies using matched candidates indicated that "discrimination adversely affected non-white job seekers in more than one job application in five."[13] A 2002 study, also using matched pairs of job applicants, found that even for entry level jobs being black created more of a liability than having a criminal record.[14]

Some actions may not be designed to discriminate against people of color but, nevertheless, may have disproportionately adverse consequences for minorities. Practices or laws that appear to be race neutral may be unfair in their implementation. Considerable documentation shows different treatment of whites and non-whites throughout the criminal justice system. Recent reports have documented the validity of black complaints about the problem of "driving while black." A 2002 study of sixty-five jurisdictions in Minnesota found widespread racial profiling against blacks, Latinos, and American Indian drivers. Police stopped and searched them more often in almost all of the jurisdictions. In several cities blacks were stopped 239 percent more often than would have been expected, given their proportion of drivers, and searched 70 percent more often. In suburban cities, Latinos were stopped 170 percent more often and searched 190 percent more often. A more realistic approach would have been to stop more white drivers since those searches produced the highest rates of contraband related to the drug trade. Similar patterns of racial profiling have been found in other states, including Maryland where 70 percent of the drivers stopped by the Maryland State Police on Interstate 95 were black, although they comprised less than 18 percent of the speeders.[15]

Statistics show that, once arrested, minorities are treated more harshly than whites for similar offenses at every step in the judicial process. They are more likely to be arrested rather than given a warning, less likely to be granted bail that would enable them to prepare a defense, less likely to be offered substance abuse treatment rather than jail, less likely to be offered plea bargains, more likely to be jailed rather than given probation. They receive longer sentences and are given the death penalty more often.[16]

Non-Hispanic whites comprise the largest group of crack users, but a very small number of them are prosecuted for crack offenses. Blacks and whites sell drugs at approximately the same rate as their proportion in the population. Blacks comprise 13 percent of the drug users, but almost 40 percent of those arrested for drug offenses, almost 60 percent of those convicted and 74 percent of those sentenced to prison.[17]

In many situations, a crack offender can be tried in either the state or the federal system, with more severe penalties in the latter. In one six-year period, the United States Attorney in the Los Angeles area prosecuted hundreds of blacks and Hispanics in federal court but no whites. The hundreds of white offenders were tried in state courts. This difference in treatment for similar offenses matters. One black man arrested with seventy grams of crack received the minimum mandatory federal sentence for selling more than fifty grams, ten years in prison. A white man, also charged in Los Angeles, was arrested with sixty-seven grams, more than the minimum for a mandatory sentence in the federal system, but he was tried in state court and received a jail sentence of less than a year. In 1992 the U.S. Sentencing Commission Report showed that in over half of the federal judicial districts, *only* minorities were prosecuted for crack cases.[18]

Stereotypes affect public opinion and, therefore, both the development of public policies and the way in which they are implemented. The discrepancy in treatment in the judicial system is not caused by the fight against crack use, often considered to be a black phenomenon. Between 1991 and 1993 whites were twice as likely to have used crack as blacks and Hispanics combined. Moreover, each race tends to purchase drugs from members of their own race. Yet the War on Drugs has disproportionately affected minorities. Drug use rates among black youth have actually been *lower* than those among whites for several decades. But nationally from 1986 to 1991 the arrests of white youth for drugs decreased by one-third while those for minority youth increased by almost 80 percent. Although the majority of juveniles arrested were white, three-fourths of the young people sentenced to prison with adults were people of color. Some experts have found that juveniles in adult prison are more likely than those in juvenile protection facilities to be raped, beaten, or commit suicide.[19] These very different experiences with the police and justice systems may account for the split in national opinion polls between white and black views on widely publicized legal cases. The extent and seriousness of racial discrepancies in the treatment of drug cases have recently been noted both by the Supreme Court and the U.S. Sentencing Commission.

Studies carefully controlled to eliminate the effects of factors other than race and ethnicity show that discrimination also exists in housing. Historically, institutions and individuals have assumed that a good neighborhood is a white neighborhood. Until the U.S. Supreme Court ruled them illegal in 1954, sales of property included covenants legally restricting future sales to non-Jewish Caucasians. Developers built separate neighborhoods for "colored." Even after restrictive covenants had been outlawed, realtors maintained segregation by steering applicants to certain neighborhoods. An ugly process of "turning neighborhoods" included realtors encouraging panic selling by whites to realtors, who then resold the homes at inflated prices to blacks. The Federal Housing Administration (FHA) mortgages that helped finance the creation of the new suburbs after World War II originally required bankers to loan only to racially homogeneous neighborhoods. In the 1980s the instructions to those who carried out the environmental review process for such housing still contained phrasing suggesting that racial, ethnic, or income diversity could be considered an environmental problem.[20]

The pattern continues. Careful studies show that bankers refuse home mortgages to blacks more frequently than to whites, even when the black applicants match the whites in terms of income, credit history, and other criteria. Real estate agents also continue widespread "steering" of black applicants to less desirable homes or apartments, announcing that a unit is "unavailable" but then showing it to a white family with the same income and other characteristics. A number of studies, covering some two dozen metropolitan areas, have found that until very recently blacks faced housing discrimination more than 50 percent of the time.[21] The practice has lessened but still hinders black renters one-fifth of the time and Hispanic renters one-fourth of the time.[22] The costs of the subprime mortgage crisis will fall most heavily on minorities since such mortgages were made more often in communities of color. Minority homeowners are more likely to be given higher interest rates than whites even if equally qualified.[23]

Scholars, the media and policy makers often perpetuate the idea that a good neighborhood is racially and ethnically homogenous. Two of the fathers of American urban sociology, Robert Park and Ernest Burgess, described the ethnic neighborhoods of Chicago, providing a basis for interpretations that continue today about the important role of homogeneity in neighborhood stability. However, as another sociologist, Gerald Suttles, points out, many of the areas that formed the basis for Park's work never represented the homogeneity often assumed in later discussions of his theories. Moreover, many of those neighborhoods actually developed their ethnic identity after the fact as a result of Park's study.[24]

Code Words and Confusion

The problem of perceptions by outsiders raises another crucial but complex issue, the accuracy of observations in situations involving race and the use of code words. Whites generally don't "see" people of color accurately. Most whites automatically overestimate the numbers of blacks present or involved in a situation or program. Given the unconscious assumption that the world normally consists of white people, one notices the presence of blacks. People inclined toward prejudice will note an undesirable action by a black person but ignore a similar action by a white person. One adult remembers hearing her mother comment every time a driver cut her off, "I bet he's black." If her bet turned out to be correct, she commented, "See, I told you so." Yet if her bet turned out to be mistaken, she never commented.

Since whites rarely have the experience of being in the minority, any concentration of blacks can be felt as threatening. Often ethnic neighborhoods, or even those with a significantly non-white population, become stigmatized by outsiders. Scholars, planners, real estate agents, the media, and others often assume that at some magic "tipping point" the numbers of minorities in the neighborhood will lower property values, ignoring the fact that whites are present in much larger numbers.

Another aspect of intergroup relations relates to the confusion between race and class. Class generally refers to a person's type of work, income, education, and, in some cases, family background. Certain behaviors, knowledge, speech, and types of posture generally are considered to identify a person with one class or another. Historically, white Americans have classified anything connected to the style, habits, music, dancing, or verbal expressions typically used by African Americans as lower class. Some aspects of African American expression, such as jazz in the early part of the twentieth century or rock music later, became widely acceptable only after being performed by white musicians.

Confusing race and class enables whites to ignore the extent of ongoing racial prejudice and discrimination. Such confusion also creates the belief that programs to assist persons of lower income primarily help people of color.[25] In one integrated community, white residents consistently perceived the subsidized housing residents as being "80 or 90 percent black," although the correct figure was less than half that number.[26] Nationally people have thought of welfare as a program for blacks, although most recipients have been white.[27]

Researchers studying integrated communities have found that code words enable whites to make racist statements without seeming to do so.[28] Herbert Gans provides a perceptive analysis of the problems of labels that become code words through lumping different types of behavior and people together and implying a lack of morality on the part of those so labeled. He notes that the word "underclass" can be used to hide anti-black or anti-Latino attitudes. Using the word "underclass accommodates contemporary taboos against overt prejudice, not to mention hate speech. Such taboos sometimes paper over—and even repress—racial antagonisms that people do not want to express openly."[29] Using code words nearly always is intended to mask prejudice. The reader should consider whether code words are playing a part in the current debate about immigration. I asked a friend to respond to a sequence of words. The words with his response follow: Hispanic—Mexican American; Mexican—immigrant; immigrant—illegal; illegal immigrant–overcrowding.

Even when the user is not glossing over personal prejudice, the use of code words often inhibits anyone from asking whether, in the particular circumstances, race is an issue. Separating the issue, which may be quite real, from the myths and word games can free neighbors and neighborhood organizations to address problems realistically. Are black teenagers, for example, acting out resentment about perceived or real prejudiced treatment? Do those with lower incomes hang out by the stores because there are no parks nearby? Whites who ignore misbehavior or problems for fear of appearing prejudiced can offend their black neighbors and complicate problem solving. Reluctance to expect appropriate behavior from children of color insults them and their parents. One parent indignantly complained of racism on the part of a teacher who let her child play in school rather than perform her work; the mother felt that the teacher did not expect the same performance from a black child that she would have demanded from a white one.[30]

Whites often fall into the trap of assuming that all blacks think and act alike and share identical opinions. An African American man on an otherwise white community board objected to being considered an authority on all matters relating to blacks. When a problem occurred involving blacks, other board members would look to him for help. Sometimes he would look away. His attitude was, "Don't look at me as if I'm the savior. I didn't want them to think that I was there to deal with the black problem. I was there elected to the board just like they were." In addition, he felt it "crippled the white people on the board for them not to have the opportunity to deal (with the problem)."[31]

A white teacher with only one African American student in her class took the student aside early in the semester to tell her that, while her contributions would be welcome, she did not have to comment during presentations about race. The teacher did not want the student to be forced to become the "token expert." Several times during intense inquiries from white students, the teacher realized how easy it would have been to simply turn to the one minority student, abdicating her own responsibility as instructor.

A Sophisticated Conversation, and Back to Sticks and Stones

During the second half of the twentieth century, the dynamics of intergroup relations partially revolved around who has the right to decide what behavior is classified as acceptable. The debate within the black community ranged from promoting black pride via certain fashions or hairstyles to debates over whether a highly placed black official or politician had been co-opted and now "acts white," from philosophies favoring separatism to debates about what being black means today.

Issues about race have plagued the United States since its founding and continue to affect national politics and local communities. The conversation at times has dominated our politics and our streets, as during race riots and the Civil Rights Movement of the 1960s. Decent people can differ about the meaning or importance of specific incidents or facts, but no community can safely ignore the issue of race. At an individual level it affects what you say to a child watching television, how you react when meeting a person of a different race, who you hire or sit with at the office, and how you vote. At a community level, it affects zoning, policing, loitering laws, choice of classroom textbooks, and selection of people as board members of community organizations. At a national level it affects our decisions about law enforcement, treatment of people making minimum or low wages, media coverage of news events and immigration laws.

Racism is not unique to America. During a six-month trip to Asia, I encountered racism in country after country, each time directed at a different despised and distrusted group. When I returned to the U.S., I was proud of America's race relations for the first time. Not because we have solved the problem but because we were actually grappling with the complex issues.

Each individual community and neighborhood must decide for itself how best to respond to the issues raised here. One community may tackle people's perceptions, holding educational sessions or diversity training or working to make sure that the local media avoid negative stereotyping and cover positive events in all neighborhoods. Another community may examine zoning laws that have discriminatory effects or monitor the hiring recruitment practices of major employers.

Groups and individuals will view these issues very differently. Because those who engage in the national, televised conversation often reflect the views of people who take extreme positions or those jockeying for political favor, I will take the risk of pointing out some potential pitfalls for us all.

Much of the national conversation has been polarized. The recent upsurge in immigration has reactivated an anti-immigration sentiment. Debates roar about how to treat various ethnic groups in history books and on campuses. Blacks and whites react quite differently to reports of alleged police brutality. People question whether displays of ethnic pride or use of a native language hinder people from becoming true Americans. Others wonder whether assimilation is desirable or, for those of a different skin color, even possible.

Both individuals and whole communities may want to discuss these issues and participate fully in the national debate. But caustic debates may divert us from mobilizing to tackle together issues that have nothing to do with race or ethnicity, as well as honestly addressing those that do.

Most of this chapter was written as a result of personal experience gained over many years. In writing this book, however, I did delve into some of the current literature, attended a training course on racism, and listened to a number of television lectures by current authors. There is an immense body of research and much scholarly debate about these issues as well as discussion in the more popular media. The following comments make no claims to fairly represent it. But I have come across a number of statements and terms that could polarize discussions unnecessarily. If whites can avoid immediate defensive reactions, and instead probe the emotions, facts and exact meaning behind the statements, and listen respectfully, the ensuing discussion may result in an informative dialogue.

Whites may simply dismiss the comments on the next several pages as an apology for blacks. Blacks may object, claiming "here is another white interpreting what we mean," or feel that I am ignoring their truth. Those of Hispanic, Asian, Native American, Middle Eastern, or other heritages may feel ignored and resent the fact that this discussion is mostly framed in terms of black/white relations. Although Hispanics now are the largest minority in the United States, many of the issues are similar, and the black/white issues have not disappeared. To those who feel that this chapter does not reflect their concerns or feelings, I can only quote another author, Robert Putnam, who prefaced his discussion on racial issues with the comment, "It is perhaps foolhardy to offer a brief interpretation of those issues here, but it would be irresponsible to avoid them."[32]

"All whites are racist." Many whites react to this comment with defensiveness, anger and denial. They feel attacked for attitudes that they feel that they do not hold and actions that they did not take. But since the issue of racism will not disappear, it behooves people to understand their neighbors' attitudes, even if they disagree with them. Richard Davis, President of the Madison, Wisconsin, Institute for the Healing of Racism, suggested a rephrasing that seemed to me more acceptable, "We have all been affected by our racial conditioning."[33] No one grew up in the United States without receiving a variety of messages, mostly negative, about blacks and other ethnic groups. Since much of people's racial conditioning becomes part of their unacknowledged belief system, it affects their reactions to current situations unless they acknowledge and examine those beliefs.

"Blacks are racist too." Whites read about blacks attacking Korean store owners or hear Louis Farrakhan attacking Jews. Or they, or a friend of theirs, were unfairly yelled at by a black, presumably just because they were white. But then they hear someone comment, "Blacks can't be racist." It certainly is true that there is hostility among various ethnic groups that could be classified by some as racist. But communities may avoid bogging down in unhelpful debates if whites realize that when some blacks claim that "blacks can't be racist," they are interpreting the word racist to mean not individual attitudes but institutional racism, the systematic pattern of major organizations treating blacks differently from whites in the housing industry and other institutions. A black declared to the author that blacks couldn't be racist since racism was institutional, and they were the ones who suffered from it. Debating the exact meaning of the term might be useful if it occurs in a safe environment as part of an honest exploration, but not when made as an off-the-cuff comment at 10:30 P.M. after a hot county council hearing on parks. Arguments about definitions also can be a way for people to distance themselves from the issue and avoid authentic dialogue.

"White privilege." White privilege is the term blacks use to refer to the advantages every white enjoys simply by having white skin. Here again, the reaction of many whites will be denial and contemptuous dismissal if not resentment, even anger. Even those acknowledging that past and/or present discrimination exists will be reluctant to admit or even realize that they personally benefit from their white skin. However, when I stopped to think about the issue, I realized that if I go into a store, it is extremely unlikely that anyone will even consider accusing me of shoplifting or follow me around to make sure I do not. Yet this is an indignity many minorities face regularly. Moreover, if a clerk is rude, I may be annoyed, I may even wonder if I did anything to provoke the rudeness, but I will not have to agonize over whether the conduct was because of who I am as a human being, that is, white. I will not have to spend energy deciding whether or not to make an issue of it, or consider what to tell my child who witnessed the insult.

White privilege also refers to the advantages flowing to whites from opportunities provided to them and their ancestors but denied blacks and other racial/ethnic groups. These range from membership in all-white clubs where news of the latest job opportunities are exchanged, to denial of a mortgage. The gap in wealth between whites and blacks results partly from a discrepancy in "generational wealth." Laws and national policies that prohibited blacks from entering certain universities or buying homes in the areas most likely to increase in value reduced the older generation's ability to achieve wealth, reducing their ability to finance college educations for their children or leave a sizeable legacy to their children or grandchildren. Indeed, two-thirds of the personal wealth enjoyed by the fortunate comes not through their own efforts and success but from transfers from one generation to another either directly or through payment of college expenses.[34]

This leads to the complicated question of whether an individual is privileged or discriminated against based on someone's attitude toward them individually or because they inadvertently were affected by a pattern of discriminatory actions by institutions. And, in either case, what is the appropriate remedy or action? This question underlies not only the discussion about reparations to people of color for past harmful actions, but also debates about affirmative action. The affirmative action question involves still another issue--whether having a diverse employment force or educational institution is an appropriate goal, and how we all can benefit from our country's diversity.

"The United States should apologize for slavery and pay reparations." The author's initial response to this was, "Nonsense, no one in my family owned slaves and half of my grandparents weren't even in the country." Communities need to be aware that the argument is more sophisticated than this. The proponents claim that the legacy of slavery, providing assistance to whites that was denied to blacks in government programs, and denying blacks access to jobs, housing, and education was accepted government policy until after the Civil Rights Movement. Thus, the parents and grandparents of blacks living today were denied opportunities that would have enabled them to accumulate assets and provide advantages to their children. The ongoing nature of the legacy is clear in this example: the policies of prestigious colleges that attempt to provide spaces for children and grandchildren of alumni assist those white descendants and reduce the number of spaces available for people of color whose forefathers would have been denied admission to the college. Proponents of reparations also point out that the United States government provided an apology and reparations to Japanese interred during World War II and actively pursued reparations from Germany for Jews and others forced into slave labor in concentration camps.[35]

Individuals can differ about whether reparations are due, whether other groups discriminated against also deserve them, or the amounts or the form that reparations should take. But people in every community need to understand the logic behind the national debate. Otherwise they may be tempted to dismiss all complaints about discrimination or racial injustice as part of an absurd claim, automatically reacting defensively or with hostility if a person of color raises the issue, rather than with honest inquiry about the individual's feelings and thoughts.

Given America's diverse population and an increasingly interconnected world, living in a racially or ethnically diverse neighborhood, whether from choice, lack of alternative or because a community is changing, can offer residents and their children a positive and useful experience. It may be helpful, however, to consider some myths and some realities.

Myths, Realities and Possibilities

Myth One: America Is, Has Been, Can Be, or Should Be Racially, Ethnically, and Religiously Homogeneous

Many people might innocently deny that they hold this belief but still make statements indicating that the myth holds an attraction for them. Frequently social and economic problems, from crime to downturns in the economy, are blamed on increased diversity, the assumption being that such problems would not exist if America consisted of white, Norman Rockwell families. The underlying attitude reflected in such comments is the unconscious assumption that "good people look like me." Yet any accurate history of America must include the story of diversity with its racial, religious, and ethnic conflicts. My mother, who spent her early childhood on an Indian reservation in South Dakota, remembered that she and all the other white people slept behind the walls of a stockade for safety. She recalls hearing the then accepted evaluation of Indians, "the only good Indian is a dead Indian."

I also remember my ninety-year-old grandmother suddenly sitting up in her bed in a nursing home and complaining about "those damn shanty Irish." She was about to vote for the Irish-American Jack Kennedy but still harbored attitudes that she must have absorbed as a child in Washington, D.C., probably in the 1880s, when many people strongly resented the influx of poor Irish immigrants.

Even when whites do not object to living near or having their children attend school with minorities, there is frequently a tipping point of tolerance. If the numbers of minorities become too high, many whites become uncomfortable and withdraw. "Normal" seems to them to be a situation where whites are in a clear majority. Historically, the country's immigration policy has reflected a marked preference for whites from Northern European countries.

Although Americans do acknowledge and celebrate diversity, frequently this recognition remains superficial. We tend to forget that whites' reaction to diversity over time has included lynching, riots, broken treaties, herding Indians into reservations and Japanese Americans into concentration camps, slavery, restrictive immigration laws, and turning away shiploads of Jews fleeing Nazi Germany. Whites' response to diversity also has encompassed the less clearly brutal but still damaging laws and practices of segregation that resulted in restricted access to education, housing, and jobs.

The homogeneous image of America, in terms of race and ethnicity never accurately reflected reality. Before the Europeans came, the numerous Native American tribes spoke different languages, worshiped different gods, and practiced different customs. Before the Pilgrims landed, French fur traders and Spanish missionaries had arrived. A black man was the first person killed fighting for American independence. The choice has never been whether America will be diverse but rather how we will handle the diversity that exists.

Myth Two: Minorities are Homogeneous

In recent years, the differences within the black and other racial and ethnic communities have become increasingly clear. Minorities, like members of the majority, differ along lines of income, religion, education, and tastes in food, music, and art. They choose different occupations and vote for different candidates and political parties. Some people of color express prejudices and tensions toward other ethnic groups as well as toward whites. Is this surprising given the worldwide existence of intergroup conflicts?

Myth Three: Healthy Neighborhoods are Naturally Homogeneous and Caucasian

Several factors have led to this perception, held at least unconsciously by many. First, racism can cause whites to assume that any neighborhood with a high proportion of minorities must be inferior. Second, some neighborhoods with a high proportion of minorities are in fact blighted. They may suffer from overcrowding, high concentrations of single parent families of all races, and inferior government services. Predatory businesses concentrate in such areas. Zoning often permits such uses as adult video stores; police tend to ignore prostitutes and drug dealers. Whenever possible, minorities as well as whites flee such neighborhoods. Third, frequently the real estate, banking, and insurance industries have fostered the idea that good neighborhoods are homogeneous and white, and they have practiced differential policies among neighborhoods based on racial and ethnic composition.[36]

Resources from local, state, and federal sources have flowed on an unequal basis into neighborhoods inhabited primarily by whites. Businesses have located near white suburban workers, providing them with access to jobs and consumer conveniences, and increasing their community's tax base. The new businesses make their corporate contributions to the suburban charities. Banks, real estate agents, and insurance agents have practiced differential policies among neighborhoods based on racial and ethnic composition.

Despite the perceptions, healthy neighborhoods have existed whose residents primarily consisted of Italians, African Americans, Mexican Americans, Puerto Ricans, Poles, Swedes, Chinese, and many other groups or combinations as well as Caucasians. Numerous healthy diverse neighborhoods exist. Some, such as the Hyde Park-Kenwood neighborhood in Chicago, have continued as diverse neighborhoods for decades. In other situations, such neighborhoods last for a while, then gradually become more homogeneous. Residents of neighborhoods that are racially or ethnically diverse, even for a short period of time, have a somewhat unique opportunity. One means of evaluating the success of such a community may be the quality of the experience of interracial or interethnic contact. The success of diversity looked at in this way is not measured solely by the length of time the neighborhood maintains a certain numerical count of persons of different characteristics, but by the effect on those individuals who have had an experience not frequently found in the United States.[36]

Myth Four: Successful Diverse Neighborhoods and Communities Experience No Tensions or Problems

The view that all contact among diverse people should be problem-free may not be helpful. The fact that diversity may involve some tension does not negate its value. It is important to be sensitive to the nuances of diversity, its richness as well as its problems. One definition of success might be comfortable physical proximity; unhampered access by all residents to services and facilities; lack of tension among neighborhood residents; an opportunity to make friends with unlike neighbors; and no more interracial, ethnic, or class conflict or discomfort than exist elsewhere in society.

This definition does not require that blacks and whites or Hispanics and blacks become friends, merely that they have the opportunity to do so. Nor does this definition require that all conflicts cease. In such a community, as in any community, some residents will not like each other; others will disagree on a range of community issues. Some residents will not get along with members of another race or ethnic group. But some residents do not get along with members of their own race. Some residents of diverse communities may not welcome living next to a person of another race, but many of them would not enjoy living next door to their own adult children.

One sociologist suggested that judging communities only by their communal aspects is less appropriate than emphasizing the quality of their civic life.[37] The Americans who now have or will have neighbors of different races, ethnic backgrounds, and incomes need to know how to maintain appropriate public behavior, build community spirit, and develop the cooperative relationships that will enable them to effectively tackle community issues. Openly addressing questions of differences can provide a greater freedom in recognizing the predominance of our common traits, abilities, and desires. Such open-mindedness can help us focus on how we can work together to better our communities.

Why should anyone wish to live in a diverse neighborhood or actively encourage participation by all groups? Some do so for idealistic reasons. Some do so because the chosen home happens to be in a diverse area. Others are unwilling to flee if minorities move into their previously white area or to leave their homes when their neighborhood undergoes gentrification. Some, such as public housing residents, lack alternatives. Others recognize the advantages to their children in growing up with diversity since they will enter a diverse work force, and visit cities and nations where they will not be in the majority.

Understanding differences may ease relationships among individuals of different races. A key to neighborhood harmony, however, rests in recognizing the vast similarities of Americans, whatever their race or ethnicity. Each of a neighborhood's families and individuals will be affected by the area's success at building community and building strong community-based organizations that can effectively tackle issues of concern to all neighborhood residents and families.

Notes

1. Except where otherwise noted, the examples are based on the author's personal experience or information provided to her by the individual involved. The examples are drawn from living and working in Chicago, Illinois, Washington, D.C. and Madison, Wisconsin as well as material from my dissertation studies in Columbia, Maryland, and Reston, Virginia. Since I have not undertaken current research on either community, I use examples from that material only when they illustrate an attitude or example of something that I also have observed elsewhere more recently. Despite my use of negative examples from these communities, my research and that of others indicate that their inhabitants then enjoyed and continue to enjoy better diverse relationships than in many places. Wireman, P. (1984.) Urban neighborhoods, networks, and families: New forms for old values (Chapter 7). Lexington, MA: D.C. Heath and Company. Wireman, P. (1976). *Meanings of community in modern America: Some implications from new towns.* Dissertation Abstracts International, 38(03), 1672A. (UMI No. 7718716). Eversley, M. (1997, July 25). In Maryland city, planning spawned integration success. *Detroit Free Press.* Retrieved April 1, 2005, from http://www.freep.com/news/race/qco125.htm.
2. Keyes, R.. (2006). *The quote verifier: Who said what, where, and when.* New York : Saint Martin's Press. Retrieved March 27, 2007, from http://www.ralphkeyes. com/pages/books_old/quote/excerpt.htm.
3. Gilman, R. C. (2000). *Spinning into butter: a play.* New York: Faber and Faber.
4. Hopper, G. K. (Ed.). (1995). *Action plan: Multicultural initiative in Texas museums.* Austin: Texas Association of Museums.

5. Wireman, P. (1984). *Urban neighborhoods, networks, and families: New forms for old values.* Lexington, MA: D.C. Heath and Company.
6. Williams, L. (2000). *It's the little things: The everyday interactions that get under the skin of blacks and whites.* New York: Harcourt, Inc.
7. Wireman, P. (1984). *Urban neighborhoods, networks, and families: New forms for old values.* Lexington, MA: D.C. Heath and Company.
8. Wireman, P. (1984). *Urban neighborhoods, networks, and families: New forms for old values.* Lexington, MA: D.C. Heath and Company.
9. Quillian, L. and Pager, D. (2002). Black neighbors, higher crime? The role of racial stereotypes in evaluations of neighborhood crime. *American Journal of Sociology. 107*(3), 717-767.
10. U.S. Department of Justice, Bureau of Justice Statistics. (2001, March 18). *Differences in rates of violent crime experienced by whites and blacks narrow* (p.1). Retrieved October 22, 2003, from http://www.ojp.usdoj.gov/bjs/pub/press/vvr98pr.htm.
11. Lanker, B. (1999). *I dream a world: Portraits of black women who changed America* (Rev. Ed.). New York: Stewart, Tabori & Chang.
12. Bendick, M., Jr., Jackson, C. W., & Reinoso, V. A. (1997). Measuring employment discrimination. In J. H. Skolnick, & E. Currie.. (Eds.). *Crisis in American institutions.* (10th ed.), (pp. 150-162). New York: Addison-Wesley Educational Publishers, Inc.
13. Bendick, M., Jr., Jackson, C. W., & Reinoso, V. A. (1997). Measuring employment discrimination. In J. H. Skolnick, & E. Currie.. (Eds.). *Crisis in American institutions.* (10 th ed.) (pp. 150-162) [Quotation on p. 155]. New York: Addison-Wesley Educational Publishers, Inc.
14. Pager, D. (2002). The mark of a criminal record. *American Journal of Sociology, 108* (5), 937-975.
15. Council on Crime and Justice and Institute on Race and Poverty.(2003). *Minnesota racial profiling study.* Retrieved September 24, 2003, from http://www. crimeandjustice.org/Pages/Publications/Reports/Racial%20Profiling%20Study/ Summary%20of%20Findings.pdf. Leadership Conference on Civil Rights/Leadership Conference Education Fund. (2002). *Justice on trial: Racial disparities in the American criminal justice system* (p.2). Washington, DC: Author. Retrieved October 2, 2003, from www.civilrights.org/publications/reports/cj/justice.pdf.
16. Leadership Conference on Civil Rights/Leadership Conference Education Fund. (2002). *Justice on trial: Racial disparities in the American criminal justice system* (pp. 1-30). Washington, DC: Author. Retrieved October 2, 2003, from www.civil-rights.org/publications/reports/cj/justice.pdf.
17. Leadership Conference on Civil Rights/Leadership Conference Education Fund. (2002). *Justice on trial: Racial disparities in the American criminal justice system* (pp. 5, 7). Washington, DC: Author. Retrieved October 2, 2003, from www.civil-rights.org/publications/reports/cj/justice.pdf.
18. Leadership Conference on Civil Rights/Leadership Conference Education Fund. (2002). *Justice on trial: Racial disparities in the American criminal justice system* (p. 13). Washington, DC: Author. Retrieved March 26, 2007, from http://www. civilrights.org/publications/reports/cj.justice.pdf.
19. Leadership Conference on Civil Rights/Leadership Conference Education Fund. (2002). *Justice on trial: Racial disparities in the American criminal justice system* (pp. 13-14, 37-38, 40). Washington, DC: Author. Retrieved October 2, 2003, from www.civilrights.org/publications/reports/cj/justice.pdf.
20. The author was an advisor on environment at the U.S. Department of Housing and Development at the time.

21. Feagin, J. R. (2000). *Racist America: Roots, current realities, & future reparations* (pp. 155-156). New York: Routledge. Turner, M. A. Ross, S. L. Galster, G. & Yinger, J. (2002, November 7). *Discrimination in metropolitan housing markets: national results from phase I HDS 2000. Final report.* Washington, DC: The Urban Institute. Retrieved January 19, 2007, from http://www.urban.org/UploadedPDF/410821_Phase1_Report.pdf.

22. Turner, M. A. Ross, S. L. Galster, G. & Yinger, J. (2002, November 7). *Discrimination in metropolitan housing markets: national results from phase I HDS 2000. Final report.* Washington, DC: The Urban Institute. Retrieved January 19, 2007, from http://www.urban.org/UploadedPDF/410821_Phase1_Report.pdf.

23. Schloemer, W., Ernt, K., & Keest, K. (2006, December). *Losing ground: Foreclosures in the subprime market and their cost to homeowners.* Durham, NC: Center for Responsible Lending. Retrieved Decmber 13, 2007, from http://www.responsiblelending.org/pdfs/foreclosure-paper-report-2-17.pdf.

24. Suttles, G. D. (1972). *Social construction of communities* (p. 21-43). Chicago: The University of Chicago Press.

25. Rank, M. R. (1994). *Living on the edge: The realities of welfare in America.* New York: Columbia University Press.

26. Burkhart, L. C. (1981). *Old values in a new town: The politics of race and class in Columbia Maryland.* (p. 4). New York: Praeger.

27. Rank, M. R. (1994). *Living on the edge: The realities of welfare in America.* New York: Columbia University Press.

28. Anderson, E. (1990). *Race, class and change in an urban community* (pp. 214-215). Chicago: The University of Chicago Press.

29. Gans, H. J. The underclass label. In J. H. Skolnick, & E. Currie. (Eds.). (1997). *Crisis in American institutions* (10th ed.) (pp. 125-137) [Quotation on p. 126]. New York: Addison-Wesley Educational Publishers, Inc.

30. Wireman, P. (1984). *Urban neighborhoods, networks, and families: New forms for old values.* Lexington, MA: D.C. Heath and Company.

31. Wireman, P. (1984). *Urban neighborhoods, networks, and families: New forms for old values* (p. 103). Lexington, MA: D.C. Heath and Company.

32. Putnam, R. D. (2000). *Bowling Alone: The collapse and revival of American community* (p. 361). New York: Simon & Schuster.

33. The author attended sessions of Dr. Davis' workshops in the spring of 2003. For information about similar workshops, see http://www.richarddavis.org/rap/hr-main.html, http://www.nrchr.org/default.asp, or http://www.centerhealingracism.org/.

34. Rank, M. R. (2004). *One nation, underprivileged. Why American poverty affects us* all. p. 72. New York: Oxford University Press.

35. Feagin, J. 2001). *Racist America: Roots, current realities & future reparations* (p. 264). New York: Routledge.

36. Turner, M. A. Ross, S. L. Galster, G. & Yinger, J. (2002, November 7). *Discrimination in metropolitan housing markets: national results from phase I HDS 2000. Final report.* Washington, DC: The Urban Institute. Retrieved January 19, 2007, from http://www.urban.org/UploadedPDF/410821_Phase1_Report.pdf. U.S. Department of Housing and Urban Development. (2006, October 26). *HUD charges Erie Insurance Group with race discrimination.* Retrieved January 24, 2007, from http://www.hud.gov/news/release.cfm?content=pr06-142.cfm.

37. Beach, M., & Beach, O. S. (1978). *Interracial neighborhoods in the urban community* (p. 56). Rochester, NY: Unpublished Manuscript.

38. Bender, T. (1978). *Community and social change in America* (p. 148). New Brunswick, NJ: Rutgers University Press.

Part 2

What Can Neighborhoods and Local Communities Do?

7

Building Community and Social Capital

Community involvement takes many different forms, leading to confusion about the nature of community-based solutions to problems. Self-help, volunteering, community organizing, community development, citizen participation and many other words have been used over the past fifty years to describe a variety of activities that can support families and neighborhoods. This chapter clarifies the differences between these terms and describes the role each can play in helping families function well. We give special attention to the development and role of Community Development Corporations, which remain an important force in many communities.

A prevalent notion in conservative political thought suggests that these efforts can effectively support families without the need for government involvement. To disabuse the reader of this mistaken idea, the chapter presents an evaluation of the limitations of community organizing and the need for complementary federal action. While local action is necessary to address problems and to create family-friendly environments, state and national commitment is clearly needed as well. The chapter concludes with a framework that can be applied to any family issue a community faces.

Self-Help

Self-help can mean several individuals getting together to discuss a mutual problem and to give each other emotional support, or it can mean neighborhood action. According to Robert Putnam, at any one time approximately 2 percent of Americans participate in self-help or support groups that address individual or family concerns. Well over a million people participate in Alcoholics Anonymous (AA) and Al-Anon.[1] Self-help groups support neighborhoods both through the direct assistance provided to residents and the indirect benefits from expanded personal relationships and networks. The latter probably only occurs if the group meets in the neighborhood. However, people may not want to discuss intimate concerns with others whom they will meet on the street the next day. When discussing the need for an AA group at a neighborhood center in Madison, for example, the author realized that going to such a meeting at the busy center would publicize a participant's condition to the neighborhood. Neighborhood organizations can support self-help groups by providing a public meeting space when appropriate, helping to find facilitators, and using the area's formal and informal channels to publicize meeting times and places.

In addition to participating in individual self-help efforts, people can join together to combat neighborhood problems. Depending upon the activity and the desires of those involved, such group self-help activities can facilitate the growth not only of individual friendships but also of casual recognition, casual acquaintances and intimate secondary relationships. People can learn new skills as well as ways to work together. The activities can provide the experience, confidence, and networks needed for more ambitious projects.

The resources needed for self-help activities will vary: often a computer and minimal funds for paper and postage will suffice. A public meeting place can be crucial, especially if people want to involve others of different incomes or ethnic or racial backgrounds.

Volunteers

Millions of Americans volunteer to help individuals, families, and their communities. They give blood, tutor children, serve as museum docents, and provide companionship for the elderly. They lead the governing boards of numerous nonprofit organizations, and serve on advisory boards at all levels of government. The immediate response to September 11, 2001, and to Hurricane Katrina demonstrated the depth of American citizens' generosity and willingness to help.

Without volunteers many community efforts would be impossible. Nearly one half of all Americans claim to volunteer by assisting a neighbor or helping at a hospital or other organization. Putnam estimated that 93 million Americans volunteered 20 billion hours in one year alone.[2] Volunteers render actual services from coaching soccer to writing grant applications. They provide one-to-one service and participate in community projects. Through their volunteer work, they build the informal relationships, networks, and community organizations that contribute to an area's social capital. Volunteer organizations also monitor government and business activities.

The type of volunteering matters. Providing direct service may broaden personal networks but does not contribute to the community's ability to undertake major projects or influence business or government. Do people volunteer as a result of their membership in a civic organization, such as the Rotary or the PTA, or does their volunteering stem from their relationship with a church? Members of civic organizations who volunteer are more likely to undertake community projects and to volunteer more frequently than people who attend church but not civic organizations. Volunteering as part of a religious connection is more likely to focus on one-to-one service and less likely to involve people beyond the church community or lead to volunteering in a civic organization.[3] Faith-based volunteering is likely to strengthen bonding capital between members of the church, synagogue, or mosque, but not bridging capital among different groups in the community.

According to Putnam, volunteering generally now has shifted away from community projects to direct one-on-one-service. Moreover, he claims that the rise in volunteering per se results from increased volunteering by the generation born before World War II who have recently retired. They have been more active and more likely to participate in community projects at each stage of their life cycle than other generations. Thus, when these people become less physically able to volunteer or as they die, the current surge of volunteer activity may well decrease.[4]

Community Organizing

The term "community organizing" has had many different meanings and interpretations and frequently is used interchangeably with the term "community development." In this book it refers to any effort to organize residents in a geographic area to identify needs and work to meet them. Community organizations tend to focus on all aspects of the entire neighborhood and to stress open-ended democratic decision-making.

The scope of a community organization can vary. At the modest end it might involve a block club formed to plant trees. Or it might entail establishing a non-profit with a multi-million dollar budget that sponsors an array of enterprises for broad-based community improvement. Common internal purposes include promoting friendly recognition, developing neighborly networks, and improving racial or ethnic relationships. Community organizations often run painting and repair campaigns, operate programs such as after-school activities, and sponsor community centers. A community organizing effort may aim to obtain and/or monitor services from nonprofit organizations, government agencies and businesses. Moving beyond the immediate neighborhood, the objective may be to forge local partnerships or to weigh in on state and national policies that effect residents. A neighborhood organization may engage in all of these activities at the same time or at different periods in its history. The organizational structure may comprise a group of individual members who live on the same block, a simple coalition of block groups, or a group of organizations. The latter were the basis for the most well-known community organizing model, Saul Alinsky's Industrial Areas Foundation (IAF).[5]

Often community organizations form with the encouragement of financial support and professional organizers from a school of social work, another organization, such as the IAF, or a government entity. Many grew out of the government-mandated citizen participation efforts that began with the Great Society programs in the 1960s and spread to subsequent government programs.[6]

As groups begin to undertake extensive improvement projects or to participate intensely in government programs, they generally open an office and hire staff. At this point tensions may arise between different, and sometimes conflicting, organizational goals. Is the organization's primary goal to encourage residents to develop their organizational and other skills, to lobby city government for improvements, or to undertake a specific project such as an after-school program or housing rehabilitation? An organization may take on all these goals simultaneously, but must recognize the potential for conflict about staff priorities and methods as well as allocation of resources.

If the major organizing objective is to encourage community interaction, people's self-development, or the growth of local leaders, ongoing efforts will be needed to continually involve new people in the organization, nourish their participation, and support their projects, even those that may not seem important to some leaders. For example, in a dispute about potential cuts in staff at a community center in Maryland, the neighborhood residents protested that those allocating funds did not understand all aspects of their work. Staff would spend considerable time helping a woman who had a skill but no teaching experience to organize her class and recruit students. They felt that the value of their program lay as much in assisting residents in developing new skills as in offering programs.[7]

A similar emphasis on process can be seen in the effort to ensure that everyone at meetings has an opportunity to talk, even if this leads to lengthy and diffuse discussions. During the early days of the Civil Rights movement, one participant complained to a meeting organizer, "Why did you let that man ramble on and on? What he said wasn't important." The organizer snapped back, "It was important to him."

Such an approach can lead to multiple meetings that cover the same ground because new people may arrive at any meeting. If they do not feel heard, they will not come again. But those who were at previous meetings may become bored, resentful about having to repeat the same discussion, and stop attending. I once used slides to overcome this problem. At the beginning of a second community meeting, I showed slides that presented those aspects of community life that residents had identified the previous week as their vision for the future. I then asked the new people if they had additional suggestions. After they made a few comments, the meeting quickly moved on. The use of the visual display eliminated a repeat of the previous meeting.

Conditions that enhance any grassroots community organizing effort include a clear philosophical commitment set forth in a written mission statement, a community tradition of democratic involvement rather than domination by a few leaders, paid staff with a community organizing philosophy, and at least minimal organizational resources, including office space, supplies, a copying machine, and seed money for new projects. A strong community group also needs a democratic governing board and a structure that permits participation by a variety of people with different interests and skills. A facilitator from an organization outside the community can be helpful, even crucial. The facilitator often brings an objective eye to the community and its longstanding disputes or rivalries. But, even then, neighborhood conflicts and politics can become as petty or heated as those in any other setting. An IAF organizer once commented that, "When I take a job in a community, the first thing I do is put six months salary in the bank. Then I can afford to be fired."

Despite the frustrations that can occur, grassroots participation can lead to satisfaction and personal growth as well as community improvement. Although staff may be important, community organizing also depends upon volunteers to help in the office, serve on governing boards and committees, provide the leadership and person power for large and small projects, lobby city and county agencies, and obtain assistance from businesses.

Citizen Participation

The belief that citizens should be involved directly in the organizations that affect them is part of the American democratic tradition. The term "citizen participation" came into widespread use during the 1960s after the law establishing the War on Poverty's Community Action Agency required that programs be developed with "maximum feasible participation" of those affected. Initially the rules required that the programs be run by local boards of directors, the majority of whose members represented the poor. Soon, however, local politicians, bureaucrats, and Congress reacted, making it clear that citizen participation was to be only advisory. Some observers concluded that any meaningful participation of the poor had ended, leaving only "maximum feasible manipulation."[8]

Nevertheless, the belief that those citizens most directly affected by government programs should have a major influence over their design and implementation remained strong both at the grassroots level and among many government officials. The extent of citizen participation requirements in federal government programs actually increased markedly in the 1970s after the official demise of the Great Society. The number of programs requiring citizen participation rose from sixteen to eighty-seven under President Richard Nixon. Some citizen groups received more than one million dollars a year to organize community participation in urban areas.[9]

Although critics complained that the participation in these efforts generally involved affluent and better educated community members, perhaps with special interests to protect, in some cases residents did achieve real changes in program administration. Most important, the efforts trained a new generation of leaders. Many of those on local boards or staff were young, minority, or female. They gained leadership experience at a time when few businesses would consider hiring them and when government agencies often were staffed with older, white men.[10]

Because of the limitations of government-mandated citizen participation and major program cutbacks under President Ronald Reagan during the 1980s, many local activists shifted their emphasis. Some began building or rehabilitating houses, both to improve their neighborhoods and to earn money to replace the loss of federal funds. Many reached out to local governments and businesses for financial support and partnerships.

Ensuring that citizens have a structured influence on government policy and programs remains an important challenge. Conditions conducive to success include:

1. The mandate for citizen participation must be clear, preferably based on Congressional or state legislation.
2. The affected citizens must have sufficient organizational power to command the right to participate.
3. The organization must be acknowledged by government officials as a legitimate spokesperson for the area or the people affected by the programs.
4. The organization must have effective input into the program's budget process.
5. The organization must have ongoing access to information and to decision makers throughout the decision-making process. Participation at a public hearing usually comes too late.
6. The organization must be able to turn to the federal or state government or the courts if local officials deny it the right to participate.
7. The organization must have access to technical experts who are accountable to the group.
8. The organization must have sufficient operating funds so that its energies are not absorbed by fund-raising.
9. Those active must be able to function well together and must understand the administrative and technical requirements of the relevant programs or laws.

Many city governments have established neighborhood councils that embody some or all of the above attributes. Some provide funds to neighborhood groups to create local plans and staff experts to assist them. Others allocate funds to neighborhood councils for operating expenses or for undertaking small projects. Portland, Oregon, for example, supports an extensive network of ninety-five neighborhood organizations, seven neighborhood offices and associations and thirty-four neighborhood business associations. The city budgets millions of dollars to provide technical assistance, to contract with neighborhood offices for services and to provide a staff person in each office. The city's Web site contained extensive information useful to any locality concerned with increasing the effectiveness of its community organizations.[11]

Community Development and Community Development Corporations

In this book, the term "community development" is taken to mean local efforts that concentrate on changing the structural conditions within a neighborhood through programs run by neighborhood-based organizations. The original mandates in the anti-poverty efforts of the sixties, including those for the Community Action and Model Cities Program, called for tackling community problems on a holistic basis. Many of the community-based efforts which have developed since have taken this approach. A survey conducted by the National Congress for Community Economic Development in 2005 estimated that 4,600 organizations existed that served low and moderate income areas and were engaged in some form of economic or housing development. Many of these organizations grew out of the citizen participation efforts mandated by government programs in the sixties and seventies. A number of the strongest organizations existing today were started by the leaders trained during that period. Indeed, one-half of the executive directors are more than fifty years old and one fifth are over age sixty. Even though the majority of organizations were started later, two-thirds of them engage in community organizing and advocacy. Their community-building activities range over almost every aspect of community life and include community safety, homeowner counseling, job-readiness training, child care, arts and culture, education and training, youth programs, and prisoner re-entry programs.[12]

Organizations engaged in community development included Community Action Agencies, Neighbor/Works/National Housing Services organizations, community development housing organizations, community development financial institutions, local development corporations and Community Development Corporations. About one-fourth were faith based. Together these groups in 2005 built more than a million units of housing, 126 million square feet of commercial or industrial space and created almost 800,000 jobs.[13]

The ability of the local groups to operate effectively has depended partly upon assistance from a variety of national organizations which have provided technical assistance and training. These vary from those that stress community organization and advocacy to those designed to help with rehabilitating housing. The Industrial Areas Foundation with fifty-seven affiliates in twenty-one states and several countries proclaims that it is "non-ideological and strictly non-partisan, but proudly, publicly, and persistently political." Their organizers were behind the first living wage campaigns. The thirty-five-year-old Association of Community Organizations for Reform Now, ACORN, claims a membership of 350,000 low and moderate income members in more than one hundred cities. For over a decade both organizations have been actively involved in assisting local groups fight for living wage measures which would require those receiving local government contracts to pay decent wages and benefits. ACORN played a major role in obtaining the passage of the Community Reinvestment Act (CRA) in 1977 which requires banks to invest in low-income and minority neighborhoods and then lobbied banks and the government for effective implementation.[14] On the other hand, a number of national organizations have relied heavily on government funding which prohibited them from lobbying.

The most prominent examples of local community organizations are Community Development Corporations, or CDCs. The genesis for CDCs was a 1966 visit by Senator Robert Kennedy to the Bedford-Stuyvesant area of New York City that led to the federal creation of the Bedford-Stuyvesant Restoration Corporation. Although the majority of CDCs have focused on housing, either the rehabilitation of existing units or the construction of new ones, many now have expanded to offer economic development or social services.[15]

Both supporters and critics of CDCs have noted the crucial need for a reliable source of operating funds, which are, unfortunately, the most difficult for any community development organization to obtain. Many foundations and other funders prefer to offer seed money for a pilot project, expecting that the local organization will find a means of supporting the project if it provides successful. This too often leaves the organization with increased overhead costs without a long-term source of increased operating funds. Paying an accountant to prepare tax statements or hiring a janitor may be sound practice, but do not provide appealing publicity photos for funders to use for their own promotion needs. CDCs often have complex structures with a variety of subsidiaries, partly to satisfy the conditions for grants from different sources. Further complicating the issue is the fact that, as a community-based organization, the CDC may be expected to hire local people who may require special training and extensive supervision.

CDCs must balance the philosophy and goals of a community-based grass-roots organization with the requirements of operating a business with deadlines and a payroll. CDCs not only build housing, they often manage the rental units they build. If they evict a tenant for non-payment of rent, they may be considered as uncaring by the neighborhood members on their board of directors. Yet if they do not collect the rents, they cannot pay the building's mortgage. To the extent that the organization stresses grassroots participation in decision-making, it reduces its ability to make business decisions promptly or to respond quickly to a grant opportunity.

This conflict between efficiency and community building can affect goals, management structures, hiring decisions, and financing. Grant requests must specify, for example, whether the funds will be used for staff to hold community meetings or for staff with expertise in packaging real estate deals. Managers may be constrained in their ability to hire non-residents. What happens when a position is posted with educational requirements that most local residents are unlikely to meet? A director who fires a local resident for non-performance may face political flak. The CDC's housing program should clearly prioritize its goals, whether to house existing residents in subsidized low-income rental housing, or to provide a new image for the area by attracting higher income homeowners. The point is not that one approach is necessarily better than another, but that any one organization embodying such conflicts will face difficulties.

The grassroots nature of CDCs also is limited by the demands of their funders and the need to maintain cordial relationships with city officials, bankers and other members of the business community. In order to have access to financial and legal expertise, a CDC may add knowledgeable outsiders to their governing boards. While this may strengthen its business capacity, it opens the CDC to criticism about outsiders with superior education and experience dominating the local residents. Perhaps more important, to the extent that a CDC depends upon city governments or businesses for funds and access to institutional decision-makers, it may be hindered from criticizing those entities. Furthermore, CDCs are rightly proud of their achievements, and fund-raising requires touting an organization's successes. But reports of CDC successes may divert attention from critical problems that need to be addressed at a state and national level such as low wages and reduced federal funding for housing.

Despite these caveats, Community Development Corporations have developed into one of the most important vehicles for community involvement, neighborhood improvement, and local institutional change. During the 1990s many CDCs expanded their operations to include commercial and business development, workforce developments, youth programs, open space projects such as gardens or parks, and providing facilities such as health clinics and community centers.[16]

In 1991 a major effort began to address the limitations of CDCs, a partnership that eventually included nine foundations, six banks, and the U.S. Department of Housing and Urban Development. It provided millions of dollars in pooled funds to undertake a multi-year effort in twenty-three cities. The program was designed to increase CDC capacity, promote institutional change, and build new and more effective linkages between CDCs and local stakeholders.[17]

The partnership used two established intermediary organizations, the Local Initiatives Support Corporation and the Enterprise Foundation, to create local collaborative relationships. These collaborations fostered partnerships and allocated funds to 300 CDCs. The intermediary organizations provided ongoing technical assistance to the local collaborations and to the individual CDCs. The use of substantial amounts of outside money and the prestige of the funders provided leverage that encouraged local stakeholders to cooperate. Funders could provide multi-year funding for the CDCs (extraordinarily helpful for organizational stability and effectiveness) and require performance standards for efforts to build organizational capacity, for community outreach, and for specific projects.[18]

Results have included significant improvements in the numbers of projects, expansion by the CDCs into areas other than housing, growth in organizational capacity, recognition of the CDCs as reliable, significant players in their larger communities, and development of greater cooperation with and among local stakeholders.[19] Clearly, strong neighborhood organizations with excellent relations among community-wide stakeholders will be the most effective in implementing the neighborhood's visions.

An Evaluation of Local Community Organizing

Politicians and others have lauded community-based and self-help efforts as an alternative to government programs, especially the "failed" programs of the 1960s. Such conclusions are unwarranted and undermine the need for supportive policies at the federal and state levels.

First, although some Great Society programs were unsuccessful, others produced significant results. Many lost funding when government expenditures shifted to the Vietnam War. Second, the philosophy and rhetoric of those advocating local involvement and self-help programs actually represent part of the legacy of the government-sponsored efforts of the 1960s and 1970s. Organizations that later emerged as leaders in the community development corporation movement often had begun as advisory groups for those earlier programs. Third, the idea of involving the people served in the design and operation of programs spread to a number of fields. For example, rhetoric similar to that of the Great Society can be found in nursing textbooks that stress the need for community involvement.[20] Fourth, activists and staff from the government-funded grassroots programs often entered government service, influencing policies at local, state and federal levels. Finally, for forty years, much of the funding for local self-help efforts has come directly or indirectly from the federal government.[21] As late as 2007, funds used to operate neighborhood centers in Madison, Wisconsin, came mostly from the federal Community Development Block Grant program.

Many government critics also like to tout community development organizations as examples of boot-strap grassroots effectiveness, in contrast to top-down efforts. The claims may be overstated, however. Even the larger CDCs that produce significant numbers of residential units cannot resolve the overall housing problem. CDC efforts may be important—they may be the only game in town—but they do not address the magnitude of the housing problem. Nor do they tackle the underlying regional and national economic, institutional, and political issues. This does not diminish the importance of CDC successes. Buying and rehabilitating one house or small apartment building on a block can make a major neighborhood impact if it removes an eyesore or a crack house. Any such effort helps to build local social capital through the relationships formed.[22]

Many of the community development organizations are not large, incorporated, well-funded Community Development Corporations. They are small operations constantly struggling to keep their doors open and retain the professional expertise and capital needed to accomplish their goals. One half of them have only seven or fewer full-time employees.[23] Both the larger CDCs and other community development organizations have relied heavily on outside funding, primarily from foundations and the federal government. Eighty-eight percent of the community organizations responding to a survey in 2005 each received over $50,000 that year from over forty different federal programs. Thirty-eight of them obtained funds from state governments and 30 percent received funds from their local governments, some of which came indirectly from the federal government programs such as through the Community Development Block Grant program.[24]

Many local community development organizations have received assistance from national and regional intermediaries. Intermediary organizations differ in organizational form, goals and financing. Some, like ACORN and the Industrial Areas Foundation, stress community organization and political activism. Some, such as the Local Initiatives Support Corporation and the Enterprise Foundation serve as a means of helping local organizations tap into the resources of national foundation and government funding sources. Others, like the government-created Neighborhood Reinvestment Corporation focus primarily on housing.[25]

Intermediaries also offer technical assistance and training. The federal government also has played an important role in supporting intermediaries. For example, during a two year period in the mid-1980s, the Economic Development Administration provided a million dollars in funding to a number of national organizations to provide technical assistance and training to local community development organizations.[26]

Many of the intermediaries have served as conduits not only for foundation and government money, but also for private sector funds. The 1986 Tax Reform Act enabled intermediaries to pool corporate investments for low-income housing projects through syndication. This provided community development organizations indirect access to the mainstream capital market. The complicated "deals" that the CDCs structure to finance housing depend heavily upon the use of tax credits granted as a reward for investing in such housing, investments which pay a high rate of return. [27] Thus, even the private investments in low-income housing are largely financed by the taxpayers.

While CDCs play an important community role, their continued viability depends upon a constant influx of outside financing. Although CDCs do gain income from their projects, the projects they undertake, after all, are to provide housing and other amenities or services that the private market has determined are basically unprofitable.

Maximizing Success: A Framework for Methodical Action

Given the constraints and limitations of local action, how can an individual or group give their best shot at addressing, perhaps even solving, a community problem? This chapter has pointed out that community organizing can mean many different things, but also that there are certain common aspects in focus and process. These suggest a framework for guiding action in a methodical fashion that will minimize conflict and maximize the chances for positive impact. This framework provides the basis for considering, in the chapters to follow, community-based action for each of the six fundamental family tasks. The framework entails issue identification, stakeholder analysis, asset inventory, the use of outside resources, and taking a systems approach.

Issue Identification

Each neighborhood and local community must determine for itself what problems it wants to tackle, carefully considering what issues are most important for its families, and clearly identifying the scope and scale of possible actions. Do people want to address nutrition issues affecting only children, or do they also concern themselves with the widow living down the street? It often helps for residents to try envisioning their future. When working in a run-down area in a small city near Chicago, I had people close their eyes and think about what they wanted the area to look like in five years. Then they considered what they would hear, then how they would feel. They wanted to see clean streets, hear friendly greetings, feel safe and welcome. I assembled a short slide show symbolizing their vision using pictures from their neighborhood and others.

The scope of a problem may change as root causes are probed and the group considers all the actors who need to be involved in the solution. Without careful analysis, simple approaches may be seized upon, blaming others will prevail, and solutions will fail or not last long. In a single day I once heard spontaneous, separate complaints about trash from the tenants in a public housing development, the housing authority staff, and the city manager. Each complained about the other; each felt that the solution was simple if only "they" would act appropriately. Viewed carefully, however, there were really eleven separate problems, each contributing to the overall situation: some tenants did not pick up trash, some outsiders used the area as a dumping ground, the garbage cans would not hold a week's garbage, the city had reduced pick-up to every other week, dogs overturned the garbage cans, an ice cream truck left children with sticky paper but no nearby trash cans. Everyone was willing to do their part, but without properly identifying the contributing factors and all of the involved parties, the necessary joint coordinated action was impossible. Thus, thorough and accurate analysis of the problem is crucial. Otherwise, overly narrow solutions will be adopted and fail, leaving only discouragement, blame and abandonment of effort.

In choosing an issue, be aware that some issues have a built-in scale: trash on the street may affect only a few families or blocks, while crime potentially has spillover effects on everyone in the area. Both issues and potential actions may impact people unequally, leading neighbors to differ about goals and solutions. Some people will not get what they want or will be harmed by actions that benefit the rest of the neighborhood. For example, the desire by many neighborhoods for exclusivity has made it difficult for other families to satisfy their housing needs.

Addressing family concerns raises a possibly sensitive issue of scale, that is, whose family matters. The geographic area of concern for some may be limited to families on their block, or to a several block area, or extend to the larger neighborhood. Others may concern themselves with everyone in their town or county, while still others would love to impact the lives of every family in the state or nation. Do neighbors consider the well-being of all young children or only their own? What if they don't have children? One condominium owner I knew objected strongly to children playing in the pool; she demanded peace and quiet declaring, "I've raised my children."

The geographic level of concern matters for three reasons. First, even achievements at a block level often cannot be accomplished without involving actors who do not live there. Second, the scope of geographic concern determines whether an entity will be asked to take responsibility for how its actions affect other geographic areas, as in the case of factories producing polluted air that blows to other states. Finally, a person's geographic level of concern determines his or her attitudes toward government programs, which may primarily benefit families in another part of the city, county, state or in other states.

Successfully addressing complex issues requires defining each issue carefully, taking a systems approach; in other words, tracing all the tentacles of the octopus. The following six chapters explore six complex issues, each of them representing a basic task that families are expected to fulfill. The issues addressed will affect many or most of an area's residents. The discussion does, however, intentionally touch on the specific impacts on families with moderate or low incomes, those of minority race or ethnicity, and on people at different stages of their lives. When determining appropriate neighborhood or community-based action, it is important to be aware of the needs of all of the area's residents.

Stakeholder Analysis

Who has a vested interest in the neighborhood, its children, the issues under consideration? Stakeholder analysis first requires thinking about who, exactly, lives in the neighborhood. An area might well include some young families with school children, a handful of widows, a few middle-age empty-nesters, some single mothers, and maybe several young professional couples just starting out. All of these households are served by nearby businesses and institutions, also potential stakeholders. Whether a potential stakeholder is relevant depends on what problem has been identified, its scale and scope.

In many cases a few neighbors can get together, take action and see immediate results. In other cases neighbors or a local organization can achieve their goals with very limited assistance from outsiders, perhaps obtaining a city permit to operate a child care center in a church basement or soliciting funds for soccer equipment from a local business or foundation. Often the desired results require a change in behavior by businesses, nonprofit organizations or government agencies operating in the neighborhood: the neighborhood wants them to do their jobs differently or better. Still other issues call for creation of partnerships between neighborhood residents or between neighborhood organizations and agencies or businesses. Depending upon the problem, potential key actors at the local level include: individuals, school teachers and administrators, park and recreation staff, businesses, religious institutions, police, city building inspectors, medical providers, service organizations such as the Rotary International, apartment owners, neighborhood and homeowners associations, and a variety of other government and nonprofit organizations.

The dynamics between neighborhood residents and other stakeholders, as well as within the neighborhood itself, are key. Residents may be pleased with the services offered by local agencies and government, or they may consider service workers insensitive, indifferent or even racist. Historical distrust may lead residents to withhold information the workers need to perform their jobs well. Will residents use the services, programs or facilities provided or avoid them out of fear, concern about confidentiality or a feeling of hopelessness? Cooperation between adjacent neighborhoods may be hindered due to historically negative relations and misunderstandings. Police and school principals may be viewed as adversaries. What is the history of cooperation or conflict among those who must be a part of any change?

Every neighborhood has multiple formal and informal organizations. A formal neighborhood organization may or may not be representative, respected or effective. There may be several competing organizations, each claiming to represent the "true" neighborhood sentiment. Even where formal types don't exist, informal organizations likely do: single people who meet after work at the local bar, teenagers who assemble every afternoon at the fast food restaurant, the same group of mothers who arrive with their children at the tot lot every morning.

What rewards and recognition can the neighborhood offer the stakeholders? This often overlooked question may determine long term success or failure. The key is to identify who has a personal or organizational stake in the success of the project, the program, or the neighborhood. When working on a drug prevention effort in a neighborhood in Ohio with scattered site public housing, the author talked primarily to the tenants and individuals who either worked in the area on a daily basis or who supervised those who did: the public housing authority staff, the managers of apartments in the area, the elementary school principal, ministers with churches there, the firemen at the local fire station, and staff at an organization building housing in the area. Each of these individuals had a very personal vested interest in what happened in the neighborhood. Each also had information, skills and expertise needed to address the issue. Jointly they were able to successfully request additional support from the city.

Long-term commitments matter. A university or major research hospital that makes an institutional commitment to improving the surrounding area will likely be a long term player, although its needs and desires sometimes may conflict with those of neighborhood residents. The president of the branch office of the local bank may be willing to help or contribute but also may find that a year later he has been transferred or that the bank's headquarters has decided to close that branch.

People generally assume that homeowners have a long term vested interest in the area. Often they do. But some homeowners see their present dwelling primarily as a temporary home, voicing most concern about rising property values. Often organizations fail to seriously solicit participation from tenants of rental properties, even though many remain in the same neighborhood for decades. When organizing in the Hyde Park-Kenwood neighborhood in Chicago, for example, the author found that block chairpersons generally assumed that tenants, especially students, had no interest in neighborhood improvement. Yet many of the students entered the university as freshmen and remained for graduate degrees, leaving eight to twelve years later, by which time they had children in the local school.

Asset Inventory

People need to identify the positive aspects of their neighborhood and its resources that they can enhance or build upon. All neighborhoods have assets. Identifying those assets shifts people's perceptions, enabling them to focus on a positive future rather than an endless list of problems, litanies of blame, or the failure of past efforts. When I interviewed service providers in the Allied-Dunn's Marsh neighborhood of Madison, Wisconsin, they tended to voice their frustration about problems, the difficulties of success, what they saw as the intransigence of local residents. Finally after about ten minutes of listening to one agency's staff catalogue the residents' faults, I interrupted, "I asked you what was good about the neighborhood." She paused, thought for a moment then blurted out, "They care about their kids. I think their parenting skills suck, but they care about their kids." Caring about kids is something to build on. In fact, that's something the neighborhood residents had built on: they had created an after-school drop-in program that eventually evolved into a community center.

That neighborhood actually had many assets: broad streets, parks, nearby shopping, lovely trees, residents who decorated their homes for holidays and planted flowers in the summer, a community center, two neighborhood associations, residents who cared and volunteered, and services provided by number of organizations. When I showed residents a draft of a slide show I had prepared about the area, one woman commented with surprise, "Why, we're a neighborhood just like all the other neighborhoods."

Other neighborhood assets include existing information channels, such as a local newspaper, a newsletter of a neighborhood organization, or church bulletins. The stakeholder analysis step should also highlight assets such as special expertise, potential funding, access to volunteers, and positive energy.

Systems Approach

Successful problem solving requires a systems approach. A neighborhood concerned about housing issues might, for example, decide to lobby for specific changes in the zoning laws. Indeed, the group might settle upon that course of action as a way to support families in multiple ways since zoning, neighborhood design, and the mix of housing options affect so many aspects of our lives. Zoning affects the ability of people with different housing needs to live together or near each other to share home maintenance chores and child care or to provide elder care. Can a group home or senior housing development providing congregate meals locate in the neighborhood? Can a number of unrelated individuals or a large extended family share a dwelling? Could a couple build "a granny flat?" Zoning regulations impact the ability of an older couple to rent a small apartment near their children and the ability of a divorced man to find an apartment near his former spouse in order to share parenting more easily. Zoning influences the location of services and the possibility of having a home-based business.

Even if agreement exists within the community about the nature of problems, is there agreement about the solutions? For example, while most Americans would agree that children should not go hungry, they differ on what to do about child hunger. If the idea of feeding children broadens to include feeding them healthy food, even more disagreement may arise. Neighborhood residents concerned with food issues, therefore, will need to define what they consider to be requirements for eating well, and determine the extent of agreement among others in the community. Only then can they move on to determining which entities have specific responsibility for solving the problem. In this example, there may be a reason not only to involve parents and planners of school lunches, but also to lobby state and national agencies, and the media.

When exploring potential actions, the Internet can prove invaluable by providing examples of other neighborhoods' efforts to address similar problems. Community improvement ideas can be trendy. Too often a well-publicized success becomes a national model without sufficient research or consideration of the special circumstances that made it appropriate for one place but not another. Federal agencies, foundations, and national nonprofit organizations have excellent evaluation data and materials on proven best practices including "how-to" guides that can be downloaded from their Web sites, often without cost. In some cases the information cites a contact person who will respond to e-mail requests for clarification or additional data.

It may be necessary to solicit outside funds or request changes in local, state or even national laws or procedures. Neighborhood groups can increase their effectiveness by sharing information and action with other neighborhood groups and with regional or national groups concerned with similar issues. A neighborhood organization that lacks the resources or inclination to tackle non-local key players can still undertake three important roles in supporting others to do so: (1) the group can join coalitions; even paying minimal membership dues helps those willing to be more active since they can legitimately claim that they represent a larger number of individuals and a greater geographic area; (2)

the group can keep individuals in the neighborhood informed on issues so that they can follow through if they wish; (3) finally, and most important, the group can make sure that local residents register and vote and can educate residents about candidates' positions on policies affecting the neighborhood.

In one city of 30,000 in Michigan, the public housing director complained that he could not get the support and services he needed from the city. Yet the residents in the public housing area potentially controlled 10 percent of the city's votes. Furthermore, the city council members were elected at-large rather than by district, thus increasing the public housing area's potential for influence if they only would vote. Voting turnout for local elections, and especially for primaries, often is very low, increasing the power of every voter.

Outside Resources

The author recalls with frustration asking an agency for classes in parenting skills for a neighborhood center only to be met with the response that the agency would provide them if the neighborhood center could pay $3,000. Effective agencies do set their own agendas and must establish limits on what they can provide; they also must meet obligations of their funding sources and professional or government monitors. Some, however, can modify their plans to fit neighborhood requests. If they cannot honor a request, they may be able to contribute something: funds, data, access to volunteers, or help in writing a proposal. They may be willing to include the requested service in next year's plans and funding requests.

Information represents a vast resource. Facts matter. Effective neighborhoods gather them, both to fully understand a problem and to provide supporting data to show others. The planning departments of cities and counties have demographic data as well as current information on a range of issues. Banks conduct economic analyses. Realtors track housing sales; hospitals track medical information. Schools forecast changing population trends. Area-wide planning organizations exist for many issues such as economic development or services for seniors. The Sierra Club and similar organizations provide information on the environment. College and university faculty often conduct research relevant for neighborhoods. Some will supervise student research related to a particular neighborhood problem.

State and national organizations of all types conduct research, much of which is readily available on the Internet. Federal government agencies provide a wealth of free information available by census tract or Congressional district. Congressional legislators and state governmental legislative research bureaus have reports of government agencies, background information, and studies.

If computer technology overwhelms you, ask local high school students; they know how to surf the Internet. The local public librarian has Internet access and staff who will help you conduct an efficient search. Libraries also can obtain any needed books via interlibrary loan. All states, most cities, and many universities are Federal Depositories, the official holders of federal government reports and documents. Reference librarians will help you find and interpret the relevant data and evaluate its accuracy. The evaluation step is key. Since anyone can post information on the World Wide Web, information can be misleading, inaccurate, or based on philosophies that differ from those of your neighborhood residents.

Finally, the analysis of resources should include consideration of what outside stakeholders bring to the table. Neighborhoods should carefully consider what each potential stakeholder might be able to offer, how to put together a team of people whose interests, skills and abilities complement each other, and how to obtain the rest of what's needed.

Grassroots efforts alone, however, often lack needed resources and power. Some key aspects of performing the tasks cannot be controlled at a neighborhood level, yet neighborhoods often can take ameliorative action and assume leadership in advocating for societal changes needed. The next chapters examine both local and non-local aspects of key family tasks. Neighborhoods and local communities can, and have, played major roles in helping families fulfill the six tasks. Many neighborhood organizations have expanded their scope to create successful partnerships with the private sector, nonprofit organizations, and government agencies. When reading the text chapters, the reader should keep in mind the framework for action suggested in this chapter. Additional specific suggestions both for organizing a neighborhood, promoting better racial and ethnic relationships and potential neighborhood actions affecting each task are considered in the *Community Action Guide* (see Author's Note, pp. xv-xvi).

Notes

1. Putnam, R. D. (2000). *Bowling alone: The collapse and revival of American community*. New York: Simon & Schuster, p. 150.
2. Ibid., p. 118.
3. Ibid., pp. 77-78.
4. Ibid., p. 133.
5. Alinsky, S. A. (1946). *Reveille for radicals*. Chicago: University of Chicago Press.
6. Wireman, P. (1987). Citizen Participation. In *Encyclopedia of Social Work* (18th ed., pp. 275-280). Silver Spring, MD: National Association of Social Workers.
7. Wireman, P. (1984). *Urban neighborhoods, networks, and families: New forms for old values*. Lexington, MA: D. C. Heath and Company, p. 91.
8. Arnstein, S. R. (1969, July). A Ladder of Citizen Participation. *Journal of American Institute of Planners, 35,* 216-224.
9. Wireman, P. (1987). Citizen Participation, pp. 275-280.
10. Ibid.
11. City of Portland Office of Neighborhood Involvement. (2007, January). *Neighborhood Involvement Directory*. Retrieved March 23, 2007, from http://www.portlandonline.com/shared/cfm/image.cfm?id=65925. City of Portland Office of Neighborhood Involvement. (2007, February 5). *FY 2007–08 Requested Budget.*

Retrieved March 23, 2007, from http://www.portlandonline.com/shared/cfm/image.cfm?id=147816 City of Portland Office of Neighborhood Involvement. (2007). *Toolbox of Resources for Citizen Involvement.* Retrieved March 23, 2007, from http://www.portlandonline.com/oni/index.cfm?c=cjaca.

12. National Congress for Community Economic Development. (2005). *5th National Community Development Census. Reaching New Heights. Trends and Achievements of Community-Based Development Organizations.* (pp. 4, 7, 9). Washington DC: National Congress for Community Economic Development. Retrieved September 10, 2007, from http://www.ncced.org/documents/NCCEDCensus2005FINALReport. pdf.

13. National Congress for Community Economic Development. (2005). *5th National Community Development Census. Reaching New Heights. Trends and Achievements of Community-Based Development Organizations.* (pp. 4, 8). Washington, DC: National Congress for Community Economic Development. Retrieved September 10, 2007, from http://www.ncced.org/documents/NCCEDCensus2005FINALReport. pdf.

14. Industrial Areas Foundation. (n.d.). *About IAF. Who are we?* Chicago, IL. Industrial Areas Foundation. Retrieved September 10, 2007, from http://www.industrialareasfoundation.org/iafabout/about.htm. Association of Community Organizations for Reform Now. Inc. (n.d.). *What is ACORN?* Retrieved September 10, 2007, from http://www.acorn.org/index.php?id=2703. Dreier, P. (1997). Philanthropy and the Housing Crisis: The Dilemmas of Private Charity and Public Policy. *Housing Policy Debate 8(1): 235-293.* p. 261.

15. Stoutland, S. E. (1999). Community Development Corporations: Mission, strategy and accomplishments. In R. F. Ferguson & W. T. Dickens (Eds.). *Urban problems and community development* (pp. 193-240). Washington, DC: Brookings Institution Press. Living Cities: The National Community Development Initiative. (2002). In B. J. Whiting (Ed.). *The first decade: 1991-2001. Something is working.* Retrieved from http://www.livingcities.org/new_look/Images/pdf/something_is_working.pdf.

16. Knitzer, J. and Adely, F. (2002, January). National Center for Children in Poverty. *The role of Community Development Corporations in promoting the well-being of young children* (p. 13). Columbia University, MD: Mailman School of Public Health. Living cities: The national community development initiative. (2002). In B. J. Whiting (Ed.). *The first decade: 1991-2001. Something is working...* Retrieved from http://www.livingcities.org/new_look/Images/pdf/something_is_working. pdf.

17. Walker, C. (2002). *Community Development Corporations and their changing support systems.* Retrieved from http://www.urban.org/uploadedpdf/310638_ChangingSupportSystems.pdf.

18. Walker, C. (2002). *Community Development Corporations and their changing support systems.* Retrieved from http://www.urban.org/uploadedpdf/310638_ChangingSupportSystems.pdf.

19. Walker, C. (2002). *Community Development Corporations and their changing support systems.* Retrieved from http://www.urban.org/uploadedpdf/310638_ChangingSupportSystems.pdf.

20. Spradley, B. W. & Allender, J. A. (1996). *Community health nursing: Concepts and practice.* Philadelphia: Lippincott Publishers, p. 488.

21. The author had direct experience with this both at the U.S. Department of Housing and the U.S. Department of Commerce.

22. Rubin, H. J. (2000). *Renewing hope within neighborhoods of despair: The community-based development model.* Albany: State University of New York Press.

23. National Congress for Community Economic Development. (2005). *5th National Community Development Census. Reaching New Heights. Trends and Achievements of Community-Based Development Organizations.* (p. 9). Washington, DC: National Congress for Community Economic Development. Retrieved September 10, 2007, from http://www.ncced.org/documents/NCCEDCensus2005FINALReport.pdf.

24. National Congress for Community Economic Development. (2005). *5th National Community Development Census. Reaching New Heights. Trends and Achievements of Community-Based Development Organizations.* (p. 19). Washington DC: National Congress for Community Economic Development. Retrieved September 10, 2007, from http://www.ncced.org/documents/NCCEDCensus2005FINALReport.pdf.

25. Dreier, P. (1997). Philanthropy and the Housing Crisis: The Dilemmas of Private Charity and Public Policy. *Housing Policy Debate 8(1): 235-293.* p. 261. Association for the Study and Development of Community. (2002, April 12). *Building Community Capacity: An Initial Inventory of Local Intermediary Organizations.* Battle Creek, MI. W. K. Kellogg Foundation. Retrieved September 19, 2007, from http://www.capablecommunity.com/pubs/INTERMEDIARY%20MONOGRAPH.pdf. Liou, Y. T. and Stroh, R.C. 1998. Community Development Intermediary Systems in the United States: Origins, Evolution, and Functions. *Housing Policy Debate 9(3): 505-594.*

26. The author directed the program at the time.

27. Liou, Y. T. and Stroh, R. C. 1998. Community Development Intermediary Systems in the United States: Origins, Evolution, and Functions. *Housing Policy Debate 9(3): 505-594.*

8

Earning an Income

The National Context

The economic future for millions looks grim. Over two-thirds of the job growth projected to occur before 2016 will be in jobs which have a median income that will not provide a decent living for the Norman Rockwell family of four. This chapter describes the realities of current economic trends, their impact on working families and the future outlook for U.S. workers. We discuss the implications of these national economic trends for neighborhoods and communities. In the final section we explore community level actions that can help families obtain adequate incomes, including an extended section on how neighborhoods and communities can begin and operate local economic development programs.

For millions of American workers the key changes since the 1970s have been either the loss of well-paid, blue collar, unionized jobs that enabled a worker to support a family or the downsizing of middle management positions that ended many individuals' lifetime climb up a stable corporate ladder. For decades during the last part of the twentieth century, the wages for the majority of workers, 60 percent, either fell or remained flat after adjusting for inflation. Between 1979 and 1995 only 40 percent of the workers received any increases in pay, and most of those increases were modest. During the sixteen-year period, only the top 5 percent of wage earners received increased wages of over 14 percent.[1] Total family incomes often remained stable, but usually only because wives took jobs and workers increased their hours. Although wages rose during the 1990s, especially for lower income workers, since 2000 the wages for entry-level workers, including those with college education, have fallen.[2] In other words, for millions of workers wages have stagnated, increasing more slowly than the cost of living.

One reason for stagnation of wages has been the decline of labor unions. Eighty percent of non-farm American workers are employed in production or in non-supervisory positions. Union workers earn approximately 20 percent more and are more likely to receive health insurance and pensions.[3] A variety of factors have contributed to the lower proportion of workers covered by unions but it cannot be explained simply by the increase in service jobs. The rate of unionization of blue-collar men fell by over one-half between 1978 and 2005.[4] The decrease in unionization has not been accidental but a result of anti-union activity by employers and withdrawal of the government from protecting the rights of workers to organize.[5]

The overall picture is worse for those at the bottom of the economic ladder. In 2000 the federal minimum wage was $5.15 an hour. A full-time minimum wage worker took home $10,712, over $3,400 less than the amount needed at that time to support a family of three at poverty level ($14,150) in 2000.[6] At the beginning of 2007, the minimum wage was still $5.15 an hour but the cost of living had risen. A full-time worker would still earn $10,712 but because of inflation would now earn over $6,400 less than the $17,170 needed to support a three-person family at the poverty level in 2007.[7] Although the minimum wage was raised to $5.85 per hour effective July, 2007, using the standard calculations for full time work of 2080 hours, a worker will receive an annual salary of $12,168. This is $1,522 less than the $13,690 needed to support two people *even* at a poverty level. The full extent of the minimum wage raise will not be effective until the summer of 2009. At that point it will reach $7.25 an hour, for an annual full-time salary of $15,080 which will support two people, but not three, at a poverty level assuming no inflation before 2009.

Although public debate frequently focuses on the fact that many minimum wage earners are teenagers, this obscures the real difficulties faced by minimum wage workers. Those earners actually provide almost 60 percent of their family's income, and in over 40 percent of the cases provide all the family earnings.[8] Most minimum wage workers are not teenagers. Approximately one-half are over twenty-five years old. Another one-quarter are young adults who presumably are setting up independent households although many now continue to live with their parents for financial reasons. It is true that about one-quarter of the minimum wage workers are teenagers, sixteen to nineteen years old.[9] But many of them are not working for spare cash for entertainment but to supplement their family's income or to save for college expenses. Even attending public high school requires money for school supplies and other expenses such as fees for certain courses or to participate in sports or other extra-curricula activities.

Another major cause of the wage disparity among workers is the way productivity increases are being distributed. The wage structure has become increasingly skewed, with those at the top receiving significantly greater increases in wages and benefits, such as health insurance, stock options, bonuses, and retirement plans. While the cost of perks for C.E.O.s continues to rise astronomically, employees at the bottom and in the middle of the corporate ladder are receiving an increasingly smaller share of that economic pie. Productivity rose by 33 percent between 1995 and 2005, but only about one-third of that increase was passed on as wage increases for the typical worker.[10] Between 1979 and 2000 the real income of households in the bottom one-fifth rose six percent, those in the middle one-fifth had increases of 12 percent while those in the top one-fifth jumped by 70 percent. The very top one percent received increases of 184 percent.[11]

Millions of workers face another problem: cuts in benefits, with fewer workers receiving employer-provided pensions or health care coverage than twenty-five years ago. Only about half now receive employer-provided health insurance, and employees are paying a larger share of the costs.[12] The share of workers with defined-benefit retirement plans, promising a specific amount of payment per month during the retired person's lifetime, has fallen to less than one-fifth of workers.[13] Some firms have discovered that they can avoid paying promised pension benefits by declaring bankruptcy. If present trends continue, the long-term outlook for millions of Americans, working or retired, remains grim.

We can glimpse the future income prospects of millions of workers by looking at the wages offered in today's high-growth occupations.[14] The discussion which follows is based upon the Bureau of Labor Department's calculations of projected job growth between 2006 and 2016 which are the latest projections available. Fifty percent of the new jobs projected to have the greatest increases in workers between 2006 and 2016 will be found in only twenty-eight job categories, as shown in table 1. One-half of the new jobs will be found in occupations other than the twenty-eight with the highest growth. While some of these occupations will offer high pay, the wages in many of these other occupations will be low.

Concentrating on the twenty-eight occupations that will cover one-half the projected employment growth provides a glimpse into the future faced by millions of families. The discussion here and below is based on the median wage for each of the twenty-eight high-growth occupations in 2006. By definition, one-half of the workers in those occupations will receive a wage higher than the median, but one-half will receive a lower wage that in many cases will be significantly lower. For example, looking at the occupation that will hire the second most new workers, retail salesperson, 10 percent of workers selling expensive products such as automobiles, will receive an annual income of $38,438, but the lowest paid 10 percent of salespersons will receive only $14,123. Fifty percent of the new retail workers will be paid between $16, 245 and $26,686 annually.[15] Thus, using the median wage for considering how the jobs in an occupational category affect the potential for family life is a reasonable proxy for a more detailed job-by-job analysis.

What does this mean for the future of the American workers and their families? We will consider how the projected jobs will affect family life by considering two standards, the poverty level and a self-sufficiency standard. Over the years, a number of researchers have analyzed the deficiencies in the official

Table 1

Economic Prospects for Workers in High Growth Jobs (2006-2016)[1]

Rank	Category	Projected growth 2006-2016 (workers)	Projected growth of category 2006-2016 (%)	Median annual full-time pay ($US 2006[1])	Persons supported by the median income at the poverty level[2]	Persons supported by the median income at a self-sufficiency standard[3]	Percentage of total additional jobs	Cumulative percentage of total growth
1	Registered nurses	587,349	23.5%	$57,280	14	6	3.8%	3.8%
2	Retail salespersons	556,824	12.4%	$19,760	3	1	3.6%	7.3%
3	Customer service representatives	545,161	24.8%	$28,330	6	2	3.5%	10.8%
4	Combined food preparation and serving workers, including fast food	451,919	18.1%	$15,050	2	0	2.9%	13.7%
5	Office clerks, general	403,557	12.6%	$23,710	5	1	2.6%	16.3%
6	Personal and home care aides	388,538	50.6%	$17,770	3	0	2.5%	18.8%
7	Home health aides	383,620	48.7%	$19,420	3	0	2.5%	21.3%
8	Postsecondary teachers	382,248	22.9%	$56,120	14	6	2.5%	23.7%
9	Janitors and cleaners, except maids and housekeeping cleaners	344,936	14.5%	$19,930	3	1	2.2%	25.9%
10	Nursing aides, orderlies, and attendants	263,643	18.2%	$22,180	4	1	1.7%	27.6%
11	Bookkeeping, accounting, and auditing clerks	263,535	12.5%	$30,560	7	2	1.7%	29.3%
12	Waiters and waitresses	254,678	10.8%	$14,850	2	0	1.6%	30.9%
13	Child care workers	247,779	17.9%	$17,630	3	0	1.6%	32.5%
14	Executive secretaries and administrative assistants	239,053	14.8%	$37,240	9	3	1.5%	34.1%
15	Computer applications software engineers	225,759	44.6%	$79,780	21	9	1.4%	35.5%
16	Accountants and auditors	225,575	17.7%	$54,630	14	6	1.4%	36.9%
17	Landscaping and groundskeeping workers	221,272	18.1%	$21,260	4	1	1.4%	38.4%
18	Business operation specialists, all other	218,243	20.9%	$55,650	14	6	1.4%	39.8%
19	Elementary school teachers, except special education	209,173	13.6%	$45,570	11	4	1.3%	41.1%

(continued on the next page)

Table 1 (cont.)

Rank	Category	Projected growth 2006-2016 (workers)	Projected growth of category 2006-2016 (%)	Median annual full-time pay ($US 2006[1])	Persons supported by the median income at the poverty level[2]	Persons supported by the median income at a self-sufficiency standard[3]	Percentage of total additional jobs	Cumulative percentage of total growth
20	Receptionists and information clerks	202,000	17.2%	$22,900	4	1	1.3%	42.4%
21	Truck drivers, heavy and tractor-trailer	193,012	10.4%	$35,040	8	3	1.2%	43.6%
22	Maids and housekeeping cleaners	185,999	12.7%	$17,580	3	0	1.2%	44.8%
23	Security guards	175,467	16.9%	$21,530	4	1	1.1%	46.0%
24	Sales representatives, services, all other	150,530	27.9%	$48,100	12	5	1.0%	46.9%
25	Carpenters	150,000	10.3%	$36,550	8	3	1.0%	47.9%
26	Management analysts	148,651	21.9%	$68,050	18	8	1.0%	48.8%
27	Medical assistants	147,675	35.4%	$26,290	5	1	0.9%	49.8%
28	Computer systems analysts	145,940	29.0%	$69,760	18	8	0.9%	50.7%

1. Shniper, L.; Dohm, A., *Occupational employment projections to 2016: Appendix: Employment by occupation,* 2006 and projected 2016. Monthly Labor Review, November 2007. Retrieved January 30, 2008, from ftp://ftp.bls.gov/pub/special.requests/ep/ind-occ. matrix/mlrappendix.zip. Bureau of Labor Statistics. (2007). Occupational Employment, Training, and Earnings: Occupation Report. Retrieved from http://data.bls.gov/oep/ servlet/oep.noeted.servlet.ActionServlet?Action=emprprt&Occ=XXXXXXXXXX&N umber=All&Sort=earn&Base=2006&Proj=2016&EdLevel=&Search=List&Type=Occ upation&Phrase=&StartItem=0. In this analysis, the 28 occupations with the most new jobs were considered. These occupations represent 50.7% of additional jobs.

2. Leavitt, M.O. (2006, January 18). *Annual Update of the HHS Poverty Guidelines.* Federal Register 71(15): 3848-9. Retrieved January 30, 2008, from http://aspe.hhs. gov/poverty/06fedreg.pdf. In 2006, the poverty level in the continental United States was $9,800 for the first person, and $3,400 for each additional person in a family.

3. Waldron, T., Roberts, B., & Reamer, A. (2004, October). *Working hard, falling short. America's working families and the pursuit of economic security.* p. 30. Prepared for The Working Poor Families Project. Chevy Chase, MD: Authors. Retrieved January 30, 2008 from http://www.aecf.org/upload/publicationfiles/working%20hard.pdf. A number of experts use a value of two times the poverty level as an estimate of an economic self-sufficiency standard. This value has been used here. In 2006, a self-sufficiency standard in the continental United States was $19,600 for the first person, and $6,800 for each additional person in a family.

poverty guidelines. These guidelines have been out-of-date for decades. While the numbers have been revised to account for inflation, they have not been updated to reflect changes in the real cost of goods or services. They are based on the cost of food, which has fallen, and do not take into account the disproportionate increases in the costs of housing and medical care or the fact that as more mothers have entered the labor force their need for purchasing child care has risen. Moreover, even the original calculation for the food costs was based on a budget designed for only temporary emergency use, not adequate for providing a permanent nutritious diet.[16] The poverty guidelines also do not vary by geographic areas or take into account the needs of people at different ages, such as growing teenagers or older persons who may have special dietary requirements.

Because the poverty guidelines are unrealistic, alternative approaches have been developed to define a modest standard of living for a family. Wider Opportunities for Women (WOW) has developed a self-sufficiency standard based on the needs of families in different circumstances and in different areas of the country. The standard provides for basic expenses including child care and transportation. It does not include funds, however, for *any* meals outside of the home, recreation, entertainment, or savings, and includes only one automobile trip per week for shopping and errands.[17] The standard would provide families basic necessities without depending upon government programs or private charity. Because of the complexity of the WOW standards, this discussion instead uses numbers based on twice the poverty level, an amount that experts agree approaches a modest standard of living which is self-sufficient, that is, does not require additional funding or services from the government or charitable organizations.[18]

To see how families taking the new jobs will fare, we first consider those jobs which will only provide poverty level wages. When considering how many people each job will support, we used the Poverty Guidelines as of 2006 to make the comparisons consistent with the data from the 2006-2016 projections and the median wage for each job category as of 2006. Clearly both the wages in some job categories and the cost of living will have risen since 2006, but the basis analysis remains valid. In fact, the increases in wages for the majority of the occupational categories projected for fast growth are low-wage jobs where increases in pay frequently lag behind inflation.

Eight of the twenty-eight jobs in the highest growth occupations will *not* support the Norman Rockwell family *even* at a poverty level. Table 2 shows the relationship between family size, the income projected for high growth jobs, and the poverty level. The median wages paid in two occupations, waiters and waitresses and a category labeled combined food preparation and serving workers including fast food (those who both prepare and serve food), would support only two people, for instance a couple or a single parent with one child even at the poverty level. Wages paid in six occupations would support a three-person family such as a couple with one child or a single parent with two children.

These jobs include retail salespersons, as well as child care workers, home health aides, personal and home care aides, maids and housekeeping cleaners, and janitors and cleaners. These are jobs that must be performed and cannot be outsourced.

If we consider the income needed for the very modest living provided by a self-sufficiency standard, table 3 shows us that about a fifth of the job categories, six of the twenty-eight, pay a median income less than that necessary to support even one person decently. Employees in another eleven occupations fare better, but one half of them still take home wages that would only support one person at the self-sufficiency standard. The median wage at two other occupations would support a couple or a single person with one child. Three other occupations pay a median income that would support a three-person family, a couple with one child or a single parent with two. Only less than one-third, nine of the twenty-eight fastest growing occupations have median wages that pay more than the $40,000 necessary to support a family of four at this self-sufficiency standard. Thus, the median income produced by over two thirds of the fastest growing occupations will not support the ideal Norman Rockwell nuclear family even at a modest standard of living.

We might conclude that many people performing the work needed for our nation to function—caring for our preschool children, stacking our groceries, taking a glass of water to our mother in the nursing home—these workers should never have *any* children unless they are willing to raise those children in poverty or at least very restricted circumstances. They should plan to tell their children that they cannot pay the fee for them to participate in high school sports, go to the movies with a friend, or ever eat a Big Mac.

In order to enjoy even the modest standard of living provided by the self-sufficiency standard but have more than two children, both members of a couple would need to work at jobs paying more than $20,000, unless one of them held one of the eight higher paying high growth jobs: registered nurse, post-secondary teacher, business operation specialist, certain types of sales representatives, computer systems analyst, accountant or auditor, computer software applications engineer, or management analyst. Again, job openings will occur in other occupations that pay well, but the opportunities will be more limited than in the twenty-eight categories discussed above.

Frequently discussion about job opportunities, especially that referring to minimum wage jobs, suggests that individuals can take these jobs as an entry-level position in order to prepare for the next step on an upwardly mobile employment ladder. The problem is that for the majority of workers the next step on the ladder does not exist. In most cases the prospect of upward mobility is constrained for reasons that have nothing to do with the individual's ability or willingness to work hard. The pyramid structure of the job market means that there are limited number of places for those who potentially might want to move

Table 2
High growth jobs (2006-2016) and poverty[1]

The twenty-eight occupations listed here represent 50.7% of the total job growth projected between 2006 and 2016[1]. Values by each occupation represent the median annual full-time income for the occupation in 2006. In 2006, the poverty level in the continental United States was $9,800 for one, $13,200 for two, $16,600 for three, $20,000 for four, and $23,400 for five persons per family.

Occupations where median income is sufficient to support only two individuals at the poverty level

Waiters and waitresses	$14,850
Combined food preparation and serving workers, including fast food	$15,050

These two occupations represent 707,000 jobs or 4.5% of total additional jobs.

Occupations where median income is sufficient to support only three individuals at the poverty level

Maids and housekeeping cleaners	$17,580
Child care workers	$17,630
Personal and home care aides	$17,770
Home health aides	$19,420
Retail salespersons	$19,760
Janitors and cleaners, except maids and housekeeping cleaners	$19,930

These six occupations represent 2.11 million jobs or 13.5% of total additional jobs.

Occupations where median income is sufficient to support only four individuals at the poverty level

Landscaping and groundskeeping workers	$21,260
Security guards	$21,530
Nursing aides, orderlies, and attendants	$22,180
Receptionists and information clerks	$22,900

These four occupations represent 862,000 jobs or 5.5% of total additional jobs.

Occupations where median income is sufficient to support five or more individuals at least at the poverty level

Office clerks, general	$23,710
Medical assistants	$26,290
Customer service representatives	$28,330
Bookkeeping, accounting, and auditing clerks	$30,560
Truck drivers, heavy and tractor-trailer	$35,040
Carpenters	$36,550
Executive secretaries and administrative assistants	$37,240
Elementary school teachers, except special education	$45,570
Sales representatives, services, all other	$48,100

(continued on the next page)

Table 2 (cont.)

Accountants and auditors	$54,630
Business operation specialists, all other	$55,650
Postsecondary teachers	$56,120
Registered nurses	$57,280
Management analysts	$68,050
Computer systems analysts	$69,760
Computer software engineers, applications	$79,780

These sixteen occupations represent 4.23 million jobs or 27.2% of total additional jobs.

---

1. Shniper, L.; Dohm, A., *Occupational employment projections to 2016: Appendix: Employment by occupation, 2006 and projected 2016.* Monthly Labor Review, November 2007. Retrieved January 30, 2008, from ftp://ftp.bls.gov/pub/special.requests/ep/ind-occ. matrix/mlrappendix.zip. Bureau of Labor Statistics. (2007). *Occupational Employment, Training, and Earnings: Occupation Report.* Retrieved from http://data.bls.gov/oep/servlet/oep.noeted.servlet.ActionServlet?Action=emprprt&Occ=XXXXXXXXXX&Number=All&Sort=earn&Base=2006&Proj=2016&EdLevel=&Search=List&Type=Occupation&Phrase=&StartItem=0. In this analysis, the 28 occupations with the most new jobs were considered. These occupations represent 50.72% of additional jobs.
2. Leavitt, M.O. (2006, January 18). *Annual Update of the HHS Poverty Guidelines.* Federal Register 71(15): 3848-9. Retrieved January 30, 2008, from http://aspe.hhs.gov/poverty/06fedreg.pdf. In 2006, the poverty level in the continental United States was $9,800 for the first person, and $3,400 for each additional person in a family.

---

up the pay ladder. For example, between 2006 and 2016 there will be 71,000 new jobs for first-line supervisors and managers of retail sales workers. However, there will be 544,000 new retail sales workers reporting to these supervisors. This "retail sales workers" category includes the previously mentioned "retail salespersons" category in addition to similar positions such as cashiers. Moreover, approximately one-third of the supervisors are store owners, thus reducing the number of potential positions available for upwardly mobile workers to about 47,000. That is, for every twelve retail sales workers available for advancement to a management position, there will be an opportunity for only one. Furthermore, the median pay for first-line supervisors was $33,925. So about one-half of those who successfully advance would still barely make enough money to support a wife and a child or to rent a two-bedroom apartment.

Another alternative for a new worker would be to leave the retail industry and apply for one of the nine high-growth occupations that will pay a median wage sufficient to support a couple with two children at a self-sufficiency standard. However, as seen in table 4, a college degree is required for five of the nine, all except sales representative and registered nurse. The demand for registered

Table 3
High growth jobs (2006-2016) and a self-sufficiency standard[1]

The twenty-eight occupations listed here represent 50.7% of the total job growth projected between 2006 and 2016[1]. Values by each occupation represent the median annual full-time income for the occupation in 2006. In 2006, a self-sufficiency standard (two times the poverty level) in the continental United States was $19,600 for one, $26,400 for two, $33,200 for three, and $40,000 for four, and $46,800 for five per family.

Occupations where median income is not sufficient to support one individual at a self-sufficiency standard

Waiters and waitresses	$14,850
Combined food preparation and serving workers, including fast food	$15,050
Maids and housekeeping cleaners	$17,580
Child care workers	$17,630
Personal and home care aides	$17,770
Home health aides	$19,420

These six occupations represent 1.91 million jobs or 12.3% of total additional jobs.

Occupations where median income is sufficient to support only one individual at a self-sufficiency standard

Retail salespersons	$19,760
Janitors and cleaners, except maids and housekeeping cleaners	$19,930
Landscaping and groundskeeping workers	$21,260
Security guards	$21,530
Nursing aides, orderlies, and attendants	$22,180
Receptionists and information clerks	$22,900
Office clerks, general	$23,710
Medical assistants	$26,290

These eight occupations represent 2.32 million jobs or 14.8% of total additional jobs.

Occupations where median income is sufficient to support only two individuals at a self-sufficiency standard

Customer service representatives	$28,330
Bookkeeping, accounting, and auditing clerks	$30,560

These two occupations represent 809,000 jobs or 5.2% of total additional jobs.

Occupations where median income is sufficient to support only three individuals at a self-sufficiency standard

Truck drivers, heavy and tractor-trailer	$35,040
Carpenters	$36,550
Executive secretaries and administrative assistants	$37,240

These three occupations represent 582,000 jobs or 3.7% of total additional jobs.

(continued on the next page)

Table 3 (cont.)

Occupations where median income is sufficient to support only four individuals at a self-sufficiency standard

Elementary school teachers, except special education	$45,570

This occupation represents 209,000 jobs or 1.3% of total additional jobs.

Occupations where median income is sufficient to support five or more individuals at least at a self-sufficiency standard

Sales representatives, services, all other	$48,100
Accountants and auditors	$54,630
Business operation specialists, all other	$55,650
Postsecondary teachers	$56,120
Registered nurses	$57,280
Management analysts	$68,050
Computer systems analysts	$69,760
Computer applications software engineers	$79,780

These eight occupations represent 2.08 million jobs or 13.4% of total additional jobs.

---

1. Shniper, L.; Dohm, A., Occupational employment projections to 2016: Appendix: Employment by occupation, 2006 and projected 2016. Monthly Labor Review, November 2007. Retrieved January 30, 2008, from ftp://ftp.bls.gov/pub/special.requests/ep/ind-occ. matrix/mlrappendix.zip. Bureau of Labor Statistics. (2007). Occupational Employment, Training, and Earnings: Occupation Report. Retrieved from http://data.bls.gov/oep/ servlet/oep.noeted.servlet.ActionServlet?Action=emprprt&Occ=XXXXXXXXXX&N umber=All&Sort=earn&Base=2006&Proj=2016&EdLevel=&Search=List&Type=Occ upation&Phrase=&StartItem=0. In this analysis, the 28 occupations with the most new jobs were considered. These occupations represent 50.72% of additional jobs.

2. Waldron, T., Roberts, B., & Reamer, A. (2004, October). Working hard, falling short. America's working families and the pursuit of economic security. p. 30. Prepared for The Working Poor Families Project. Chevy Chase, MD: Authors. Retrieved January 31, 2008 from http://www.aecf.org/upload/publicationfiles/working%20hard.pdf. A number of experts use a value of two times the poverty level as an estimate of an economic self-sufficiency standard. This value has been used here. In 2006, a self-sufficiency standard in the continental United States was $19,600 for the first person, and $6,800 for each additional person in a family.

---

nurses will be high, second only to that for retail sales persons. Since such nursing does not require a four-year college degree, at first glance it might seem that home health aides and personal and home care aides might look forward to advancement in their own field. However, even obtaining the necessary credentials through an associate degree program may be very difficult for those working to support themselves or their family. Associate degrees in nursing require two to three years of study. In addition to costs, workers may face problems of a mismatch between the hours for classes and their job requirements and sometimes a long waiting list for availability of required clinical classes.

Although much of the media and political rhetoric focuses on the need for an educated work force capable of competing in the global marketplace, increasingly college graduates may find that the work available to them does not require a college education. As shown in table 4, over 43 percent of the total projected job growth will occur in twenty-three occupations that do not require a college degree. The competition for the highly paid positions that do require a degree will be high. Those without college degrees will find themselves competing for advancement slots with college graduates, even in cases where a degree is not technically necessary.

Finally, if all the millions of workers performing the jobs at the bottom of the pay scale either quit or were promoted, the nation could not function. Our schools, hospitals, stores, and nursing homes would face an enormous crisis. Clearly our nation has an interest in making it feasible to support a healthy family with the income earned in these highly important vocations.

Workers' ability to support their families is further limited by the structure of the workplace. Often employees today cannot work and receive pay for a forty-hour week at a single job. The nation's largest employer, Wal-Mart, classifies workers as full-time if they work as few as thirty-four hours a week. Moreover, an internal 2005 memo from Wal-Mart's executive vice president in charge of human resources suggested using more part-time workers. It also recommended requiring that all jobs include some physical activity, a move likely to decrease the number of long-term employees with health problems commanding higher wages because of seniority.[19]

The scenarios painted above are unfortunately too optimistic. They assume that workers can work full-time, year-round, will not face temporary unemployment and will be able to work continually until retirement age. For millions of workers, including those in middle or even upper management, this is not a realistic expectation. Many men in top management positions are losing their positions due to company reorganization. Such men, often in their fifties, may find it difficult or impossible to find a similar management position in another company. They also may be considered overqualified for many lower-level jobs.

One response to the changing job market has been self-employment. However, despite the glamour and hype associated with entrepreneurship and its occasional real successes, small businesses have a high failure rate,

Table 4
Educational Characteristics of High Growth Jobs (2006-2016)[1]

The twenty-eight occupations listed here represent 50.7% of the total projected job growth between 2006 and 2016. In 2006, the poverty level for a family of four in the continental United States was $20,000, and a self-sufficiency standard (two times the poverty level) in the continental United States was $40,000.[2]

High Growth Jobs Available to Those Without a Four-year College Degree
The following twenty-three occupations are projected to grow by 6.72 million workers or 43.1% of the total projected increased workforce. Only four of these occupations have a median annual full-time income sufficient to support a "Norman Rockwell" style family of four at a self-sufficiency standard.

	Number of New Jobs, 2006-2016	Median Annual Income in 2006
Jobs insufficient to support a family of four even at the poverty level		
Waiters and waitresses	254,678	$14,850
Combined food preparation and serving workers, including fast food	451,919	$15,050
Maids and housekeeping cleaners	185,999	$17,580
Child care workers	247,779	$17,630
Personal and home care aides	388,538	$17,770
Home health aides	383,620	$19,420
Retail salespersons	556,824	$19,760
Janitors and cleaners, except maids and housekeeping cleaners	344,936	$19,930

The eight occupations above represent 2.81 million workers or 18.0% of the total projected increased workforce.

	Number of New Jobs, 2006-2016	Median Annual Income in 2006
Jobs sufficient to support a family of four at the poverty level		
Landscaping and groundskeeping workers	221,272	$21,260
Security guards	175,467	$21,530
Nursing aides, orderlies, and attendants	263,643	$22,180
Receptionists and information clerks	202,000	$22,900
Office clerks, general	403,557	$23,710
Medical assistants	147,675	$26,290
Customer service representatives	545,161	$28,330
Bookkeeping, accounting, and auditing clerks	263,535	$30,560
Truck drivers, heavy and tractor-trailer	193,012	$35,040
Carpenters	150,000	$36,550
Executive secretaries and administrative assistants	239,053	$37,240

The eleven occupations above represent 2.80 million workers or 18.0% of the total projected increased workforce.

(continued on the next page)

Table 4 (cont.)

Jobs sufficient to support a family of four at a self-sufficiency standard	Number of New Jobs, 2006-2016	Median Annual Income in 2006
Sales representatives, services, all other	150,530	$48,100
Business operation specialists, all other	218,243	$55,650
Registered nurses[3]	587,349	$57,280
Computer systems analysts[4]	145,940	$69,760

The four occupations above represent 1.10 million workers or 7.1% of the total projected increased workforce.

High Growth Jobs Typically Requiring a Four-year College Degree
The following five occupations are projected to grow by 1.19 million workers or 7.6% of the total projected increased workforce. All have a median annual full-time income sufficient to support a "Norman Rockwell" style family of four at a self-sufficiency standard or higher.

Jobs sufficient to support a family of four at a self-sufficiency standard	Number of New Jobs, 2006-2016	Median Annual Income in 2006
Elementary school teachers, except special education	209,173	$45,570
Accountants and auditors	225,575	$54,630
Postsecondary teachers	382,248	$56,120
Management analysts	148,651	$68,050
Computer applications software engineers	225,759	$79,780

The five occupations above represent 1.19 million workers or 7.6% of the total projected increased workforce.

1. Shniper, L.; Dohm, A., *Occupational employment projections to 2016*: Appendix: Employment by occupation, 2006 and projected 2016. Monthly Labor Review, November 2007. Retrieved January 30, 2008, from ftp://ftp.bls.gov/pub/special.requests/ep/ind-occ.matrix/mlrappendix.zip. Bureau of Labor Statistics. (2007). Occupational Employment, Training, and Earnings: Occupation Report. Retrieved from http://data.bls.gov/oep/servlet/oep.noeted.servlet.ActionServlet?Action=emprprt& Occ=XXXXXXXXXX&Number=All&Sort=earn&Base=2006&Proj=2016&EdLevel=&Search =List&Type=Occupation&Phrase=&StartItem=0. In this analysis, the 28 occupations with the most new jobs were considered. These occupations represent 50.7% of additional jobs.

2. Leavitt, M.O. (2006, January 18). *Annual Update of the HHS Poverty Guidelines*. Federal Register 71(15): 3848-9. Retrieved January 30, 2008, from http://aspe.hhs.gov/poverty/06fedreg.pdf. In 2006, the poverty level in the continental United States was $9,800 for the first person, and $3,400 for each additional person in a family. Waldron, T., Roberts, B., & Reamer, A. (2004, October). *Working hard, falling short. America's working families and the pursuit of economic security.* p. 30. Prepared for The Working Poor Families Project. Chevy Chase, MD: Authors. Retrieved January 30, 2008 from http://www.aecf.org/upload/publicationfiles/working%20hard.pdf. A number of experts use a value of two times the poverty level as an estimate of an economic self-sufficiency standard. This value has been used here.

3. This occupation typically requires a post-secondary certificate.

4. Occupants often have some college.

generally considered to be 80 percent within the first five years. As director of a state-financed small business development center, I noted the limitations of self-employment as a means to upward mobility. While the program did help some people start businesses that grew and employed others, many of the new businesses provided only a marginal income for the owners. Much of the program's contribution consisted of helping people preserve their life savings and their homes by encouraging them not to start businesses that were doomed to failure. Moreover, turning to entrepreneurship generally deprives individuals of the opportunity to access health insurance at a reasonable cost.

Thus, many of the Americans who depend upon their jobs to pay their bills will face difficulties. A few lucky ones will inherit a fortune, receive soaring employee stock options, or win the lottery. Others can supplement their earned income with money from rental property, investments, government transfer payments such as Social Security, and, to a diminishing degree, from pensions. A booming economy does not necessarily translate into higher wages and job security for millions of workers. The increases in productivity and profits have been shifted from providing higher wages and benefits to workers to paying extremely high salaries and benefit packages to top executives and providing increased profits for stockholders.

Here again, the average worker has lost out. The media coverage of the booming stock market during the late twentieth century conveyed the impression that this growth benefited most families. In 1998, even before the drop in the stock market, 60 percent of those who owned stock had portfolios worth only $4,000 or less.[20] Although approximately one-half of American households own stock, most have small holdings, including those in their pension plans. In 2004, only one-third of Americans who owned stock had holdings worth more than $5,000.[21] Workers with 401(k) pensions must worry whether their hopes for a comfortable retirement will disappear during a recession or vanish in an Enron-like debacle, which has happened in more than one company. Thus, the majority of families will continue to depend upon paid wages for sustenance.

The national discussion is beginning to acknowledge that a rising stock market does not translate into increased earnings for most Americans and that the new economy does not promise job security for millions. In fact, many Americans have faced economic insecurity for decades. An analysis based on information between 1968 and 1997 concludes that a majority of Americans will face poverty during at least one year of their adult life. Sociologist Mark Rank calculates that by the age of seventy-five almost sixty percent of adults will have been poor for at least one year and 30 percent will have experienced poverty on five or more occasions.[22]

The Local/Community Level

What relevance does this gloomy analysis hold for real life at the local level? Many of the recent and projected economic changes will affect small towns, suburbs, and edge cities as well as city neighborhoods. Communities now vary greatly in the extent to which they provide decent jobs for their residents. During the first half of the twentieth century, businesses generally located near their workers; workers often found affordable housing near their employment. The fifties, sixties, and seventies saw business after business relocating to suburban sites. During the eighties and nineties the outward movement continued, with firms moving to edge cities and small towns. Businesses also began contracting with firms located in Mexico, South America, and Asia for work previously performed in city neighborhoods and in small towns. Older suburbs began to suffer the same types of job loss previously experienced by inner-city neighborhoods. Often the jobs that remained provided only entry-level wages without benefits, insufficient to support a family. Rural areas also suffered as the ability of families to support themselves by farming declined, leaving 98 percent of the country's farmers dependent upon off-site jobs for at least part of their income.[23]

Three sets of key players affect the ability of residents in any community to earn an income. The first set includes those who influence the overall state of the economy, from the chairman of the Federal Reserve Bank and the executives at major corporations to the rulers of nations controlling oil prices. The second set of players determines not whether jobs are available but their safety, wages, benefits, and other working conditions. Those players include Congress and other legislatures that set minimum wage levels, unions, the businesses themselves, and a variety of federal, state and local officials who monitor occupational safety standards and other regulations. The third set of players affects how a specific local community fares given the overall situation. Those players include local businesses and governments, organizations like the Chambers of Commerce that work to promote economic development, unions, technical colleges, and universities that provide training and research, the local school system, and the government agencies and foundations that fund technical assistance, job readiness and economic development programs. These actions facilitate or hinder the availability of jobs, the creation of home-based businesses, and the access to reliable transportation. Many of these factors are beyond local control, such as corporate decisions about whether to shut down branch offices. Residents can influence other decisions only with great difficulty: convincing banks, for example, to provide credit needed by businesses for starting, expanding, and operating.

Local jobs not only provide an income to families, they also play a significant role in the development of social capital and the network fabric of the community. Neighborhood businesses play an important role in family life, introducing children to the work world. Children need local businesses for an opportunity to observe that world. Local businesses can provide children with after-school, summer, and entry-level jobs as well as knowledge of different kinds of occupations and a range of role models. In *The Way We Really Are,* Stephanie Coontz found that when men over sixty talked about what had helped them become responsible workers and adults, they recalled the on-the-job informal mentoring from the older men with whom they worked side by side.[24] "The senior men teased the youngsters, sending them out for a left-handed hammer or making them the butt of sometimes painful jokes, but they also showed the kids the ropes and helped protect them from the foreman or boss. They explained why 'putting up with the crap' was worth it." She noted that the men agreed "that the loss of non-parental male mentoring may be a bigger problem for boys today than the rise of single mother homes."[25]

Even in communities and neighborhoods where businesses exist, increasingly they are no longer owned by residents or managed by long-time neighbors. A television documentary, "Store Wars," focused on the conflict in the small town of Ashland, Virginia, when Wal-Mart decided to locate one of its megastores there. Despite the fears of existing business owners, opposition of many residents and an initial adverse vote by the city council, Wal-Mart eventually prevailed.[26] At the beginning of the twenty-first century, Wal-Mart announced that in several years it planned to be opening one store a day.[27] In towns and cities across America, the business landscape is similar, with national chains edging out locally owned retail establishments, restaurants, movie theaters, and grocery stores.

After Madison, Wisconsin hit the lists in national publications as one of the best places to live in the country, a number of national chains started opening coffee shops and other stores there. This can hurt neighborhoods, since the absentee owners lack long-term relationships with the area and its residents. Mobile managers do not have a significant investment in the economic and social viability of any specific neighborhood. They gain little long-term career benefit from taking a few moments to chat with area children, contribute money to the local basketball team, grant employees time off to participate in community activities, or play an active positive role in improving the community. Recently an ominous trend has occurred with outside business forces interfering in local concerns, not to improve or benefit the community but to lower the taxes of their local branches or to push their political agendas. In 1997, for example, during the final days of an election for the Wisconsin Supreme Court, a newly formed organization raised and spent $200,500 on a get-out-the-vote effort to re-elect Justice Jon Wilcox. The funds came mostly from people and organizations outside of Wisconsin. One New York businessman contributed $7,500.[28]

Community Action

Communities and neighborhoods should understand the particular needs of different types of households, both to predict how changes in the economy will affect them and to design approaches that better meet their needs. What do your residents need? Available local jobs can reduce the time crunch of employed parents who must prepare dinner, help their children with their homework, and arrange for their supervision after school. Adults with skills commanding high salaries are not as financially dependent on jobs nearby or public transportation since they own cars and probably do not punch a time clock. They may, however, want to conduct businesses in their homes, which could require changes in zoning or condominium regulations.

Persons without access to jobs paying high wages depend more frequently on jobs within walking distance or those accessible by public transportation. Like families with higher incomes, they also may want to conduct a home-based business but are less likely to have the skills and/or the equipment to operate one solely via telephone, facsimile machine, and modem. Some of the types of businesses they may likely want to operate, such as a child care center or catering service, may require a degree of tolerance from neighbors, as well as permission from zoning authorities and approvals from health departments and other licensing bodies.

Many retired persons do not need paid employment, although some would like convenient full or part-time jobs for supplemental income, social contacts and the opportunity to use their skills. Older workers' need for jobs may increase due to forced retirement or company downsizing as well as the increasing cost of health care. When corporations such as Enron collapse or restructure, their older employees may lose both their jobs and the value of the investments in their pension plans. Even now, many persons need additional money badly, a situation that began before the stock market crash. In 1998 over five million Americans aged sixty-five or older had incomes below or near the poverty level.[29] In 2005, ten percent of individuals over age sixty-five had incomes below the poverty level.[30] Communities should keep in mind all household types as they consider possible actions to strengthen their neighborhoods and better support their families.

There are major ways neighborhoods can become active to support families' access to a decent income. The *Community Action Guide* (see Author's Note, pp. xv-xvi) discusses lobbying, information and referral and provides some questions to ask when planning a local effort. Here we address an issue not always considered by those concerned with helping people obtain a decent job: transportation. We then explore possibilities for local community-level economic development efforts.

Transportation to Local and Non-Local Jobs

If the jobs have moved to the suburbs or beyond, why don't city neighborhood residents follow them? Some do, often leaving the neighborhoods with fewer adult role models and fewer community leaders. Others cannot move, due to a lack of moderate income housing near the suburban jobs or the continued existence of racial discrimination in the housing market. Some fear living in a possibly prejudiced environment, or simply like their current neighborhood and prefer not to lose close relationships with family, friends, and neighbors there.

People in declining rural areas may be reluctant to relocate from communities where they, and perhaps their parents and grandparents, grew up. Moreover, people who own homes in areas with a declining real estate market face losing their investment and the security provided by at least having a place to live. The linkages and approaches we discuss here assume that the neighborhood or community wishes to preserve and strengthen itself, not see itself disintegrate and dissolve. Therefore, providing transportation from cities and towns to distant jobs may offer an important way to mitigate the negative impacts of unavailable local employment.

For residents of towns and cities, access to the millions of jobs located in suburbs, edge cities, outlying industrial parks, or even just on the other side of town, depends upon car ownership or convenient public transportation. Despite America's love affair with the car, 16 percent of the nation's households lack a vehicle of any kind. More significantly, almost three-and-a-half million households headed by someone between twenty-five and forty-four years old, the prime years for raising a family, lack their own transportation.[31] These ownership numbers underestimate the difficulty. Many low-income individuals possess cars that break down frequently, requiring costly repairs. Without reliable transportation, a worker often misses work, or shows up late—with the same excuse—time after time. When available, public transportation works, but often requires several transfers and considerable expense. It generally takes longer than driving. Using public transportation becomes even more difficult for a parent needing to drop off a toddler at a child care center before heading to work.

Public transportation can also be unreliable or unavailable during certain hours. A woman I knew graduated from the Madison Area Technical College as a welder but could not apply for an available job in a nearby rural town because she lacked a car. Another Madison woman quit her job because she was afraid to stand alone waiting for a bus in a rough neighborhood at midnight, a possible safety issue for men as well.

Transportation planning at the local level should be based in part on the impact that routes and the timing of construction will have on the lives of low-income families. The crime problems of Washington, D.C., gained national attention in the mid-1990s; the young men in one of the most seriously troubled sections of that city grew up in an area without jobs for their parents. When an excellent subway system was built, uniting the city with the Virginia and Maryland suburbs, the link between the poor, mostly black, areas of the city and the affluent, mostly white, suburbs was the last one to be completed. Thus, for many years the beautiful, efficient subway served tourists and whisked well-to-do suburban residents from Maryland and Virginia to highly paid jobs in downtown Washington, D.C. The new rapid transportation system created building booms and job development around the suburban subway stops but left the low-income residents in the District's Anacostia neighborhood with no access to those jobs. What would Washington, D.C., be like today if thousands of the parents of today's teenagers had held those suburban jobs?

Operating Economic Development Programs

Many neighborhoods have successfully operated a wide variety of economic development projects. Some established Community Development Corporations (CDCs) that began by rehabilitating one building that was a community eyesore; they now run multimillion dollar businesses providing commercial or retail space and other services. Such organizations provide jobs directly and through the businesses they bring into the area. Over 4,000 Community Development Corporations in both rural and urban areas provide housing, job training and placement programs, social services and enterprise development.[32]

Almost all cities, counties and even small towns or rural areas sponsor economic development projects. But creating jobs, especially ones that will support a family, takes concentrated effort over years. Those interested should carefully evaluate the best place to focus. The type of effort most appropriate for a given community or neighborhood depends upon a variety of factors, especially the state of the overall local economy and the size of the area.

Given the wealth of existing economic development experience, any neighborhood interested in pursuing a specific project or approach can easily locate successful models. They can tap into this expertise, read the evaluation studies to avoid pitfalls, and purchase already developed and tested worksheets and financial models. The recent annual meeting announcement of the National Association of Development Organizations Research Foundation includes networking "Brown Bag" lunches on ecotourism, business recruitment, forming a nonprofit, workforce development, housing, cultural programs as an economic strategy, and working with consultants. The International Economic Development Council, the Council for Urban Economic Development, and a variety of other groups host similar conferences as well as specialized workshops. Several organizations provide excellent week-long training on specific aspects or techniques such as housing or commercial development. The training schedule of the National Development Council, which has been providing economic development training for over thirty years, includes business development finance and job creation programs, rural economic development, and housing development finance.

Because economic development efforts are complex, require specialized expertise and skills and demand ongoing effort over years, a neighborhood may not want to undertake its own programs. They may prefer to work with existing efforts. Or they may concentrate on lobbying others to undertake certain programs. As indicated above, in some cases neighborhoods might more profitably spend their energies on creating convenient transportation options to jobs elsewhere, or concentrate on developing ameliorative programs to help people survive despite the availability of only low wage jobs. These approaches are not more important than economic development, but success may be more easily attained. The average child care worker, for example, may not be able to afford summer care for her own children. In the short run, it may be easier to obtain funds from businesses or foundations to provide summer care scholarships than to tackle raising the salaries of the area's child care providers, desirable as that might be. That said, economic development constitutes a major approach for neighborhoods to use in addressing their job needs, so we include below a special, more detailed section on how an ambitious neighborhood should approach economic development.

Identifying Assets

All communities, and even many neighborhoods, have some assets that can be used for job development efforts. Investigate the conventional wisdom about what makes for success, but also use your community's collective imagination. People only recently began recognizing and building upon the potential assets of museums in a major way. Indeed, in the early 1990s while planning a conference to help museums and economic development officials in Northwest Wisconsin work more effectively together, I initially found that neither side wanted to attend. Yet museums have now been recognized as an important part of cultural and heritage tourism, the most profitable segment of the market.[33]

For years conventional wisdom indicated that businesses could not profit with central city locations. Firms avoided those areas, flocking to the suburbs. Recent research has documented tremendous overlooked market opportunities in inner-city areas, even ones commonly considered to be "depressed." The Boston-based Initiative for a Competitive Inner City claims that the retail market of American inner-city residents equals that of Mexico.[34]

The higher density of cities, including areas with poor residents, provides more total retail sales potential than suburbs with wealthy residents living in single family houses on large lots. John Pawasarat and Lois Quinn note that the usual sources of marketing estimates are based on Census information that is inevitably out-of-date and typically undercounts inner-city residents. Marketing firms generally group neighborhoods together and label them based on their demographic characteristics. When Pawasarat and Quinn used other records, such as the number of households filing state income tax returns, they found that the adjusted gross income and estimated retail spending per square mile in an inner-city area compared favorably with that of surrounding suburban areas.[35]

The 405 households in the suburban area referred to as "Family Ties," for example, had an adjusted gross income per square mile of $20 million with an estimated annual retail spending of $5.4 million. With population densities ranging from 2,197 to 4,376 people per square mile, gross incomes in the inner city "Difficult Times" ranged from a low of $36.9 million to a high of $116.9 million with an estimated annual retail between four to nine times greater than that of the "Family Ties" area. Pawasarat found that many of the areas considered poor risk for a hardware store, for example, actually had two to three times as much potential as some of the wealthier areas.[36] After all, how many hammers does one household need?

Pawasarat also criticized the widespread use of catchy but loaded names to label areas. Not only do the labels mask real economic facts, they also reflect race, ethnicity, and class prejudices. Contrast "Young Immigrant Families" and "Hispanic Mix" with "Blue Blood Estates." Such names reinforce stereotypes and people's negative perceptions of the inner city.

The Pawasarat report details how neighborhoods can assemble the necessary data by themselves or with the help of local community colleges or universities. Neighborhoods attempting to attract new retail businesses into their area should download the study and familiarize themselves with similar work being conducted elsewhere.[37]

Commercial crime indices used by marketing firms further reinforce negative images. The indices make assumptions about the crime in an area based on the demographics of people living within several miles.[38] They do not reflect actual crime rates compiled from accurate data.

Developing a neighborhood's potential requires paying attention to image and working to counter negative stereotypes. You also may have many assets that are not recognized by outsiders or even by most residents. For example, does your community have a "can do" spirit? Do you have a track record of working together, getting projects completed? Is there racial, class, and ethnic harmony? Is there cooperation and stability within government or does a new city council overturn every decision of the previous one?

Choosing the Issue and the Opportunity for Impact

Shifts occurring in the geographic requirements of businesses may help or hurt your particular locale. In his book *Hot Towns*, Peter Wolf outlines five waves of migration in America: the initial settlements near the coasts, the movement into the Midwest and West, the concentration of people in the growing industrial cities, the growth of the suburbs, and now a movement to smaller towns and rural areas. Government policies encouraged these migrations by providing or assisting in the development of the railroads in the nineteenth century and the highways in the twentieth. Wolf argues that the development of the facsimile machine, one-day package delivery systems, and the Internet now provide many businesses the option of locating almost anywhere. Some members of his "fifth migration" have specific requirements such as location near a major university, but their options remain wide.[39]

Although the data will vary for specific businesses, general information on occupational growth trends can be found easily via the Internet. The Department of Labor's Bureau of Labor Statistics publishes the *Occupational Outlook Handbook*, which describes the employment prospects for individual occupational categories ranging from executives to home health aides. It provides details about working conditions, benefits, health hazards, education and other qualifications needed for entry, and advancement prospects. Within each occupation, it gives the range of wages both for various jobs and for various kinds of employers.

Neighborhood organizations themselves often fail to provide decent working conditions. They frequently are underfunded, scrambling to fulfill multiple and sometimes conflicting goals, and are dependent upon volunteers. Volunteers may not understand why a paid staff member resists working unpaid overtime. Nonprofit organizations serving the neighborhood often fall into the same trap, sometimes depending upon poorly paid residents for unlimited and on-call outreach services. Neighborhood organizations can push government and other funders to provide sufficient money to hire enough staff and provide decent salaries, benefits and working conditions.

Any neighborhood should recognize the long-term nature of its task and take the time to do its homework. It should start by clarifying objectives. Most economic development efforts involve both costs and benefits, which may not be distributed equally among members of the community. Creating wealth does not necessarily mean creating additional jobs for existing residents. A large nonprofit medical complex may create wealth for the original land owners and for the doctors who own and operate the complex but, at the same time, remove land from the tax rolls. In a small town such a complex might need to recruit newcomers to fill low-paying service jobs. Those newcomers will need housing and schools. Increased tourism may create wealth for certain business owners but will increase tax expenditures for traffic control and street repairs. Providing new industry with tax breaks or space in a publicly financed industrial park or giving tax breaks to those businesses locating in a downtown area may create new jobs but can also reduce the locality's ability to finance its schools. Although communities have used each of these techniques successfully, localities considering them need to understand potential problems and develop a plan for managing the risks and undesirable spillover effects.

Communities will need to manage any physical growth involved through land use and transportation planning. They also must calculate the costs of new infrastructure and increased services as well as potential tax benefits or losses. The effects of potential rises in land values and housing costs need to be considered. Undertaking long-term economic development also may require creating new leadership capacity, encouraging more effective citizen involvement, developing more systematic measurement and evaluation methods, and creating procedures for managing community conflict.

Approaches to Economic Development

Economic development is *very* trendy. This year's most popular solution may not be appropriate for an individual community, nor may it prove viable five years hence. Approaches to economic development that have been successfully undertaken by neighborhoods and small towns as well as larger entities include: (1) starting and growing new small businesses; (2) retaining and expanding existing businesses; (3) recruiting businesses and industry; and (4) attracting tourists or retirees. All of these approaches are considered in Appendix 3. (See Author's Note, pp. xv-xvi).

Any community should at least briefly review the wide range of approaches, the research evaluating their success, and the "how-to" manuals. In most cases excellent training and technical assistance programs at reasonable costs are available through state and national government agencies or nonprofit organizations. For example, for decades the Economic Development Administration of the U.S. Department of Commerce operated a multi-million dollar research and technical assistance economic development grant program that provided studies of best practices and financed development of training programs and technical assistance materials.[40]

Local economic development efforts may help families to earn a decent living. Having an adequate income largely determines a worker's ability to feed and house a family. These basic responsibilities will be considered next, along with ways local communities and neighborhoods can help.

Notes

1. Mishel, L., Bernstein, J. & Allegretto, S. (2006). *The state of working America 2006/2007*. p. 6. Washington, DC: The Economic Policy Institute. Retrieved January 11, 2007, from http://stateofworkingamerica.org/swa06-00-toc-exec-intro.pdf.
2. Mishel, L., Bernstein, J. & Allegretto, S. (2006). *The state of working America 2006/2007*. p. 7. Washington, DC: The Economic Policy Institute. Retrieved January 11, 2007, from http://stateofworkingamerica.org/swa06-00-toc-exec-intro.pdf.
3. Mishel, L., Bernstein, J. & Allegretto, S. (2006). *The state of working America 2006/2007*. p. 7. Washington, DC: The Economic Policy Institute. Retrieved January 11, 2007, from http://stateofworkingamerica.org/swa06-00-toc-exec-intro.pdf.
4. Mishel, L., Bernstein, J. & Allegretto, S. (2006). *The state of working America 2006/2007*. p. 7. Washington, DC: The Economic Policy Institute. Retrieved January 11, 2007, from http://stateofworkingamerica.org/swa06-00-toc-exec-intro.pdf.
5. Shulman. B. (2005). *The betrayal of work: How low wage jobs fail 30 million Americans and their families*. New York: The New Press, pp. 125-139.
6. Federal Register, Vol. 65, No. 31, February 15, 2000, pp. 7555-7557. As reported by the U.S. Department of Health & Human Services in *The 2000 HHS poverty guidelines: One version of the [U.S.] federal poverty measure*. Retrieved January 24, 2007, from http://aspe.hhs.gov/poverty/00poverty.htm.
7. U.S. Department of Health & Human Services in *The 2007 HHS poverty guidelines: One version of the [U.S.] federal poverty measure*. Retrieved January 24, 2007, from http://aspe.hhs.gov/poverty/07poverty.shtml.
8. Mishel, L., Bernstein, J. & Allegretto, S. (2006). *The state of working America 2006/2007*. p. 7. Washington, DC: The Economic Policy Institute. Retrieved January 11, 2007, from http://stateofworkingamerica.org/swa06-00-toc-exec-intro.pdf.
9. U.S. Department of Labor: Bureau of Labor Statistics. *Labor force statistics from the current population survey*. Retrieved January 15, 2007 from http://www.bls.gov/cps/minwage2005tbls.htm.

10. Mishel, L., Bernstein, J. & Allegretto, S. (2006). *The state of working America 2006/2007*. p. 5. Washington, DC: The Economic Policy Institute. Retrieved January 11, 2007, from http://stateofworkingamerica.org/swa06-00-toc-exec-intro.pdf.
11. Mishel, L., Bernstein, J. & Allegretto, S. (2006). *The state of working America 2006/2007*. p. 2. Washington, DC: The Economic Policy Institute. Retrieved January 11, 2007, from http://stateofworkingamerica.org/swa06-00-toc-exec-intro.pdf.
12. Mishel, L., Bernstein, J. & Allegretto, S. (2006). *The state of working America 2006/2007*. p. 6. Washington, DC: The Economic Policy Institute. Retrieved January 11, 2007, from http://stateofworkingamerica.org/swa06-00-toc-exec-intro.pdf.
13. Mishel, L., Bernstein, J. & Allegretto, S. (2006). *The state of working America 2006/2007*. p. 6. Washington, DC: The Economic Policy Institute. Retrieved January 11, 2007, from http://stateofworkingamerica.org/swa06-00-toc-exec-intro.pdf.
14. The U.S. Department of Labor Bureau of Labor Statistics develops occupational projections every two years. The most recent version covers the period 2006-2016, and the base data was released December 4, 2007.[a] Along with summary reports, the data is available in various formats online.

Methodology

For our analysis, we used *Occupational employment projections to 2016: Appendix: Employment by occupation, 2006 and projected 2016* in an Excel spreadsheet format[b] and *Occupational Employment, Training, and Earnings: Occupation Report* as a database query generating an HTML table.[c]

For the most part, this data uses individual occupation codes. The notable exceptions, where Bureau of Labor Statistics groups the codes, are as follows: 25-1000 – Postsecondary teachers; 29-1060 – Physicians and surgeons; 45-1000 – Supervisors, farming, fishing, and forestry workers; and 53-4010 – Locomotive engineers and operators.

Distinct occupations were separated from occupation summary lines by the following logic: [occupational code last digit not zero] or [occupation is last in a group] → [distinct occupation]. From this, we obtained 790 distinct occupations.

To obtain rank in growth, distinct occupations were then sorted in descending order based on number of additional jobs (Numeric change, column F). The occupation with the greatest number of additional jobs was 29-1111 - Registered nurses, with 587,349 additional jobs. The occupation with the least number of additional jobs was 43-5081 - Stock clerks and order fillers, with 130,722 lost jobs.

Percentage of total was then calculated by dividing the additional jobs value for each occupation by the additional jobs value for 00-0000 - Total, all occupations.

To obtain rank in median income, 2006 median annual earnings data[c] was merged by occupation title, and the resultant table was sorted in ascending order by median annual earnings values. The lowest paying occupation was 35-3031 – Waiters and waitresses ($14,850) and the highest – Airline pilots, copilots, and flight engineers ($141,090). Median earnings data was not available for 37 distinct occupations, but this did not hamper our analysis.

To obtain persons supported by median at poverty level or persons supported by median at 2 times the poverty level, the median income value was compared with poverty level tables generated from the 2006 poverty level values. In 2006, the poverty level in the continental United States was $9,800 for the first person, and $3,400 for each additional person in a family.[d]

To determine whether the occupation meets the housing wage, the median income for the occupation was compared with the 2006 national housing wage.[e] The National Housing Wage represents the amount a full-time worker must earn to be able to afford the rent for a modest 2 bedroom apartment while paying no more than 30 percent of income for housing. In 2006, the National Housing Wage was $ $33,925.

To determine the educational characteristics of the occupation, the educational attainment cluster (column 14) was used.

   a.   Bureau of Labor Statistics. (2007, December 4). *Employment Projections: 2006-16.* Press release. Washington DC: author. Retrieved January 30, 2008 from http://www.bls.gov/news.release/pdf/ecopro.pdf.

   b.   Shniper, L.; Dohm, A., *Occupational employment projections to 2016: Appendix: Employment by occupation, 2006 and projected 2016.* Monthly Labor Review, November 2007. Retrieved January 30, 2008, from ftp://ftp.bls.gov/pub/special.requests/ep/ind-occ.matrix/mlrappendix.zip.

   c.   Bureau of Labor Statistics. (2007). Occupational Employment, Training, and Earnings: Occupation Report. Retrieved from http://data.bls.gov/oep/servlet/oep.noeted.servlet.ActionServlet?Action=emprprt&Occ=XXXXXXXXXXX&Number=All&Sort=earn&Base=2006&Proj=2016&EdLevel=&Search=List&Type=Occupation&Phrase=&StartItem=0.

   d.   Leavitt, M.O. (2006, January 18). *Annual Update of the HHS Poverty Guidelines.* Federal Register 71(15): 3848-9. Retrieved January 30, 2008, from http://aspe.hhs.gov/poverty/06fedreg.pdf. In 2006, the poverty level in the continental United States was $9,800 for the first person, and $3,400 for each additional person in a family.

   e.   National Low Income Housing Coalition. (2006, December 12). *Out of Reach 2006.* Introduction. pp. 3-4. Retrieved January 20, 2007, from http://www.nlihc.org/oor/oor2006/introduction.pdf.

15. U.S. Department of Labor: Bureau of Labor Statistics. *Occupational outlook handbook.* Retrieved January 15, 2007 from http://www.bls.gov/oco/ocos121.htm.

16. Wu, K. B. (2004, February). *Poverty using official and experimental measures.* Issue Brief 66. Washington, DC: AARP Public Policy Institute. Retrieved January 24, 2007, from http://assets.aarp.org/rgcenter/econ/ib66_poverty.pdf. Waldron, T., Roberts, B., & Reamer, A. (2004, October). *Working hard, falling short. America's working families and the pursuit of economic security.* p. 30. Prepared for The Working Poor Families Project. Chevy Chase, MD: Authors. Retrieved January 24, 2006, from http://www.aecf.org/publications/data/working_hard_new.pdf.

17. Kuriansky, J., & Brooks, J. eds. (2003). *Setting the standard for American working families. A report on the impact of the Family Economic Self-Sufficiency Project nationwide.* p. 2. Washington DC: Wider Opportunities for Women. Retrieved January 24, 2007, from http://www.wowonline.org/docs/FINAL_FESS_report_072103.pdf.

18. Waldron, T., Roberts, B., & Reamer, A. (2004, October). *Working hard, falling short. America's working families and the pursuit of economic security.* p. 30. Prepared for The Working Poor Families Project. Chevy Chase, MD: Authors. Retrieved January 24, 2006, from http://www.aecf.org/publications/data/working_hard_new.pdf.

19. Greenhouse, S., Barbaro, M. (2005, October 26)Wal-Mart memo suggests ways to cut employee benefit costs. *The New York Times.* Retrieved January 15, 2007 from http://nytimes.com/2005/10/26/business/26walmart.ready.html. Wal-Mart. *Corporation Facts: Wal-Mart By the Numbers.* Downloaded on January 26, 2007 from http://www.walmartfacts.com/FactSheets/1292007_Corporate_Facts.pdf.

20. Mishel, L., Bernstein, J., & Boushey, H. (2002). *The state of working America 2002-2003* (p. 22.). Washington, D.C.: The Economic Policy Institute. Retrieved February 5, 2003, from http://www.epinet.org/books/swa2002/index.html.

21. Allegretto, S. *Economic snapshots: Dow's all-time high inconsequential for most Americans.* The Economic Policy Institute. Washington, DC. Retrieved January 31, 2007 from http://www.epi.org/content.cfm/webfeatures_snapshots_20061011.

22. Rank, M. R. (2004). *One nation, underprivileged: Why American poverty affects us all.* New York: Oxford University Press, pp. 93-94.
23. Dunn, J. (2001, September). *Back to the future: The Farm Bill and rural economic development.* Economic Development Digest. National Association of Development
24. Coontz, S. (1997). *The way we really are: Coming to terms with America's changing families.* New York:Basic Books.
25. Coontz, S. (1997). *The way we really are: Coming to terms with America's changing families.* New York: Basic Books, p. 16
26. STORE WARS: When Wal-Mart Comes to Town. Television program aired on Public Broadcasting Stations. Directed and produced by Micha Peled. See PBS-STORE WARS: When Wal-Mart Comes to Town. Retrieved February 10, 2003, from http://www.pbs.org/storewars/stores3.html.
27. STORE WARS: When Wal-Mart Comes to Town. Television program aired on Public Broadcasting Stations. Directed and produced by Micha Peled. See PBS-STORE WARS: Wal-Mart Facts. Retrieved February 10, 2003, from http://www. pbs.org/storewars/stores2.html.
28. Murphy, B. (2001, February). Dirty Hands. *Milwaukee Magazine,* pp. 54-64, 86.
29. Administration on Aging. (2001). *A profile of older Americans:2001: Poverty.* Retrieved October 15, 2002, from http://www.aoa.gov/aoa/sta. Bond, J. T., Galinsky, A., & Swanberg, J. E. (1998). *The 1997 National study of the changing workforce: Executive summary* (p. 7). New York: Family and Work Institute. Retrieved April 15, 2003, from http://fwi.igc.org/summary/nscw.pdf. ts/profile/2991/8.html.
30. U.S. Census Bureau. (2006, September 6). *Historical Poverty Tables. Table 3. Poverty Status of People, by Age, Race, and Hispanic Origin: 1959 to 2005.* Retrieved March 22, 2007, from http://www.census.gov/hhes/www/poverty/histpov/hstpov3.html
31. U.S. Census Bureau. (2000). *Detailed tables: H45. Tenure by vehicles available by age of householder [35] - Universe: Occupied housing units. Data set: Census 2000 summary file 3 (SF 3) - Sample data.* Retrieved February 13, 2003, from http://factfinder. census.gov/servlet/DTTa...id=D%mt_name=DEC_2000_SF3_U_H045&_lang=en.
32. Ford Foundation. (n.d.). *Seizing opportunities: The role of CDCs in urban economic development* (p. 32). Washington, DC: Author. Retrieved April 11, 2003, from http://www.fordfound.org/publications/recent_articles/docs/fordcdc.pdf.
33. Wireman, P. (1997). *Partnerships for prosperity: Museums and economic development.* Washington, DC: American Association of Museums.
34. Winfield, C., Deitz, R., & Garcia, R. (2001, Summer). *Conference explores inner-city business development* (p. 2). The Regional Economy of Upstate New York (Newsletter of the Buffalo Branch of the Federal Reserve Bank of New York). Retrieved April 15, 2003, from http://www.ny.frb.org/maghome/regional/sumr2001.pdf.
35. Pawasarat, J., & Quinn, L. M. (2001). *Exposing urban legends: The real purchasing power of central city neighborhoods* [Discussion paper]. Washington, DC: The Brookings Institution. Retrieved April 15, 2003, from http://brook.edu/dybdocroot/ es/urban/pawasarat.pdf.
36. Pawasarat, J., & Quinn, L. M. (2001). *Exposing urban legends: The real purchasing power of central city neighborhoods* [Discussion paper]. Washington, DC: The Brookings Institution. Retrieved April 15, 2003, from http://brook.edu/dybdocroot/ es/urban/pawasarat.pdf.
37. Federal Reserve Board of New York. (2001). Rediscovering inner-city markets. *Capital Connections, Vol. 3*(3). Retrieved October 20, 2002, from http://www. federalreserve.gov/dcca/newsletter/2001/fall01/innercity.htm.

38. Pawasarat, J., & Quinn, L. M. (2001). *Exposing urban legends: The real purchasing power of central city neighborhoods* (pp. 12-13) [Discussion paper]. Washington, DC: The Brookings Institution. Retrieved April 15, 2003, from http://brook.edu/dybdocroot/es/urban/pawasarat.pdf.
39. Wolf, P. (1999). *Hot towns: The future of the fastest growing communities in America.* New Brunswick, NJ: Rutgers University Press.
40. Research and National Technical Assistance, Economic Development Administration. (2001). *Economic studies of the Economic Development Administration: An annotated bibliography, 1995-2001.* Washington, D.C.: U.S. Department of Commerce. Retrieved from http://www.eda.gov/ImageCache/EDAPublic/documentts/pdfdocs/1g3_5f22_5fedaeconstudies_2epdf/v1/1g3_5fedaeconstudies.pdf.

9

Housing, Community Boundaries, and Neighborhood Design

Families provide shelter, a home for themselves, their children, and sometimes aging parents or other relatives. When children first establish a separate
household, often as full-time students, many parents cosign a lease to assure
a landlord that their child will pay the rent. Parents provide temporary shelter
for an adult child undergoing a divorce or major surgery. They drive across
the country to help their daughter move. Children visit nursing homes to help
parents or other elderly relatives find one that suits them. When people die, they
will their houses to their children or grandchildren.

Neighborhoods have played major roles in the provision of shelter: opposition, creation, and modification of the rules of the game. Neighborhood
influence on housing frequently has consisted of NIMBYism, standing for
Not In My Back Yard. Neighborhoods lobby and use direct action to prevent
"undesirables" from moving in. At various times and places these undesirables
have been people with children, the aged, members of minority groups, people
with lower incomes, rental units, small houses on small lots, halfway houses, or
group homes. Other neighborhoods voice concern about housing their current
residents as their older homes deteriorate or when rising prices and taxes force
long-term homeowners from the area. They realize that their children could not
afford to buy or rent in the neighborhood in which they grew up. People may
want a place in their current neighborhood where they, or their neighbors or
parents, can move as they age.

This chapter briefly discusses the housing system, that complex combination of people and rules that together govern housing type, location, and
price. Addressing the entire range of housing and neighborhood design issues
lies beyond the scope of this book. Neighborhoods need only be aware that a
complex system exists and that it will affect their ability to tackle any question
of housing or neighborhood development. We then examine three issues: why
trends in adjacent communities matter to every neighborhood; how neighbor-

hood and local community design influence the ability of families to thrive; and types and affordability of housing.

The Big Picture: National Trends and Major Players

Whether a family can find a decent home in a nice neighborhood may seem to depend only upon income. But it is more complicated than that. The rules for determining the boundaries of communities, the layout of neighborhoods and the affordability of housing are each determined by a complex network of decisions by local, state, and federal government agencies, developers, banks, realtors, and individual builders.

For example, the methods used to determine the safety of non-wood building materials have a key impact on housing prices. Whether a local builder can use a new material depends upon an elaborate system of research, testing, securing approval from professional groups such as engineers and architects, and perhaps obtaining changes in local building codes. The parties involved have different professional loyalties and sometimes follow financial agendas that may prevent adoption of the most effective materials or procedures needed to produce safe, inexpensive housing. The author once helped a congressman structure the board of an organization designed to pull the parties together to make testing and adoption of new materials easier. Representatives of the lumber industry visited the congressman in an attempt to ensure that the directors of the new organization would be controlled by those favorable to the lumber industry.

A variety of government, environmental, and zoning regulations govern the framework of the private housing market. Within those constraints, however, realtors, builders, and developers largely determine the pattern of land use, the attractiveness of neighborhoods, and the type and prices of housing.

The massive federal highway construction program of the 1950s opened the development of rural farmland for new suburbs. The federal housing programs' mortgage arrangements and tax laws enabled millions of families to buy homes there. Almost half of the suburban homebuyers depended upon those programs to provide them low down payments and long-term, fixed rates, low interest loans.[1] All the new homeowners gained an indirect subsidy when they calculated their income, then deducted their mortgage interest and property taxes before arriving at the amount they owed in taxes. Federal regulation of the banking industry continues to enable families to finance homes with long term mortgages. The financial institutions in turn control the availability of mortgages, construction funds, interest rates, and the criteria for approving loans.

States control the boundary lines of towns and cities. The rules for incorporation, annexation, and localities' ability to levy taxes are set by states. States, along with the federal government and localities, determine the location of roads, a major influence on housing development. States can provide tax benefits to homeowners and tax credits to builders. Some states, including Wisconsin, have passed laws and programs affecting land use. States and localities pass and implement affirmative action laws. Local government officials set zoning and building code requirements, which determine neighborhood layout, density, and whether an area contains industry, apartments, and/or single family housing. Those decisions are often influenced by trade unions and local business groups. Finally, both states and local governments may sponsor a range of housing programs.

Other entities play a more subtle role. Unions may affect housing prices through shaping acceptable practices for construction or rehabilitation, both directly through their work and indirectly through their influence on local building codes. News media can affect housing markets through highlighting the desirability or problems of individual neighborhoods. At the same time, images from entertainment media imply that most Americans live in expensive homes, thus obscuring the real housing problems of millions of Americans.

The Regional Context: No Neighborhood is an Island

The list of key players shows that obtaining the desired housing for any neighborhood may involve influencing some non-neighborhood players. Although some affluent neighborhoods may be able to maintain themselves without addressing or caring about the development of nearby areas, this eventually will prove detrimental for the community at large and the nation as a whole. Over the past one hundred years the concentration of American housing has shifted from rural and small town, to large cities, to suburbs, and now is dispersing to small towns and rural areas. People have been fleeing core cities. In too many cases this has led to deterioration of once prosperous neighborhoods and businesses, increased concentration of people of color, and left cities their historic role of providing an entry point for new immigrants without the manufacturing and the other job opportunities that historically helped immigrants move into the American mainstream. Long-time residents have faced declines in real income and job opportunities. Even more potentially damaging, those living in poverty in core cities increasingly reside in areas where everyone else is poor, businesses absent or marginal, and where underfunded schools struggle with overwhelming problems. These real difficulties are often exaggerated in media reports, fueling people's desire to leave the city.

Unfortunately in most cases the businesses and households moving to the suburbs took their core city's tax base and potential for further economic growth with them. David Rusk has undertaken an extensive analysis of the changes in housing patterns over the past forty years in 522 metropolitan areas. His analysis showed that core cities that have continued to thrive are the few that have had the political ability and will to expand, capturing the population and tax base of the areas developing on their edges. Rusk argues that the health of the entire nation depends upon maintaining viable central cities, the "core" of the regions in which they are located.[2] Or, as another scholar puts it, "There is no such place as 'away.'" Sociologist Xavier de Souza Briggs points out that the new global economy rests upon a metropolitan-wide economic base.[3]

Core cities provide the economic base for much of the surrounding area, as well as the concentration of minds and resources needed for intellectual and cultural development and enjoyment. Peter Wolf details the growth of "Hot Towns" resulting from the ability of major actors in the economic game to move their businesses to areas with good climates and abundant recreational opportunities. But he also notes that many of the "cultural creatives" making location decisions still need to locate near the concentrations of government and educational institutions in core cities and want to live within easy access of its cultural opportunities.[4] The core cities, therefore, continue to represent a positive asset for the nation.

Why does this matter to most Americans? After all, the liturgy of inner-city problems has been told for decades. Many believe that core city problems are either the fault of their residents or, at any rate, are unsolvable. Although for decades poverty has been seen as a central city problem, research shows that millions of the poor and near-poor live in rural areas. By 2005 more poor lived in suburbs than in urban areas.[5]

So why should we pay attention to Rusk's analysis? For the thousands who live in a core city and wish to develop or maintain a decent neighborhood, Rusk's analysis should provide an impetus to broaden their efforts to take a comprehensive community-wide approach, and to recognize that long-run success will involve years of effort. Why should people who live in the suburbs or a pleasant small town near the city care? Their areas could easily be impacted by the same forces. The complicated forces that have created, encouraged and supported the decline of the inner cities, are now affecting older suburbs and will soon hit areas even further out.[6] Because of the regional nature of urban economies with the dispersal of low-income jobs and people, increased poverty rates in a central city generally are reflected by increases in the poverty rates in nearby suburbs.[7]

Rusk claims that without effective leadership in countering these trends, the future holds further deterioration of the core cities, a decline of the older suburbs, increased sprawl with its toll on the environment and demands on commuters, further polarization of racial and ethnic groups, and increased separation of the "haves" from the "have-nots."[8] Although in some cities and certain neighborhoods, higher income persons have been relocating into urban areas, the overall trend remains in the opposite direction. In addition, such movements often have been directly or indirectly subsidized by government revitalization efforts and can create problems of their own, the so-called "gentrification" effect.

According to Rusk, counteracting the negative effects of these trends will require either the ability for core cities to annex their adjacent areas or some form of regional cooperation. He argues that while annexation of the surrounding areas by core cities might be desirable, in most cases it will be politically impossible. He recommends devising regional approaches to accomplish some of the same benefits, and provides examples of successful models.[9]

Neighborhood Design for Space and Activities

The design of neighborhoods and conditions in a community may support or hinder an individual family's ability to perform each of its basic tasks. Neighborhood design affects the available facilities, services, and atmosphere as well as exposure to air and noise pollution, hazardous chemicals and dangerous traffic, to which children are especially susceptible. Other design issues important to children include the availability of play areas and visual beauty.

Children need active physical play to develop their large and small muscles, strength, coordination, and balance. Through play they learn to relate to other children and have the chance to practice leadership skills and teamwork. They develop their intellectual and creative abilities. They invent things, build playhouses, act out dreams; they discover how to manipulate the physical environment and how to do things independently. Play areas should offer children a variety of activities, as well as a chance to observe and interact with children of other ages. Large yards, little-used streets and nearby woods, fields or vacant lots provided such opportunities in the past. Today cars often speed through neighborhoods; yards may be small or nonexistent; vacant lots sprout housing or businesses.

Children do not use their space or even view it the same way adults do. Kevin Lynch and other scholars talked to children in a number of countries about their lives, how they saw and used the space around them. They found that children's experiences and preferences differed markedly from those of adults, including those planning urban areas. In general the children's ideal environment "reflected constant themes: trees, friends, quiet, lack of traffic, small size, cleanliness." Some children in Lynch's studies, however, craved center-city excitement. Thus, those concerned with appropriate children's activities need to consult the children as well as plan for a variety of different interests and desires.[10]

Too frequently playgrounds are designed for preschool children only. Older children may ignore or abuse them. Some structures visually interesting to adults lack creative play opportunities. Ann Szalkowski, who builds children's playgrounds, notes that different facilities and opportunities must be created for teenagers. They will not be attracted to equipment designed for younger children but need a space for activities that test their skills and daring.[11]

Children need beauty as well as spaces for a quiet moment, contemplation, "cooling out" or talking to their best friend. The author recalls the joyous looks on some children's faces in a low-income housing area as they showed her their favorite trees in a nearby park. Neighborhood gardens, both flower and vegetable, provide beauty and a connection to the earth. Nature and beauty provide children a link to the natural environment, the larger world, awareness of the mysteries of the universe, a sense of awe. Exposure to nature can spark children's curiosity about science. A volunteer at the Allied-Dunn's Marsh Neighborhood Center provided a biweekly nature club for youngsters from the after-school program. One cold February afternoon I looked out the window and wondered what the children were doing in the freezing weather. Then I realized that they were peering with awe at the barely swelling buds on the maple tree.

While children are certainly not the only residents of a neighborhood who appreciate good design, they are among its most vulnerable. Neighborhood design that keeps its most fragile members in mind will likely be supportive of all families.

Housing Types

Just as neighborhood design should be influenced by its end users, so too should housing types. Who are the families for whom we design housing? The majority of Americans live with family members, but millions live alone or with other adults who are not family members. Of the 111 million American households, 22 percent consist of couples with children, 28 percent are couples without children, and almost an equal number, 27 percent, are people living alone. The remaining 23 percent of our households include different combinations such as a woman and her elderly mother, single parents with their children, a grandmother with her grandchildren, or unrelated people living together.[12] The legal definitions of family and local codes affect who can live together to share expenses, child care and household chores. The local housing market, for its part, should provide choices that can accommodate the variety of needs of today's families, offering a menu that includes more than just the single-family owner-occupied house.

Choosing a home is also a choice about proximity to the other things a family needs. Zoning and building codes affect not only the density and type of an area's housing, but also the location of stores, offices and community services. Zoning and land use practices have varied from the "Home is Haven" layout of the suburbs to the mixed uses found in many more urban areas and now being promoted by advocates of the New Urbanism. From the viewpoint of family tasks, a mixed use pattern has many advantages. Convenient location of a variety of stores and businesses means some individuals can work near their homes and people can accomplish the chores of household shopping more easily.

The type of shelter needed by families and individuals varies with life stage, income, health and personal preference. Families with children need more bedrooms. Elderly couples who no longer drive may require assisted living in a complex that provides meals, eliminating the problem of obtaining groceries. A mixture of housing permits an older person unwilling or unable to maintain a large house to move into a smaller apartment, a condominium or even an assisted living home but remain in their old neighborhood. People with large lots can build a "granny flat" for a parent. Since having more than one adult in a household helps when handling everyday chores and child care, and becomes critical when an adult is seriously ill, families, single individuals and society at large benefit from arrangements that allow people to more easily share households. The rules affect not only students and young workers, but also unmarried couples, those desiring to live in extended families, and people searching for community through establishing communal housing arrangements.

Owning a Home

The dream of most Americans remains homeownership, preferably in a single family house with a yard. This dream does not vary with class. An extensive study of welfare recipients in Wisconsin found that many shared this dream. "... that's what we're working towards. Being able to stand on our own feet. Being able to maybe even one day buy a house. Have our own home..."[13]

Homeownership remains a symbol of stability, reliability, and adult status. It often provides families access to more desirable communities that spend more money on schools. Thus, homeownership can help families gain educational advantages for their children likely to result in later economic gain. Homeownership provides the major means of saving for most Americans, their chief way of accumulating wealth. The median family net worth for homeowners reaches $184,400 compared with $4,000 for renters.[14] Equity in their home comprises a major proportion of most homeowners' total wealth. Neighborhoods also benefit when a large proportion of residents own their homes. Homeowners' inability to leave quickly or easily and their financial stake give them a vested interest in neighborhood affairs and maintenance.

In addition to ensuring regular payments towards a saleable asset, homeowners benefit from indirect government subsidies due to the tax advantages of home ownership. Although many people object to considering tax savings as subsidies, the money is real money. For example, a family paying $1,000 a month in rent spends $12,000 a year on housing costs. A family with the same income paying $1,000 a month in mortgage payments also pays $12,000 in housing costs. However, the home-owning family can claim part of the $12,000, the interest on the loan, as an itemized deduction when calculating their federal income taxes.

The homeowner saves even more money since he can also claim a deduction for property taxes. People often buy their first home primarily because they couldn't afford not to, since the federal government pays, albeit indirectly, for a large percentage of the investment. In Wisconsin, homeowners also gain from deductions for both mortgage interest and property taxes when calculating their state income tax. Homeowners reap another advantage because they can finance other purchases with a tax deductible home equity loan at a lower rate than available through credit cards. If the house increases in value, the homeowner also benefits from purchasing a growing asset with leveraged money.

People often say, yes, but renters don't pay property taxes or have the expense of making repairs. In fact, renters do pay for the property taxes and the repairs since landlords calculate those costs when establishing the rent. The landlord can deduct all expenses from taxes while, hopefully, the property continues to gain in value. When the owner sells the property, the profit counts as a capital gain, which may be excluded from taxation or taxed at a lower rate than income gained from employment. The wealth of many middle-income Americans today results from the rising home prices over past years combined with the tax advantages.

The indirect subsidy to homeowners costs the federal government billions of dollars. The Congressional Joint Committee on Taxation estimated a 2006 revenue loss of almost S70 billion from the deduction for mortgage interest on owner-occupied residences, almost $20 billion from the homeowners' property taxes deduction, and $24 billion from exclusion of capital gains taxes on home sales, a total of $113 billion or over three times the $36 billion provided the Department of Housing and Urban Development in FY 2007. [15]

Those who can afford to buy expensive homes and second homes benefit most. Considering the mortgage interest deduction alone, in 2005, over two-thirds of this benefit, over $42.6 billion, went to those with incomes over $100,000. The 3.2 million taxpayers with incomes of $200,000 and above received $17.5 billion in tax benefits, or $6.5 billion more than the total given the 16 million taxpayers with incomes less than $75,000.[16]

Although many note the existence of public housing complexes and read about various programs to assist lower-income people in housing, the direct and indirect benefits provided to homeowners far outweigh those programs. The cost of all of the U.S. Department of Housing and Urban Development's programs—including those providing housing for six and a half million lower income family and elderly households–was $36 billion in FY 2007. Thus, the mortgage interest benefit to the three million taxpayers with incomes over $200,000, $17.5 billion, amounted to about one-half the HUD budget. Including the projected 2006 tax loss of $24 billion due to the exclusion of capital gains on sales of principal residences, the total from these two benefits alone exceeds all the HUD budget by $5.5 billion.[17]

Many people not only ignore the real costs of the homeowner deduction to federal and state government, but also fail to acknowledge the benefits they receive. Many older people purchased their homes with a federal program such as a VA loan or FHA mortgage. Formerly rural land would never have been developed into suburban tracts without the federal government's highway program. Children rarely recognize that the help they received with their first home down payment probably came from the profits their parents realized from selling their own first home purchased years before.

Today, manufactured homes such as trailers and prefabricated houses provide shelter for increasing numbers of Americans. In fact, twice as many people live in manufactured homes as live in large apartment buildings (those with over fifty units). Manufactured homes accounted for one-fifth of new homes built in 1999. One-quarter of the units were located in rural, and to a lesser extent, suburban areas of Florida, California, and Texas.[18]

As a means of solving the housing problem, however, manufactured housing faces a number of barriers. Many suburban and urban areas strictly limit their placement to special parks and restrict the number and location of those parks. Financial institutions may consider the units personal property rather than real estate, rendering long term mortgages and credit unavailable. Units with a permanent foundation located on private land are eligible for standard mortgages, but many owners are forced to use more expensive consumer loans and forego the tax benefits of homeownership. Mobile home parks, also called manufactured home communities, can provide warm and welcoming neighborhoods for their residents. Some, however, are poorly designed or rundown, providing unattractive and unsafe environments.

Although mobile homes have suffered an image problem, improved products and the seriousness of the affordable housing shortage may make them an attractive option for communities. The industry has been changing rapidly, producing larger homes with more amenities, and more homes being placed on privately-owned individual lots.[19] In 1999, residents of manufactured housing, most of whom are owners, had a median income of $26,900. The median market value of their homes was $17,000. Between 1995 and 2000, the number of households living in manufactured homes jumped from six to over eight million. Manufactured homes are purchased disproportionally by persons aged sixty-five and older and those under twenty-five years old. From a community's viewpoint, manufactured home communities offer both low cost housing and stability. The annual turnover for both owners and renters is about 5 percent, considerably lower than the 10 percent turnover average for conventional homeowners and 60 percent for renters.[20]

Although owning their own home remains most American families' dream and would benefit them financially, many families can never hope to achieve this. Moreover, home ownership is not always an appropriate choice. Some do not want the chores connected with home maintenance, or they plan to move in the near future. Although the general trend has been for homes to increase in value, in some areas values have decreased. That can easily happen for a short period, possibly at exactly the time a homeowner needs to sell. Although the housing market soared during the 1990s, from 1975 to 1995, home prices increased only one-half percent above inflation.[21] Moreover, the homes lower income households can afford may well be in areas where the housing values are unlikely to appreciate substantially and may even decline.[22] Home ownership in a low-income neighborhood can actually harm families by limiting mobility in pursuit of a job or better schools.

In recent years, policies and programs have promoted home ownership for lower income persons. This may not be the best option for many, nor the most appropriate use of program dollars. If a lower-income person loses a job or has a medical emergency, they are unlikely to have the savings necessary to prevent foreclosure and the loss of their entire investment. This is particularly likely if they purchased their home with a subprime or predatory loan or with an adjustable rate mortgage. In 2000, defaults increased and approximately one million households lost their homes and when the economy slowed.[23] In today's economy, most lower income individuals will not graduate to jobs that pay significantly more, and thus may not be able to handle higher mortgage payments or higher property taxes. Moreover, they likely lack the knowledge and financial resources to capitalize on their home purchase by periodically selling at a profit and buying a more valuable home.

Promoting home ownership may not alleviate housing problems. In fact, almost 60 percent of low-income homeowners in both rural and urban areas have housing bills totaling more than one-third of their income.[24] Many are unable to make needed repairs on their homes. National policies have clearly supported home ownership through the tax code, the highway system, and programs to promote homeownership among low-income families. While this national policy choice may have many benefits, it also detracts from the need for affordable rental housing.

Rental Housing

The availability of decent, affordable rental housing remains crucial for America's families. Approximately one-third of American households live in rented quarters. Although 69 percent of all American households own their homes, in 2006 only one-half of those with incomes below the median household income did so. More telling, almost 60 percent of families with household heads under age thirty-five, the prime age for rearing children, rent.[25] The proportion is even higher among single parents, rising to 74 percent for single female households. The home ownership rate for household heads between the ages of twenty-five and thirty-nine is actually lower now than in 1982.[26]

Nationally, a death of good moderately-priced rental housing exists. Millions of American households cannot afford a two-bedroom unit without dipping into the money for food or other necessities. The National Low Income Housing Coalition annually publishes a national survey of the availability of rental units by state and by major metropolitan area. In 2006, in order to afford a two-bedroom unit without paying more than 30 percent of income for rent, a worker would have needed to earn $16.31 an hour or $33,925 a year. In 2006, one-half of all private sector workers earned under fifteen dollars an hour. Some 42 million households had earnings of less than $34,000 a year.[27] While in some areas of the country the "housing wage" is less, in others it is considerably higher.

The lyrics of a popular song of the 1920s extolled, "We will raise a family. A boy for you, a girl for me. Oh can't you see how happy we would be?"[28] But once the family has two children of opposite sexes, they soon will need not the two-bedroom unit discussed above but an even less affordable three bedroom one.

Minimum wage workers fare even worse. At the beginning of 2007, the national "housing wage" was over three times the existing minimum wage of $5.15. A household where the husband worked two forty-hour jobs and the wife worked one forty-hour job at the minimum wage would have a joint income eighty-six cents below the housing wage.[29] A full-time minimum wage worker could not afford even a one-bedroom apartment anywhere in the country. The National Low Income Housing Coalition found that some nine million renter households paid half or more of their income for housing.[30] In 2007, Congress raised the minimum wage. However, the new wage rate will not reach $7.25 an hour until 2009 and then will be less than one-half of the amount needed in 2006 to rent a two-bedroom apartment.

Who may have difficulty finding affordable rental housing now and in the future? Of the twenty-eight occupations likely to employ the most new workers between 2006 and 2016, several of them pay median wages below the housing wage. That is, one-half of the workers in these occupations will not be able to afford a two-bedroom apartment without paying more than 30 percent of their income for housing. The median wage in a number of the others is only slightly higher; that means the wages of many of the workers in those jobs will fall below the housing wage, which was $16.37 an hour or $33,924 a year in 2006. Those occupations include retail salespeople, customer service representatives, janitors and cleaners, waiters and waitresses, food preparation workers, food preparation workers who also serve food, home health aides, receptionists, child care workers, maids and housekeeping cleaners, medical assistants, landscaping and groundskeeping workers, security guards, and office workers. These workers perform the services upon which we all depend: the cashier at the store, the receptionist at the office, the nursing assistant bringing a glass of water to a patient, the individual taking in clothes at the dry cleaners, and the person putting out the fresh fruit at the grocery store.

Where do workers who cannot afford housing in the private rental market turn? Some can use various government programs, but available funding does not nearly meet the need. In Dane County, Wisconsin, for example, about 3,000 people have obtained assistance from the Section 8 assistance program of the federal government, which provides assistance to those who would otherwise be forced to pay more than 30 percent of their income in rent. In the late 1990s the program had a waiting list of 2,000 households, and in 2007 the waiting list had been closed for several years. Nationally, because of limited funding, the program only serves two million of the eight million households eligible.[32]

Some landlords will not accept people receiving Section 8 assistance. Indeed, landlords in Madison, Dane County's major city, vigorously fought a proposed law requiring them to consider those funds when assessing whether a prospective tenant could afford the rent. Yet thousands of respectable, conscientious workers hold jobs making them eligible for the program.

Where do families live if they are not lucky enough to obtain a moderately priced unit? Some live in temporary shelters or badly deteriorated, substandard housing, which can result in health problems such as asthma and lead poisoning, as well as safety problems from rickety staircases, torn carpets and fire hazards. Other families double up with relatives, causing stress and, in some, cases, spreading diseases such as tuberculosis, which flourishes in cramped and overcrowded living conditions.

Many families, including those with children, join the ranks of the homeless. The author remembers with pain and frustration the fate of a lovely, well-behaved child in the after-school program at the Allied-Dunn's Marsh Neighborhood Center. Her mother provided the type of positive parenting and role model society wants, displaying concern about her child and a willingness to become active in supporting the after-school program. Yet when her landlord decided to sell her building, she and her husband lost their housing. They could not find another unit in the neighborhood. They had money to pay the rent, but not enough to pay the rent plus an additional hefty security deposit. The units they could afford, including the security deposit, would not accept them because the landlord did not want to rent to a family with six children. Despite frantic efforts of the parents and the after-school director, no housing could be found. The family moved into a shelter in downtown Madison. I do not know what became of them. I do know that the neighborhood lost a potential leader.

Myths abound about the homeless. Tonight some 200,000 American children will sleep on the streets or in a shelter. Each year well over a million children will have this experience.[33] The major cause of homelessness is poverty combined with an inadequate supply of housing that is affordable to those with low incomes. Not only do people face the problem of low wages discussed in the previous chapters, but the subsidies available through welfare and housing programs have been reduced. In addition, between 1973 and 1993 over two million low-rent units were lost due to abandonment, conversion into condominiums or increases in costs. Yet between 1980 and 2003, federal support for low-income housing dropped almost 50 percent.[34] The homeless problem is often considered an inner-city issue attributable to a single man's unwillingness to work or addiction to drugs or alcohol. Today, however, almost 40 percent of the homeless are families with children. Over one-fifth of the urban homeless hold jobs. The homeless now live in affluent suburbs and rural areas as well as urban areas. In a five-year period some five to eight million Americans will be homeless for at least one night.[35]

The homeless suffer more than other Americans from chronic health problems and street crime. Children must shift from school to school, facing the stigma attached to their homeless condition. Although preschool programs contribute to children's school readiness and success, homeless children rarely obtain that assistance. Homeless parents sometimes send their children to live with relatives or friends, thus disrupting parental ties.[36]

Homelessness often results from domestic violence. Indeed, an estimated 20 to 50 percent of homeless women are fleeing violence.[37] Today many children live alone on the streets, having fled their families due to rape, incest, violence, or other troubles. The author recalls a woman telling how she left her mother's funeral and went directly to a social worker explaining that she did not want to return home with a sexually abusive stepfather. "Luckily, she believed me." That sixteen-year old was lucky, but many less fortunate or less resourceful teenagers roam our streets. Indeed, between 500,000 and 1.23 million youth and young adults aged sixteen to twenty-four are homeless. On the streets they face sexual assault, being beaten up, robbed, stabbed, and shot.[38]

Special Implications for Different Households

In addition to facing discrimination in housing markets, minorities often work at low-paying jobs, limiting their ability to meet the income ratios required by lenders for mortgages or to pay high security deposits. Actually there are more white families than minority families dependent on government subsidies such as Section 8 to pay their rents. For their size as a group, though, minority families are more often dependent upon such assistance than are white families.

Other families or individuals with potential housing problems include the elderly and those with disabilities. Many elderly face housing problems merely due to low income. Millions, especially elderly widows, subsist on Social Security, which makes desirable units unaffordable. Many others own their homes but cannot physically perform the needed maintenance, nor afford to hire outside assistance. They may also lack the funds to make the modifications in their homes needed to accommodate declining physical capacity. As people age, the availability of locally-based convenience shopping and activities grows more important, especially if the cost of maintaining a car or physical disability makes driving more difficult. Many widows depended upon their husbands for home repairs and driving. A woman in her seventies in Monona, Wisconsin, while caring for her dying husband faced a challenge in obtaining groceries by herself. Although she had a driver's license, she had not driven for thirty years.

Most older persons live in their own homes in a suburb or a rural area.[39] Experts and the elderly themselves agree that, both financially and emotionally, people fare better by living in their own homes as long as possible. A variety of groups have developed appropriate assistance programs, but they suffer from inadequate funding. Insurance policies and government programs tend to gear benefits towards professional health care delivered in nursing homes rather than in helping someone living in their own home with basic tasks.

To the extent that adequate housing for older persons requires specialized senior housing or a nursing home, the problems for anyone developing such residences overlap with those creating housing for people with disabilities or with low incomes: locating a neighborhood amenable to the idea. Reluctance to accept elderly housing may be based upon disapproval of any dwelling other than a single family home, fear of seeing elderly people considered "depressing" by many, or the assumption any government sponsored housing is undesirable. Whatever the reasons, in Madison, for example, zoning policies lump such housing with that for those who have mental or physical disabilities or who are former convicts. Some Madison neighborhoods have opposed senior housing. Others have supported it as a means of accepting their "fair share" of housing for those with special needs or low-income persons, thus avoiding providing housing for low-income families or people whose conditions seem to make them less desirable neighbors.

Discrimination

Discrimination can occur against individuals, families, or against entire neighborhoods. For over half the twentieth century, the federal government would not loan money to people buying homes in integrated neighborhoods. "Redlining" refers to bankers' practice of drawing a red line around an area to indicate that no loans should be approved in that area. The inability of some neighborhoods to obtain mortgages for new owners or funds for home repairs led Congress in 1977 to outlaw the practice. A number of banks have responded by modifying their practices and investing in neighborhoods.

Unfortunately, study after study shows that discrimination in the housing market continues to exist. Players who discriminate include banks, mortgage companies, and realtors. A study by the Federal Reserve Bank of Boston showed that the rejection rates for minorities remained higher than that of Caucasians even when they had the same wealth, employment, credit histories, and amount of debt. Minorities face discrimination at every step of obtaining a mortgage when matched with whites of identical characteristics. They are less likely to obtain helpful information from loan officers and are quoted higher interest rates.[40] Moreover, because the housing market remains largely segregated, minorities are less likely to buy homes in areas with maximum potential for increase in value.[41] Realtors sometimes play a discriminatory role, either through steering minority customers into certain areas and properties or by lying about the availability of a house. Numerous studies show that when matched home seekers approach a realtor, the minority couple too often learns that the house has been sold or removed from the market, yet a non-minority applicant finds the same property available minutes later.[42]

Partly for these reasons, minorities are significantly less likely to achieve the financial advantages of home ownership status than non-Hispanic whites. While three-fourths of white households enjoy homeownership, only one-half of minority households are owners.[43] Moreover, experts estimate that for most of the twentieth century, the homeowner gap between blacks and whites homeownership rates was between 25 and 30 percent. This left black parents with less home equity to pass on to their children for investing in their education, stocks, or their own homes. The difference in homeowner rates translates into differences in net worth since equity in their homes represents the greatest single asset of American households. Minority households have significantly less net worth than non-Hispanic whites. The median net worth of non-Hispanic whites is $79,400, compared to $7,500 for blacks and $9,750 for Hispanics. Even when minorities do achieve homeownership, the homes they buy are less likely to be located in areas with the greatest potential for appreciation.[44]

Discrimination against minority renters is even more rampant than that against potential home buyers. While blacks encountered discrimination 17 percent of the time when trying to buy a house, they faced it over 21 percent of the time when trying to rent. The discrimination faced by Hispanics was even higher, almost 20 percent of the time for those desiring to become homeowners and over 25 percent of the time for renters.[45]

Practices that seem neutral may have discriminatory effects. Concentration of bank offices in suburban communities, for example, makes it more likely that agents will loan money there rather than in inner-city neighborhoods. Landlords may use screening procedures that, while seemingly neutral, may adversely affect more minority families. Minorities more often face jail rather than warnings for minor offenses.[46] Landlords seeing the criminal record can conclude that they will be unreliable tenants and refuse to rent to them.

In Madison, for example, concentrated police drug enforcement effort for some years was directed at low-income neighborhoods with high proportions of minorities, resulting in numerous arrests, many for use of or possession of small quantities of marijuana. In the summer of 1997 the city council passed an ordinance permitting police to arrest someone for talking to a known drug dealer. Yet the prevalence of widespread illegal underage drinking, including weekly public binge drinking, by a large proportion of the mostly white students at the University of Wisconsin was ignored by policy makers and the press for years. Concerns finally arose partly in response to national publicity highlighting the University of Wisconsin's top ranking for student binge drinking and an effort to clean up the area adjacent to the campus as part of a downtown revitalization effort. In 1998, however, the Madison police softened their approach to public drinking parties near the University of Wisconsin campus. They said that while they would ticket sponsors of large parties for selling alcohol without a license and serving to minors, they would not ticket the underage partygoers. "We don't want to alienate the student population from the good service the Madison police brings to our community."[47]

"A Decent, Safe and Sanitary Home and Suitable Living Environment for Every American."

That mission statement of the U.S. Department of Housing and Urban Development (HUD) has not yet been fulfilled. While most Americans are pleased with their homes and neighborhoods, millions pay too large a proportion of their incomes for housing and millions suffer a variety of housing problems. Millions are one pay check or one health care emergency away from homelessness.

Our current situation and future potential is due to several factors. First, the private market does not pay millions of workers enough to afford the available housing without paying an unreasonable amount of their incomes in housing costs. Second, the private market will not provide large numbers of affordable housing for either purchase or rent. Third, government policy has primarily consisted of providing subsidies for the purchase of single family homes through the tax code and through providing the highways necessary to open outlying areas for development. Fourth, federal funding for new construction of affordable housing has been drastically curtailed. Fifth, funding for the maintenance and necessary rehabilitation of public housing units has been reduced sharply allowing that housing stock to deteriorate. Sixth, distrust of land use planning and the inability to apply it across governmental jurisdictions has resulted in increased geographic dispersal of housing. This can result in financial rewards to developers regardless of the costs to local governments for roads and schools. It also encourages increased commuting by car with negative impacts on the environment and the amount of time parents have to spend with their children or undertaking community projects.

Most of these causes are national in scope although they have major impacts on local communities and neighborhoods. There are, however, some actions local residents can take. Some states and localities have addressed these issues. The appendix on housing will consider a range of possible actions for communities to consider.

Notes

1.   Coontz, S. (1992). *The way we never were: American families and the nostalgia trap* (pp. 77-78). New York: Basic Books.
2.   Rusk, D. (1999). *Inside game outside game: Winning strategies for saving urban America*. Washington, DC: Brookings Institution Press.
3.   Briggs, X. de S. (2000, September 27). *Community building: The new (and old) politics of urban problem-solving in the new century.* Public address at the Second Annual Robert C. Wood Visiting Professorship in Public and Urban Affairs, University of Massachusetts/Boston.
4.   Wolf, P. (1999). *Hot towns: The future of the fastest growing communities in America*. New Brunswick, NJ: Rutgers University Press.

5. Alan Berube, A. & Kneebone, E. (2006, December). *Two steps back: city and suburban poverty trends 1999–2005.* Washington, DC: The Brookings Institution. Retrieved December 20, 2006, from http://www.brookings.edu/metro/pubs/20061205_citysuburban.pdf.
6. Rusk, D. (1999) *Inside game outside game: Winning strategies for saving urban America.* Washington, DC: Brookings Institution Press.
7. Alan Berube, A. & Kneebone, E. (2006, December). *Two steps back: city and suburban poverty trends 1999–2005.* Washington, DC: The Brookings Institution. Retrieved December 20, 2006, from http://www.brookings.edu/metro/pubs/20061205_citysuburban.pdf.
8. Rusk, D. (1999) *Inside game outside game: Winning strategies for saving urban America.* Washington, DC: Brookings Institution Press.
9. Rusk, D. (1999) *Inside game outside game: Winning strategies for saving urban America.* Washington, DC: Brookings Institution Press. National Coalition for the Homeless. *NCH Fact Sheet #3. How many people are homeless?* (p. 5). Retrieved May 26, 2003, from http.www.nationalhomeless.org/who.html.
10. Lynch, K. (1977). *Growing up in cities: Studies of the spatial environment of adolescence in Cracow, Melbourne, Mexico City, Salta, Toluca, and Warszawa* (p. 49). Paris: United Nations Educational, Scientific and Cultural Organization & The Massachusetts Institute of Technology.
11. Szalkowski, A. of Gerber Leisure Products, Inc., Madison, WI. (personal communication, October, 2001).
12. U.S. Census Bureau. (2006, August 15). *2005 American Community Survey. United States: General demographic characteristics: 2005.* Retrieved November 9, 2006 from http://factfinder.census.gov/servlet/ADPTable?_bm=y&-geo_id=01000US&-ds_name=ACS_2005_EST_G00_.
13. Rank, M. R. (1994). *Living on the edge: The realities of welfare in America* (p. 97). New York: Columbia University Press.
14. Bucks, B. K., Kennickell, A. B., & Moore, K. B. (2006, February). *Recent changes in U.S. family finances: Evidence from the 2001 and 2004 survey of consumer finances* (p. A8). Washington, DC: Federal Reserve Bulletin. Retrieved December 5, 2006, from http://www.federalreserve.gov/pubs/oss/oss2/2004/bull0206.pdf.
15. Joint Committee on Taxation. U.S. Congress. (2006, April). *Estimates of federal tax ependitures for fiscal years 2006-2010 (JCS-2-06). Table 1. Tax expenditure estimates by budget function, fiscal years 2006-2010.* p. 33. Retrieved January 20, 2007, from http://www.house.gov/jct/s-2-06.pdf.
16. Joint Committee on Taxation. U.S. Congress. (2006, April). Estimates of federal tax ependitures for fiscal years 2006-2010 (JCS-2-06). Table 3. Distribution by income class of selected individual tax expenditure items at 2005 rates and 2005 income levels. Retrieved January 20, 2007, from http://www.house.gov/jct/s-2-06.pdf.
17. Joint Committee on Taxation. U.S. Congress. (2006, April). *Estimates of federal tax expenditures for fiscal years 2006-2010 (JCS-2-06). Table 3. Distribution by income class of selected individual tax expenditure items at 2005 rates and 2005 income levels.* p. 49. Retrieved January 20, 2007, from http://www.house.gov/jct/s-2-06.pdf. U.S. Department of Housing and Urban Development. (2004, February 3). *Fiscal year 2005 budget summary.* Retrieved January 20, 2007, from http://www.hud.gov/about/budget/fy05/budgetsummary.pdf.
18. Kochera, A. (2001, May). Issues in manufactured housing. AARP Publication No. FS16R. Washington, DC.: AARP Research Center. U.S. Census Bureau. (2006, August). *American housing survey for the United States: 2005. Table 1A-1. Introductory characteristics - all housing units.* Series H150/05. Retrieved 2006-12-06

from http://www.census.gov/prod/2006pubs/h150-05.pdf. Wilden, R. W. (2000, February). *Manufactured housing and its impact on seniors*. [Final report delivered to Congress on June 28, 2002, by the Commission on Affordable Housing and Health Facility Needs for Seniors in the 21st Century]. Retrieved December 9, 2004, from www.seniorscommission.gov/pages/final_report/manufHouse.html.

19. Wilden, R. W. (2000, February). *Manufactured housing and its impact on seniors*. [Final report delivered to Congress on June 28, 2002, by the Commission on Affordable Housing and Health Facility Needs for Seniors in the 21st Century]. Retrieved December 9, 2004, from www.seniorscommission.gov/pages/final_report/manufHouse.html.

20. Wilden, R. W. (2000, February). *Manufactured housing and its impact on seniors*. [Final report delivered to Congress on June 28, 2002, by the Commission on Affordable Housing and Health Facility Needs for Seniors in the 21st Century]. Retrieved December 9, 2004, from www.seniorscommission.gov/pages/final_report/manufHouse.html. NAHB Research Center. (1998, October). *Factory and site-built housing: A comparison for the 21st century*. Washington, D. C.: U.S. Department of Housing and Urban Development. Retrieved December 6, 2004, from http://www.huduser.org/Publications/pdf/factory.pdf.

21. Hockett, D., McElwee, P. Pelletiere, D., & Schwartz, D. (2005, January). *The crisis in America's housing: Confronting myths and promoting a balanced housing policy*, p. 13. Retrieved April 12, 2005, from http://www.childrensdefense.org/familyincome/housing/myths.pdf#search='The%20Crisis%20in%20America's%20Housing'.

22. Masnick, G. S. (2001, February). *Home ownership trends and racial inequality in the United States in the 20th century*. Joint Center for Housing Studies, Harvard University. Retrieved April 12, 2005, from http://www.jchs.harvard.edu/publications/homeownership/masnick_w01-4.pdf.

23. Pitcoff, W. (2003, January/February). *Has homeownership been oversold?* In "Shelterforce online," No. 127, p. 3, National Housing Institute. Retrieved April 12, 2005, from http://www.nhi.org/online/issues/sf127.html.

24. Hockett, D., McElwee, P. Pelletiere, D., & Schwartz, D. (2005, January). *The crisis in America's housing: Confronting myths and promoting a balanced housing policy*, p. 14. Retrieved April 12, 2005, from http://www.childrensdefense.org/familyincome/housing/myths.pdf#search='The%20Crisis%20in%20America's%20Housing'.

25. U.S. Census Bureau. (2006, October 27). *Census Bureau reports on residential vacancies and homeownership*. p. 6. Retrieved December 6, 2006 from http://www.census.gov/hhes/www/housing/hvs/qtr306/q0306prss.pdf. U.S. Census Bureau. (2006, October 27). http://www.census.gov/hhes/www/housing/hvs/historic/histt15.html.

26. U.S. Census Bureau. (2006, October 27). *Census Bureau reports on residential vacancies and homeownership*. Retrieved December 6, 2006, from http://www.census.gov/hhes/www/housing/hvs/qtr306/q306prss.pdf. U.S. Census Bureau. (2006, August). U.S. Census Bureau. (2006, April 28) *Housing Vacancies and Homeownership. Table 15. Household Estimates for the United States, by Age of Householder, by Family Status: 1982 to present*. Retrieved December 6, 2006, from http://wwwcensusgov/hhes/www/housing/hvs/historic/histt15html.

27. National Low Income Housing Coalition. (2006, December 12). *Out of Reach 2006. Introduction*. pp. 3-4. Retrieved January 20, 2007, from http://www.nlihc.org/oor/oor2006/introduction.pdf.

28. Caesar, I., & Youmans, V. (1924). Tea for Two. Harms, Inc.

29. National Low Income Housing Coalition. (2006, December 12). *Out of Reach 2006*. Retrieved December 19, 2006, from http://www.nlihc.org/oor/oor2006/.

30. National Low Income Housing Coalition. (2006, December 12). *Out of Reach 2006. Introduction.* pp. 4. Retrieved January 20, 2007, from http://www.nlihc. org/oor/oor2006/introduction.pdf.

31. Bureau of Labor Statistics. (2007, December 4). Employment Projections: 2006-16. Press release. Washington, DC: author. Retrieved January 30, 2008, from http:// www.bls.gov/news.release/pdf/ecopro.pdf. In this analysis, the 28 occupations with the most new jobs were considered. These occupations represent 50.2% of additional jobs. For an explanation of the calculations see chapter 8, note. 14.

32. Center on Budget and Policy Priorities. (2003, May 14). *Introduction to the housing voucher program.* p. 2. Retrieved January 19, 2007, from http://www.cbpp. org/5-15-03hous.pdf.

33. National Coalition for the Homeless. (2006, June). *NCH Fact Sheet #2. How many people experience homelessness?* pp. 2-3. Retrieved January 19, 2007, from http://www.nationalhomeless.org/publications/facts/How_Many.pdf. McGarity, N. (2007, January 10). *First nationwide estimate of homeless population in a decade announced. Approximately 744,313 people homeless on a single night.* Washington, DC: National Alliance to End Homelessness. Retrieved January 12, 2007, from http://www.endhomelessness.org/content/article/detail/1443.

34. National Coalition for the Homeless. (2006, June). *NCH Fact Sheet #1. Why are people homeless?* Retrieved January 19, 2007, from http://www.nationalhomeless. org/publications/facts/Why.pdf

35. National Mental Health Information Center. Substance Abuse and Mental Health Services Administration. U.S. Department of Health and Human Services. (n.d.) *Facts about homelessness.* Retrieved January 17, 2007, from http:// mentalhealth.samhsa.gov/cmhs/homelessness/facts.asp. Substance Abuse and Mental Health Services Administration. U.S. Department of Health and Human Services. (2006, June) *Matrix: homelessness services. Homelessness statistics and data.* Retrieved January 17, 2007, from http://www.samhsa.gov/matrix/statistics_homeless.aspx

36. Moses, D. J. (n.d.). *America's homeless children.* Newton, MA: National Center on Family Homelessness. Retrieved January 19, 2007, from http://familyhomelessness. org/pdf/fact_children.pdf.

37. National Coalition for the Homeless. (2006, June). *NCH Fact Sheet #1. Why are people homeless?* Retrieved January 19, 2007, from http://www.nationalhomeless. org/publications/facts/Why.pdf.

38. The National Alliance to End Homelessness. (2006, August 10). *Youth Homelessness.* Fact Sheet. Retrieved January 20, 2007 from http://www.endhomelessness. org/files/1059_file_YouthFacts.pdf.

39. U.S. Census Bureau. (2006, August). *American housing survey for the United States: 2005. Table 7-1. Introductory characteristics - occupied units with elderly householder.* Series H150/05. Retrieved 2006-12-06 from http://www.census.gov/ prod/2006pubs/h150-05.pdf.

40. Feagin, J. R. (2001). *Racist America: Roots, current realities, & future reparations.* New York: Routledge Press.

41. Masnick, G. S. (2001, February). *Home ownership trends and racial inequality in the United States in the 20th century.* Joint Center for Housing Studies, Harvard University. Retrieved April 12, 2005, from http://www.jchs.harvard.edu/publications/homeownership/masnick_w01-4.pdf.

42. Feagin, J. R. (2001). *Racist America: Roots, current realities, & future reparations.* New York: Routledge Press.

43. Masnick, G.S. (2001, February). *Home ownership trends and racial inequality in the United States in the 20th century.* Joint Center for Housing Studies, Harvard University. Retrieved April 12, 2005, from http://www.jchs.harvard.edu/publications/homeownership/masnick_wo1-4.pdf.

44. Masnick, G. S. (2001, February). *Home ownership trends and racial inequality in the United States in the 20th century.* Joint Center for Housing Studies, Harvard University. Retrieved April 12, 2005, from http://www.jchs.harvard.edu/publications/homeownership/masnick_w01-4.pdf. U.S. Census Bureau. *Net worth and asset ownership of households: 1998 and 2000.* Retrieved May 26, 2003, from http://www.census.gov/hhes/www/wealth/1998_2000/wlth98-7.html.

45. Turner, M. A. Ross, S. L. Galster, G. & Yinger, J. (2002, November 7). *Discrimination in metropolitan housing markets: national results from phase I HDS 2000. Final report.* Washington, DC: The Urban Institute. Retrieved January 19, 2007, from http://www.urban.org/UploadedPDF/410821_Phase1_Report.pdf. U.S.

46. Leadership Conference on Civil Rights and Leadership Conference Education Fund. (2003). *Justice on trial: Racial disparities in the American criminal justice system.* Washington, DC.: Author. Retrieved October 2, 2003, from www.civilrights.org/publications/reports/cj/justice.

47. Mosiman, D. (1998, October 5). Police adopt softer policy on big parties near campus. *Wisconsin State Journal,* p. 1B.

10

Health

The National Context

People need five kinds of health support that generally must be provided at home or within neighborhoods, but that are affected by the decisions of many outsiders. People need protection from unintentional injury from traffic accidents, fire, and other causes. They need to live in environments with clean air and water, free from hazardous waste, excessive noise, and other forms of pollution. Individuals need the resources to develop and maintain the lifestyle habits that will promote both short- and long-term health. They need access to doctors and other care professionals, including those practicing legitimate alternative medicine, for preventive check-ups and treatment when ill. And, finally, they need someone to care for them when incapacitated either by fairly simple conditions such as the flu or a long-term, debilitating illness.

The most crucial factor determining whether neighborhood residents can access doctors, hospitals, and alternative health providers is health insurance. This, in turn, depends upon employers and programs such as Medicare, Medicaid, and state-financed special health insurance pools for those otherwise uninsurable. In 2006, well over 47 million Americans lacked health insurance. Companies increasingly have cut coverage, including that promised to their retirees.[1]

Basic demographic characteristics such as age, sex, race, ethnicity, and economic status, including income and education, at least partly determine genetic and environmental health risks, attitudes, and behavior, as well as access to both preventive measures and appropriate care.

For example, people of color have less health care coverage than whites.[2] African Americans have higher rates of infant mortality than Caucasians and lower rates of survival once diagnosed with cancer.[3] In both cases, earlier preventive medical care could lower the death rates.

Men are more likely to have better insurance coverage than women since they are more often long-term employees of large firms. To some extent, the ability of others to obtain medical treatment has been balanced by Medicaid programs for lower-income persons, making the working poor the most likely to lack insurance coverage. White males receive more attention when hospitalized and more research is devoted to their medical problems.[4] Indeed, until recently much research used only males as subjects, ignoring the possibility that women's bodies would react differently to procedures or drugs.[5] Studies have indicated that women's reports of heart problems frequently have neither been taken as seriously nor treated as aggressively as those of men.[6] Insurance companies sometimes have discriminated in terms of coverage, ironically even providing drugs to assist impotent men to have sex while refusing women coverage for birth control pills. Without health care insurance people tend to postpone routine preventive care. Postponing such visits can lead to more expensive treatments later and/or death. Regular mammograms, for example, have been shown to reduce deaths of women aged forty through sixty-nine from breast cancer by two-thirds.[7]

In 2005, over eight million American children, more than one-tenth of all children and almost one-fifth of children living in poor households, lacked health insurance coverage from either private or government sources.[8] Previous analyses showed that one in four uninsured children lack a regular health provider, compared to one out of twenty-five insured children.[9] Almost 20 percent of uninsured children under five had not seen a doctor within the previous year, even though the medical profession recommends annual check-ups to keep immunization schedules current and to screen for and treat any developmental problems. Uninsured children often need but cannot obtain needed eyeglasses, prescription drugs, dental care, or other needed medical attention.[10]

Many non-local players affect community members' health potential. Key players affecting traffic accidents and deaths include the lawmakers and traffic engineers who establish speed limits and design roads, the police and state highway patrol, the lawmakers and state motor vehicle licensing officials who determine the criteria for obtaining and keeping driver's licenses, judges who sentence traffic offenders, and automakers who determine the safety of automobiles through design and manufacturing standards. Other actors include school board members who decide whether to provide driver training courses, organizations such as Mothers Against Drunk Driving, and business, legal, and health institutions that affect misuse of alcohol, including bars and stores selling liquor to minors or those intoxicated. Insurance companies that deny treatment for alcohol and drug problems and prisons that fail to provide such treatment for their inmates contribute to the problem. Since most murders and suicides involve a gun, effective gun control probably would reduce fatalities. Attacks by family members or intimate partners are twelve times more likely to result in death if a firearm is used.[11]

Businesses play an important health role through their willingness to control environmental pollution connected with their operations. Their employment practices affect lifestyle choices, including stress and the availability of health insurance. Businesses increasingly have switched to part-time employees, temporary workers, or contract employees who do not receive any health benefits.

The media and the food, tobacco, and alcohol advertising industries may be the most influential players in determining the neighborhood residents' health habits. Other key players include grocery stores and fast food restaurants, school boards and school lunch programs. Businesses that provide forty-hour-a-week jobs with good wages and reasonable hours help indirectly by providing their workers sufficient leisure time to cook family meals and exercise. Federal agencies, nonprofit organizations, universities, and professional groups contribute through sponsoring and conducting basic research, publicizing data, setting standards, sponsoring awareness campaigns, and providing information on which to base neighborhood action.

Often those needing home care, whether nursing care or housekeeping assistance, lack a family member who can provide it. Families with funds can hire outside assistance. Some communities provide a variety of low-cost, home-based services. Medicare, however, does not cover such expenses. The likelihood of having either the income to purchase private help or private insurance that will provide it varies with income, race, sex, and ethnicity.

Healthy Lifestyles

For most Americans, key long-term health issues boil down to eating nutritious food, obtaining adequate rest and relaxation, exercising vigorously several times a week, avoiding smoking or exposure to smoke, abstaining from harmful drugs including an excess of alcohol or inappropriate use of prescription medications, avoiding risky sex, practicing good hygiene such as brushing teeth and washing hands properly, and obtaining preventive medical care for immunizations and routine check-ups.

Neighborhood cultural and social habits influence health. In Wisconsin, summer events feature bratwurst and beer. Friday nights bring fish fries. Pot luck dinners abound with rich desserts. Student parties furnish kegs of beer and often encourage excessive drinking. Such traditions create health risks for the state's residents. Wisconsin has a high rate of obesity and one of the highest rates of binge drinking in the nation, both likely to result in health problems. Furthermore, it has one of the highest rates of drinking and frequent drinking among pregnant women, a potential risk to the fetus.[12]

Few adults exercise enough for their health. Only 30 percent exercise regularly. Among young people aged twelve through twenty-one years old, only approximately one-half exercise vigorously. White males exercise the most.[13]

After years of messages about the dangers of smoking, adults have reduced their use of cigarettes, but one-quarter of America's high school students smoke. Overall smoking rates vary with sex, race and ethnicity, and education. About 20 percent of adults still smoke. Female smoking rates are slightly lower than those for males, but millions of women still smoke during pregnancy, despite the fact that it can harm the baby.[14]

In 2004, HIV infection was no longer among the top ten causes of death in the United States. However, it was the second leading cause of death for black males aged thirty-five through forty-four and fourth for black males aged twenty-five through thirty-four and forty-five through fifty-four.[15] Unfortunately, millions of Americans, both teenagers and adults, continue to practice unprotected sex.

Higher incomes help people maintain healthy habits. Fruits and vegetables cost more than pasta and cookies. Expensive stores tend to provide fresher vegetables and to offer choices that are less contaminated with pesticides. Belonging to a health club or gym makes committing to a regular exercise program much easier. Children from families with higher incomes and higher levels of education both own and use bicycle helmets most frequently.[16] Staying healthy takes know-how and money—money that's not already allocated for other basic needs.

Thus, Americans' ability to enjoy good health and needed health care rests partly upon their individual choices and behaviors but also upon decisions made by business and governments at all levels. National policies affect neighborhood health through laws and regulations governing health care and insurance, environmental hazards such as air pollution and toxic waste, and through regulating motor vehicle safety and speed limits. Businesses affect health through attention to safety and environmental factors when conducting their business and through practices regarding health benefits for employees. Here we focus on issues that affect people in every community in the country: the chief causes of death for children and their parents, environmental health hazards, and access to health care.

What Affects Families Where They Live?

From ages one through thirty-four, you are unlikely to die of any illness except a mental illness that leads to suicide. Unintentional injuries cause most deaths of children and of adults during the years when they commonly are parenting young children.[17]

Motor vehicle accidents are the leading cause of unintentional death for children older than one and adults younger than sixty-five years old.[18] Too often children die while crossing the street or playing near heavy traffic areas. Some research indicates that until age eleven or twelve many children do not have the ability to deal safely with traffic because they cannot coordinate their sight with their hearing, and their ability to distinguish right from left, fast and slow, near and far may not be fully developed. Children themselves are aware of their limitations and may suffer psychologically when forced to contend with dangerous traffic, as evidenced by poignant comments from the first graders in one study. Seventy percent of them expressed fear of the traffic. Many described physical symptoms of anxiety: headaches, pains in the stomach, sweating, and fast heartbeat. They said that they were afraid of being killed and reported such dysfunctional behavior as closing their eyes at the crossing and running so they would not see the cars.[19]

Traffic safety in residential neighborhoods is key. Children play near their homes whether or not it is safe. Very small children typically are not allowed to go beyond calling distance—about the length of a football field. Even elementary school children play in their own neighborhoods, usually within several blocks of home. They seize short snatches of time for play—before dinner, between school and soccer practice, or while waiting for their parents to take them someplace. Although these older children theoretically know how to handle traffic, they often become careless or forget. They may run after a ball or a friend or be dared into taking risks.[20]

After traffic accidents, the greatest health threat for children and young parents is homicide and "legal intervention," that is, being killed by police in the line of duty. Once you have survived problems related to defects from abnormalities at birth you are more likely to die from homicide than cancer or any other specific disease until you are thirty-five years old.[21]

Nationally homicide stands as the second greatest killer for those aged fifteen through twenty-four, third for those aged twenty-five through thirty-four, and the fourth for children aged one through fifteen. In 2004, homicide was the leading cause of death for African Americans aged fifteen through thirty-four and the second leading cause of death for Hispanics from ages fifteen through thirty-four.[22] Three-fourths of these deaths occur when someone pulls the trigger on a gun, generally someone known by the victim. For the nation as a whole, almost 80 people a day die from firearm-related injuries.[23] The use of guns also accounts for the disparity in injuries and deaths between men and women in cases of domestic violence. Men are more likely to use guns. Guns also are the instrument of choice for suicides, used almost 60 percent of the time. Some four women a day die as a result of domestic abuse, half from firearm wounds.[24]

Suicide is a major killer of children, teenagers, young adults and parents of children. It ranks as the second leading cause of death for those 25 through thirty-four and third for children over ten years old, teenagers and young adults. It ranks as the fourth leading cause of death for those aged thirty-five through forty-four, an age when many parents still have young children. Suicide falls but remains high, the fifth cause of death, for those aged forty-five through fifty-four, many of whom still have teenagers living at home who need their guidance as they move into adulthood.[25]

Race, ethnicity, and gender also influence the risk of suicide. Males commit suicide more than four times as often as females.[26] Over 90 percent of those who commit suicide are white. On the other hand, the rate for Hispanic males aged forty-five through 64 was the highest of any ethnic group.[27]

Between 1952 and 1995 suicides for young adults almost tripled. The rate for those aged fifteen through nineteen rose 11 percent between 1980 and 1997, with firearm related deaths accounting for two-thirds of the increase. The suicide rate for slightly younger children, those aged ten through fourteen, increased an astonishing 109 percent during this same period.[28]

Other leading causes of fatal injuries include drowning, fires, falls, and poisoning. More children under age fifteen die from drowning than perish in fires. Children's death rate from drowning is surprisingly high, one-half as high as childhood deaths from cancer.[29] Drowning is the third greatest cause of death for toddlers, those aged one through four. A large percentage of preschool children who drown die in residential swimming pools, almost half the time at their own home.[30] Males drown four times more frequently than females, regardless of age.[31]

In addition to unnecessary deaths, common accidents result in large numbers of injuries, some with serious life-long consequences. Even injuries with short-term physical effects result in pain, inconvenience, and medical expenses. The National Center for Injury Prevention and Control estimates that each year between one-fifth and one-fourth of all children suffer an injury sufficient to require medical attention, missed school, or bed rest.[32]

Although the causes of death discussed here result from actions of individuals and often occur within a neighborhood, actions of local, state, and the national government have an effect. Speed limits, regulations of the hours truck drivers are permitted to work without a break, requirements for air bags in automobiles, these all are governmental decisions. For example, deaths from motor vehicle accidents went down when Congress passed the fifty-five-mile-an-hour speed limit and increased when they raised it.[33] Governments provide police services, including neighborhood police officers. They regulate sale and possession of guns. Businesses influence the toll through decisions about whether to provide health care that includes coverage of mental health and alcohol and drug treatment. Governments and other institutions provide assistance for those problems as well as addressing preventive programs such as after-school activities.

Some causes of death and illness occur less dramatically than motor accidents and homicide but still take their toll. They involve environmental issues such as the air we breathe.

Environmental Health

Good health requires freedom from environmental hazards including air pollution, noise pollution and contamination from lead and other chemicals. Air pollution contributes to a variety of illnesses, including bronchitis, emphysema, and asthma. The American Lung Association estimates that over 11 million Americans suffer from chronic bronchitis, three million have emphysema and more than six million children have asthma. Air pollution problems particularly affect the elderly, for whom, to a greater extent than for younger adults, respiratory diseases can result in limitation of normal activities and even death. Dirty air also is especially harmful to children who breathe more frequently than adults because their lungs are smaller. In addition, they more often breathe through their mouths, which reduces the ability of the respiratory tract to remove both gases and particles. Children increase their exposure to airborne pollutants by playing out of doors, and may increase this risk by playing in dirt that releases pollutants.[34]

Noise pollution causes hearing loss. According to the U.S. Public Health Service, about half of the 21 million Americans with hearing problems owe their affliction to exposure to excessive noise. One authority suggests that over 138 million Americans are exposed to noise levels above those scientifically established as safe.[35] Even lesser noise levels may harm health indirectly, causing sleep loss or stress. As with air pollution, the very young and very old may be the most vulnerable. A third of older Americans suffer hearing limitations. By the age of eighty-five, half will be hearing impaired.[36] People with even partial hearing loss may experience pain or discomfort when exposed to very loud noise.[37] In addition, high noise levels bother people with hearing impairments because they cannot easily distinguish individual sounds such as voices or telephone rings from background noise. They may have difficulty hearing from a distance, leading them to withdraw from social occasions and from attending church and theaters.[38] The resulting loneliness and isolation can lead to other health problems.

The effect of noise on children's learning environments has recently been noted in a study on noise and transportation and has led to the development of acoustical performance criteria for schools. Some evidence indicates that children living in noisy environments may learn to screen out sounds—including the voices of their teachers. Noise may lead to mental and emotional stress and difficulties in language development. Children in noisy schools underachieve more than those in quiet schools regardless of socioeconomic backgrounds.[39] One evaluation found that constant exposure to noise affected children's ability to acquire language skills, resulting in lower reading abilities. Increasingly, the future hearing of youth is threatened by exposure to the volume favored by much of the popular music in bars and other venues of entertainment. Neighborhoods can inform parents about the permanent health risks their children face from prolonged exposure to high volumes of noise including that from earphones plugged into portable music devices.[40]

Chemical pollution, particularly mercury and lead poisoning, pose another serious environmental health hazard. Mercury, a fallout from burning coal, harms nerve cells. The National Academy of Sciences estimated that 600,000 infants a year are born with potentially adverse development due to mercury absorbed by the fetus. Wisconsin has issued warnings about eating large quantities of fish from any of its lakes because of the high mercury content. Massachusetts recommended that pregnant women not eat *any* fish from Massachusetts waters.[41]

Lead poisoning has a variety of harmful effects including damage to the central nervous system. It can lead to mental retardation and such learning and developmental problems as decreased attention, impulsiveness, an inability to follow directions, and aggressive behavior. Almost 900,000 American children aged one through five years old have elevated levels of lead in their blood.[42] The problem affects all socioeconomic groups although children from lower income families suffer more often, chiefly because toddlers eat paint chips from windowsills in dilapidated buildings and play in areas where they are exposed to soil contaminated with past emissions of leaded gasoline.[43]

Hazardous waste creates health problems. Toxic chemicals seep into the ground, reappearing in the water and, as in the notorious case of Love Canal, New York, in peoples' backyards. In the Love Canal community where a school and homes were built on and near a waste dump, children became ill and extraordinary numbers of miscarriages, stillbirths, and birth defects occurred. Eventually after considerable neighborhood protest, the federal government purchased the homes and relocated the families.[44] In another example, highlighted in the film *Erin Brockovich,* starring Julia Roberts, Erin discovers both the pain of innocent families watching their loved ones suffer from chemical-related cancer and the intransigence of the responsible industry. Based on a true story, that film ended with a legal victory, but cited similar cases still in court.

Care When Sick

Children, even more than adults, experience a variety of short-term illnesses that usually are managed with rest, water and/or juice, drugs that reduce fever, and the proverbial chicken soup. Obtaining this simple care can become problematic if all of the adults are employed outside the home or if a person lives alone. For example, the author, then a healthy forty-year-old living alone, became ill with a high fever. After visiting the doctor for tests, I stumbled home to bed. The next day, the doctor telephoned with a diagnosis of infectious hepatitis, instructing me to remain at home and not to allow any visitors. In my groggy state, I forgot to mention that I had little food in the house. Luckily my parents who lived nearby could drop groceries off at my door.

Thus the adequacy of home health care depends upon the availability of an adult in the home, their knowledge and nursing skills. Usually this means a female who does not hold a job or, depending upon the severity of the illness, manages to combine employment and home nursing care. While many people disrupt their lives to move near loved ones who need health care, often at considerable professional and personal sacrifice, others may not have this option.

The need for home health care will grow as more surgeries occur in doctor's offices and hospitals discharge patients still needing complicated procedures or treatment with machines. The need for such care also will grow as the population ages. Only one-tenth of those aged sixty-five through seventy-four need home care assistance, but by the time people reach age eighty-five, one-half of them will need it.[45] Although much of the care needed requires only basic assistance in food preparation, laundry and maintaining social contacts, in some cases skilled nursing assistance will be required. While initially spouses may be able to provide the help, spouses may be unable to manage either the physical or psychological demands of home nursing as they age themselves and as the severity of their partners' illnesses increases.

Moreover, one-third of those currently receiving health care live alone. Elderly widows constitute a huge growing population likely to need such care in the future. By age sixty-five almost half of all women are widowed, divorced, separated, living apart from their spouse or were never married. By the age of seventy-five, the percent of women living with a spouse drops to one-third. By age eighty-five only 12 percent of women are living with a spouse.[46] Although Medicare pays for medical services such as skilled nurses and speech therapy, it does not cover other home care or household maintenance. Many people lack private insurance, and even those with coverage often find it inadequate. People frequently need assistance merely in coordinating the various services, as well as filling out the voluminous forms for insurance reimbursements.

Although neighborhoods can develop back-up support systems for those who have no relatives nearby, an often unexamined myth underlies the rhetoric about the potential assistance from neighbors. The reservoir of potential helpful neighbors with leisure time no longer exists in many, perhaps most, neighborhoods. Those neighbors, primarily women, who used to be available now hold jobs outside of the home and may be providing health care for their own parents or spouses. Another myth assumes that people working from their homes are available to help neighbors. Home-based businesses have schedules, deadlines, and appointments just as demanding as businesses with separate offices. Even "stay-at-home moms" want control over their own time. For example, the author's niece, who chose to forgo considerable income to spend her time with her three young children, finds that she has to continually resist demands for volunteer tasks that jointly would be as time consuming as a job.

In many ways, America's health care system is broken and presents great challenges for our neighborhoods and families. Yet it is crucial that we also look for constructive solutions at a local level. The next chapters address the tasks of feeding our families, maintaining our homes, and caring for our children, which also affect health. Eating healthy and well-balanced meals, providing clean and safe homes for individuals and families, and ensuring that our children are well cared for and well-educated will go a long way toward also improving our basic health and promoting physical and emotional well-being.

Notes

1.   Nutting, R. (2007, August 29). *More lack health insurance.* Wisconsin State Journal. National Center for Health Statistics (2006, November). *Health, United States, 2006. With chartbook on trends in the health of Americans* (p. 5, 12). Retrieved December 6, 2006, from http://www.cdc.gov/nchs/data/hus/hus06.pdf. Gould, E. (2006, September 28). *Briefing paper. Health insurance eroding for working families: Employer-provided coverage declines for fifth consecutive year.* Washington, DC: Economic Policy Institute. Retrieved November 11, 2006, from http://www. epi.org/content.cfm/bp175.

2. U.S. Census Bureau Press Release (2003, September 30). *Numbers of Americans with and without health insurance rise.* Retrieved October 22, 2003, from http://www.mindfully.org/Health/2003/Census-Without-Insurance30Sep03.htm.

3. National Center for Chronic Disease Prevention and Health Promotion. (n.d.). *Chronic disease prevention: Chronic disease overview* (p. 5). Retrieved May 6, 2003, from http://www.cdc.gov/nccdphp/overview.htm. National Center for Chronic Disease Prevention and Health Promotion. *Minority and ethnic groups: Minority burden of chronic disease.* Retrieved April 18, 2008, from http://www.cdc.gov/omhd/AMIT/amh.htm.

4. American Medical Association. CSA Reports. *Women's health: Sex- and gender-based differences in health and disease.* Retrieved November 17, 2003, from http://www.ama-assn.org/ama/pub/print/article/2036-4946.html.

5. American Medical Association. CSA Reports. *Women's health: Sex- and gender-based differences in health and disease.* Retrieved November 17, 2003, from http://www.ama-assn.org/ama/pub/print/article/2036-4946.html.

6. Schulman, K. A., Berlin, J. A., Harless, W., Kerner, J. F., Sistrunk, S., Gersh, B. J., et al. (1999, February 25). The effect of race and sex on physicians' recommendations for cardiac catheterization. *New England Journal of Medicine, 349,* 618-626.

7. Tabar, L., Vitak, B., Chen, H. T., Yen, M., Duffy, S. W., & Smith, R. A. (2001, April 22-25). *Beyond randomized controlled trials: Organized mammographic screening substantially reduces breast cancer mortality.* Presented at the American Cancer Society, 43rd Science Writers Seminar, Dana Point, CA.

8. DeNavas-Walt, C., Proctor, B. D., & Lee, C. H. (2006, August). *Current population reports, P60-231: Income, poverty, and health insurance coverage in the United States: 2005,* p. 21. Washington, D.C.: U.S. Census Bureau, U.S. Government Printing Office. Retrieved December 4, 2006, from http://www.census.gov/prod/2006pubs/p60-231.pdf.

9. Pollack, R., Fish-Parcham, C., & Hoenig, B. (1997, June). *Unmet needs: The large differences in health care between uninsured and insured children.* Washington DC: Families USA Foundation. Retrieved May 13, 2003, from http://www.familiesusa.org/site/PageServer?pagename=media_reports_unmet.

10. Pollack, R., Fish-Parcham, C., & Hoenig, B. (1997, June). *Unmet needs: The large differences in health care between uninsured and insured children.* Washington DC: Families USA Foundation. Retrieved May 13, 2003, from http://www.familiesusa.org/site/PageServer?pagename=media_reports_unmet. Sullivan, J. (2006, September) *No Shelter from the Storm: America's Uninsured Children.* Washington, DC: Campaign for Children's Health Care. Retrieved January 10, 2007, from http://www.childrenshealthcampaign.org/tools/reports/Uninsured-Kids-report.PDF.

11. Saltzman, L.E., Mercy, J.A., O'Carroll, P.W., Rosenberg, M.L., Rhodes P.H. Weapon involvement and injury outcomes in family and intimate assaults. *JAMA.*1992;267:3043-7. Retrieved January 27, 2007 from http://www.jhsph.edu/gunpolicy/US_factsheet_2004.pdf.

12. Alcohol consumption among pregnant and childbearing-aged women-United States, 1991 and 1995. *Morbidity and Mortality Weekly Report, 46*(16), 346-350. Retrieved May 13, 2003, from http://www.cdc.gov/mmwr/preview/mmwrhtml/00047306.htm.

13. National Center for Health Statistics. (2006, November). *Health, United States, 2006. With chartbook on trends in the health of Americans* (p. 36). Retrieved December 6, 2006, from http://www.cdc.gov/nchs/data/hus/hus06.pdf. U.S. Department of Health and Human Services. (1996). *Physical Activity and Health: A Report of the Surgeon General.* pp. 4-6. Atlanta, GA: U.S. Department of Health

and Human Services, Centers for Disease Control and Prevention, National Center for Chronic Disease Prevention and Health Promotion. Retrieved January 22, 2007, from http://www.cdc.gov/nccdphp/sgr/chap1.htm.

14. Mathews, T. J. (2001, August 28). Smoking during pregnancy in the 1990s. *National Vital Statistics Reports, 49*(7), 1. Centers for Disease Control and Prevention. Retrieved from http://www.cdc.gov/nchs/data/nvsr/nvsr49/nvsr49_07.pdf. Centers for Disease Control. (1997, April 25). National Center for Health Statistics. (2006, November). *Health, United States, 2006. With chartbook on trends in the health of Americans* (p. 32-33). Retrieved December 6, 2006, from National Center for Health Statistics. (2006, November). *Health, United States, 2006. With chartbook on trends in the health of Americans*. Table 63. Current cigarette smoking among adults 18 years of age and over, by sex, race, and age: United States, selected years 1965–2004. (p. 266-267). Retrieved December 6, 2006, from http://www.cdc.gov/nchs/data/hus/hus06.pdf. http://www.cdc.gov/nchs/data/hus/hus06.pdf. National Center for Health Statistics. (n.d.). *Health, United States, 2004*. Table 60: Current cigarette smoking by persons 18 years of age and over according to sex, race, and age: United States, selected years 1965-2002, and Table 64: Use of selected substances by high school seniors, tenth-, and eight-graders, according to sex and race: United States, selected years 1980-2003. Retrieved January 13, 2005, from http://www.cdc.gov/nchs/data/hus/hus04.pdf. National Center for Health Statistics. (n.d.). *Health, United States, 2004*. Chartbook on trends in the health of Americans: Smoking. Retrieved January 13, 2005, from http://www.cdc.gov/nchs/data/hus/hus04.pdf.

15. National Center for Injury Prevention and Control, Centers for Disease Control. (2006, December 1). *10 leading causes of death, United States, 2004, black, non-Hispanic, both sexes*. Retrieved December 4, 2006, through a query at http://webappa.cdc.gov/sasweb/ncipc/leadcaus10.html.

16. Bicycle Helmet Safety Institute. (n.d.). *A compendium of statistics from various sources* (p. 12). Retrieved April 29, 2003, from http://www.bhsi.org/stats/htm.

17. National Center for Injury Prevention and Control, Centers for Disease Control. (2006, December 1). *WISQARS Leading Causes of Death Reports, 1999 - 2004: 10 leading causes of death, United States, 2004, all races, both sexes*. Retrieved December 4, 2006, through a query at http://webappa.cdc.gov/sasweb/ncipc/leadcaus10.html.

18. National Center for Injury Prevention and Control, Centers for Disease Control. (2006, December 1). *WISQARS Leading Causes of Death Reports, 1999 - 2004: 10 leading causes of unintentional injury death, United States, 2004, all races, both sexes*. Retrieved December 4, 2006, through a query at http://webappa.cdc.gov/sasweb/ncipc/leadcaus10.html.

19. Michelson, W., & Roberts, E. (1979). Children and the urban physical environment. In W. Michelson (Ed.). *Child in the city: Changes and challenges* (pp. 430-431). Toronto: University of Toronto Press. Pollowy, A. (1977). *The urban nest* (p. 97). Stroudsburg, PA.: Dowden, Hutchinson and Ross. Raundalen, M., & Raundalen, T. S. (1978, July). *Interviews with four thousand Norwegian girls and boys about their daily life and the future* (p.12). Paper presented at the meeting of the International Congress on the Child in the World of Tomorrow, Athens, Greece.

20. Churchman, A. (1979, June). *Children in urban environments: The Israeli experience* (p. 11). Paper presented at the MAB International Symposium on Managing Urban Space in the Interest of Children, Toronto, Canada.

21. National Center for Injury Prevention and Control, Centers for Disease Control (2006, December 1). *10 leading causes of death, United States, 2004, all races,*

both sexes. Retrieved December 4, 2006, through a query at http://webappa.cdc. gov/sasweb/ncipc/leadcaus10.html.

22. National Center for Injury Prevention and Control, Centers for Disease Control (2006, December 1). *10 leading causes of death, United States, 2004, black, non-Hispanic, both sexes* and *10 leading causes of death, United States, 2004, all races, Hispanic, both sexes.* Retrieved December 4, 2006, through queries at http://webappa.cdc.gov/sasweb/ncipc/leadcaus10.html.

23. National Center for Injury Prevention and Control, Centers for Disease Control (2000, December). *Web-based injury statistics query and reporting system (WISQARS). Atlanta, GA: Author.* Retrieved April 23, 2001, from http://www.cdc. govncip/factsheets/fafacts.htm.

24. National Center for Injury Prevention and Control. *Firearm injuries and fatalities.* Retrieved April 23, 2001, from http://www.cdc.gov/ncip/factsheets/fafacts.htm. Violence Policy Center (n.d.). *Facts on firearms and domestic violence.* Retrieved January 13, 2005, from http://www.vpc.org/fact_sht/domviofs.htm. Edward Sondik, E. (1999, October 6). *Healthy people 2000. Violent and abusive behavior progress review.* Lecture presented at the National Center for Health Statistics, Hyattsville, MD. Retrieved December 19, 2007, from http://www.cdc.gov/nchs/about/other-act/hp2000/violence/violencecharts.htm.

25. National Center for Health Statistics. National Center for Health Statistics (2006, November). *Health, United States, 2006. With chartbook on trends in the health of Americans.* Table 46. Death rates for suicide, according to sex, race, Hispanic origin, and age: United States. Selected years 1950-2003. pp. 230-232. Retrieved January 10, 2007, from http://www.cdc.gov/nchs/data/hus/hus06.pdf.

26. National Center for Health Statistics. National Center for Health Statistics (2006, November). *Health, United States, 2006. With chartbook on trends in the health of Americans.* Table 46. Death rates for suicide, according to sex, race, Hispanic origin, and age: United States. Selected years 1950-2003. pp. 230-232. Retrieved January 10, 2007, from http://www.cdc.gov/nchs/data/hus/hus06.pdf.

27. National Center for Health Statistics. National Center for Health Statistics (2006, November). *Health, United States, 2006. With chartbook on trends in the health of Americans.* Table 46. Death rates for suicide, according to sex, race, Hispanic origin, and age: United States. Selected years 1950-2003. pp. 230-232. Retrieved January 10, 2007, from http://www.cdc.gov/nchs/data/hus/hus06.pdf.

28. National Center for Injury Prevention and Control, Centers for Disease Control (2006, December 1). *10 leading causes of death, United States, 2004, all races, both sexes.* Retrieved December 4, 2006, through a query at http://webappa.cdc. gov/sasweb/ncipc/leadcaus10.html. National Center for Injury Prevention and Control. *Suicide in the United States* (pp. 1-2). Retrieved April 23, 2001, from http://www.cdc.gov/ncipc/factsheets/suifacts.htm.

29. National Center for Injury Prevention and Control, Centers for Disease Control (2006, December 1). *10 leading causes of death, United States, 2004, all races, both sexes* and *10 leading causes of injury deaths, United States, 2004, all races, both sexes.* Retrieved December 4, 2006, through queries at http://webappa.cdc. gov/sasweb/ncipc/leadcaus10.html.

30. National Center for Injury Prevention and Control. (n.d.). *Drowning prevention* (p. 2). Retrieved October 8, 2002, from http://www.cdc.gov/ncipc/factsheets/drown.htm.

31. National Center for Injury Prevention and Control. (1999). *Unintentional injury. Drowning fact sheet* (p. 2). Atlanta, GA: Centers for Disease Control and Prevention.

32. National Center for Injury Prevention and Control. (n.d.). *Childhood injury fact sheet* (p. 1). Retrieved May 4, 2003, from http://www.cdc.gov/ncipc/factsheets/childh.htm.

33. National Institute for Highway Safety. (2001, November). *Q&A: Speed and speed limits*. Retrieved April 25, 2003, from http://www.highwaysafety.org/safety_facts/ qanda/speed_limits.htm.

34. American Lung Association Epidemiology and Statistic Unit Research and Scientific Affairs. (2003, September). *Estimated prevalence and incidence of lung disease by lung association territory.* Retrieved November 14, 2003 from http://www.lungusa. org/data/ep/EstimatedPrev03.pdf. Wireman, P. (1984). *Urban neighborhoods, networks, and families: New forms for old values* (pp. 115, 129). Lexington, MA: Lexington Books, D.C. Heath and Company.

35. Suter, A. H. (1991, November). *Noise and its effects* (pp. 12,10). Report prepared for the consideration of the Administrative Conference of the United States. Retrieved April 16, 2003, from http://www.nonoise.org/library/suter/suter.htm.

36. Centers for Disease Control and Prevention. *New series of efforts to monitor health of older Americans-2001 Fact Sheet*, p.2. Atlanta, GA: National Center for Health Statistics. Retrieved from http://www.cdc.gov/nchs/releases/01facts/olderame. htm.

37. Wireman, P., & Sebastian, A. G. (1986). Environmental considerations for housing sites for the elderly. In R. J. Newcomer, M. P. Lawton, & T. O. Byerts (Eds.). *Housing an aging society: Issues, alternatives, and policy*, p. 170. New York: Van Nostrand Reinhold Company.

38. Suter, A. H. (1991, November). *Noise and its effects* (p. 13). Report prepared for the consideration of the Administrative Conference of the United States. Retrieved April 16, 2003, from http://www.nonoise.org/library/suter/suter.htm.

39. Lee, C.S.Y. and Fleming, G.G. 2002, June. General Health Effects of Transportation Noise. Final Report. U.S. Department of Transportation Federal Railroad Administration Report DTS-34-RR297-LR2 FRA/RDV-01/01. Retrieved August 30, 2007 from http://www.volpe.dot.gov/acoustics/docs/2000/dts-34-02_5.pdf. American National Standards Institute, Inc. 2002, June 26. American National Standard. Acoustical Performance Criteria, Design Requirements, and Guidelines for Schools. ANSI S12.60-2002. Retrieved August 30, 2007 from http://asastore. aip.org/.2. Suter, A. H. (1991, November). *Noise and its effects* (pp. 17-18). Report prepared for the consideration of the Administrative Conference of the United States. Retrieved April 16, 2003, from http://www.nonoise.org/library/suter/suter.htm.

40. Suter, A. H. (1991, November). *Noise and its effect,*(p. 18). Report prepared for the consideration of the Administrative Conference of the United States. Retrieved April 16, 2003, from http://www.nonoise.org/library/suter/suter.htm. Health Canada. (Original: 2002, July, Updated: 2005, January). *It's your health: Hearing loss and leisure noise.* Retrieved November 23, 2007, from http://www.hc-sc.gc.ca/iyh-vsv/environ/leisure-loisirs_e.html.

41. National Resources Defense Council. (2004, February 27). *Bush mercury policy threatens the health of women and children.* Retrieved April 24, 2004, from http:// www.nrcd.org/media/pressreleases/040227.asp. Beck, V. (2006). *Choose wisely: A health guide for eating fish in Wisconsin.* Wisconsin Department of Natural Resources publication number PUB-FH-824 2006. Retrieved March 23, 2007, from http://www.dnr.state.wi.us/fish/pages/consumption/Fish%20Advisory%20 06%20web%20lo.pdf. Daniel, M. (2001, July 25). Mercury levels in fish bring warning. *The Boston Globe.* Retrieved April 28, 2003, from http://www.eces. org/articles/static/99603720075518.shtml. U. S. Public Interest Research Group, Environmental Working Group (2001) *Reducing mercury emissions by 95 percent is critical to protecting maternal and child health* (p.1). Washington DC. Retrieved from http://www.ewg.org/reports/mercmemomay20001/html.

42. National Center for Environmental Health (2001, April 21). *What every parent should know about lead poisoning in children.* Retrieved May 20, 2001, from http://www.cdc.gov/nceh/lead/faq/cdc97a.htm.

43. National Center for Environmental Health (2001, April 21). *What every parent should know about lead poisoning in children.* Retrieved May 20, 2001, from http://www.cdc.gov/nceh/lead/faq/cdc97a.htm. American Academy of Child and Adolescent Psychiatry (1995, March). *Screening Children for Lead: Guidelines for Child and Adolescent Psychiatrists.* Policy statement. Retrieved November 22, 2003, from http://www.aacap.org/publications/policy/ps32.htm.

44. Gibbs, L. M. (1998). *Love Canal: The story continues.* British Columbia, Canada: New Society Publishers.

45. Spradley, B. W., & Allender, J. A. (1996). *Community health nursing: Concepts and practice* (p. 488). Philadelphia: Lippincott Publishers.

46. Spradley, B. W. & Allender, J. A. (1996). *Community health nursing: Concepts and practice* (p. 488). Philadelphia: Lippincott Publishers. United States Census Bureau. (2004, September 15). *Current population survey, 2003: Annual social and economic supplement.* Table A1. Marital status of people 15 years and over, by age, sex, personal earnings, race, and Hispanic origin/1, 2003. Retrieved April 26, 2005, from http://www.census.gov/population/socdemo/hh-fam/cps2003/tabA1-all.pdf.

11

Food

Throughout history, families have shared food, its gathering, production, processing, and preparation. In many countries, in fact, the standard greeting asks, "Have you eaten today?" However, even in America, when a family cannot fulfill its basic economic functions, children go hungry. Although many Americans struggle with overweight, millions of children suffer from fear of hunger, actual hunger or the lack of a balanced diet. In 2005, some 35 million Americans, including over 12 million children, lived in households that could easily run out of food.[1] Between 2002 and 2004, an average of almost 13 million households were food insecure, meaning that they faced the possibility of not having enough nutritious food. In four million of these households someone actually went hungry.[2] In most cases, the adults fed their children and went hungry themselves. Nevertheless, in 2002, one-half million American children were actually hungry due to lack of food.[3]

The ability of families to feed themselves well must be considered within the broader context of what the U.S. Department of Agriculture calls "food security" and the comprehensive system of food production and distribution. Although definitions vary, food security basically means that everyone should be able to obtain a culturally acceptable, nutritionally adequate diet at all times without resorting to emergency sources. The food system refers to the entire process of producing the food served at the family table: which crops farmers grow and which chemicals they use; how the processors prepare the food for sale; the locations of grocery stores and their prices; the network of laws, regulations and inspections; research on new products; and advertising. Readers will note the long tentacles of many of the issues affecting their neighborhood families' ability to feed themselves well. Those concerned may, however, be able to address some of the issues without engaging the entire octopus.

This chapter will outline the role of the major non-local players. It then shows how these affect the nation's eating habits and whether people have enough to eat. Finally, it considers the role of local community and neighborhood efforts.

By identifying major players and problems, readers will be able to determine where corrective and positive actions can lead to significant results.

Key Players

A systematic examination of the activities and institutions related to most people's food consumption shows the major role played by non-neighborhood actors: (1) businesses; (2) the federal government; (3) state officials; (4) city/county/school officials; (5) nonprofit organizations and religious institutions; and (6) the media.

Businesses control many aspects of whether families feed their families properly through actions that influence whether food is accessible and affordable. The wages they pay employees, including those who pick the fruit and freeze the vegetables, affect family income. The pesticides and additives they use in growing and processing affect safety. The advertising they buy affects individuals' desires and choices. Neighborhood location of a good grocery store, the products carried and their prices primarily depends upon the marketing decisions of national corporations.

Whether people can travel easily to a good grocery store depends upon decisions about roads, sidewalks, and bus routes that rest with city, county, state and sometimes federal officials. Residents' knowledge of healthy eating habits probably comes from their individual families, heavily influenced by non-local private business via advertising as well as the educational campaigns of the government and such nonprofit national organizations such as the American Heart Association.

The federal government plays a major role in overall food security through its responsibilities for food safety including control of pesticides and inspection of food processing plants. Although Americans normally take the safety of their food for granted, over 300,000 people are hospitalized and 5,000 die annually due to illnesses caused by food-borne pathogens.[4] While local officials bear responsibility for overseeing the cleanliness of restaurants and grocery stores, hamburger produced in one state quickly reaches shelves throughout the nation. Only the Food Safety and Inspection Service of the U.S. Department of Agriculture has the ability to monitor the safety of the meat and poultry crossing state boundaries.[5]

The federal government also sponsors long-term research and provides health information from experts in the Office of the Surgeon General and the Centers for Disease Control. It provides funds for food stamps, school lunches and contributes heavily to supplemental food programs operated by nonprofit and religious institutions.

States control many aspects of environmental management, affecting the safety of locally grown food and the fish caught in state rivers and lakes. Wisconsin prides itself on its many lakes which provide local recreation and serve as a major source of income from out-of-state tourists. However, the Wisconsin

Department of Natural Resources issues annual warnings telling people not to eat too many fish of certain kinds and not to eat them at all from some lakes.[6]

State governments control money. Even when funds come from federal programs, state governments decide whether to accept and how to distribute the funds and manage the programs. For example, after the traditional welfare program was eliminated in 1996, the number of people receiving food stamps dropped significantly. Often, however, this occurred not because the former recipients had found well-paying jobs that made them ineligible, but because states administered the program in a restrictive manner. People applying to the new program who were ruled ineligible for benefits were not necessarily told they might still be eligible for food stamps, nor did the recipients who obtained jobs always realize that they might be eligible to continue their food stamps.[7] Over the next five years, Food Stamp Program participation dropped by 6.5 million people. In six states, participation dropped by over one-third.[8] In Missouri, for example, although 75 percent of those who had left welfare had incomes low enough to make them eligible to receive food stamps, only 60 percent of them were receiving the benefit two and a half years later. One-third of those eligible but not receiving the benefit said that they had been unable to buy enough food at some point during the previous month. Over one-half of the former recipients did not realize that such help was still available, did not know where to obtain it, or had been denied assistance.[9] Thus, the way states administer programs can influence their effectiveness in preventing hunger.

States also educate and set policy. After the state of California issued a policy statement encouraging the creation of a garden in every school, the number of gardens in Los Angeles schools jumped markedly over the next several years.[10] Land grant universities, financed with both federal and state funds, undertake research on food issues and employ extension agents who provide advice to farmers, information on nutrition to homemakers, and assistance to community gardeners.

Local governments control zoning that affects whether housing options permit people with non-traditional household compositions to share a kitchen. They also support farmers' markets, fund a variety of nonprofit and neighborhood organizations, lobby for desired federal and state programs and monitor their implementation.

School boards determine whether school lunches provide food that educates children and their taste buds about healthy choices. School boards can prohibit marketing messages from soft drink companies and others that encourage children to develop unhealthy habits.

Local nonprofits and religious organizations, supported by their volunteers, run many of the programs that assist the neighborhoods in their food efforts. National nonprofits conduct research on food issues and lobby for policies promoting food security. They also lobby on issues affecting income, such as the minimum wage and Earned Income Tax Credit levels, as well as funding for food stamps and school lunches.

The primary role played by the media comes from advertising, largely controlled by the businesses that purchase it. The news media also plays a more objective role through reporting results of scientific studies about healthy eating or the problems of obesity and hunger and covering activities such as farmers' markets.

Healthy Eating Habits

Healthy eating habits protect people from a variety of serious illnesses, including diabetes and heart attacks. A combination of unhealthy diets and lack of exercise kills hundreds of thousands of Americans each year. The problem affects not only adults, two-thirds of whom are overweight, but also increasingly hurts children. Between 1971 and 2004 the rate of overweight children and adolescents jumped from 4 percent to 17.5 percent. About one-quarter of African American girls and boys and one quarter of Mexican American boys weigh too much for their health.[11] Overweight children tend to grow into overweight adults with the related serious health problems. Perhaps as important, their weight can lead to teasing, self-consciousness, social withdrawal, and self-esteem problems.

A study by the Institute of Medicine highlights the link between the typical American lifestyle and health. At least until recently, naturalized Mexican Americans experience heart disease and diabetes twice as often as recent immigrants. In Mexico, many lived in rural areas with better access to fruits and vegetables and less access to fast-food restaurants and other sources of junk food.[12] Kelly Brownell, a professor of psychology, epidemiology and public health at Yale, wrote, "Americans have unprecedented access to a poor diet—to high—calorie foods that are widely available, low in cost, heavily promoted, and good tasting. These ingredients produce a predictable, understandable, and inevitable consequence—an epidemic of diet-related diseases."[13]

Although recent media publicity on obesity has increased awareness of the correlation between what children consume in school and weight problems, during the 1990s, some 150 school districts in twenty-nine states signed exclusive contracts with beverage companies. The agreements often included provisions for the soft drink company to sponsor school activities with displays of the company logo. The Colorado Springs School District, for example, signed an exclusive contract with a soft drink company providing the district 8 to 11 million dollars over ten years.[14] Such arrangements can affect the children's choices between milk and sugar-laden drinks and could influence what teachers say when discussing nutrition or what message the children absorb.

School cafeterias, like grocery stores, operate within certain financial constraints. Faced with budget problems, many sell soda and other snacks to increase revenue, sign exclusive contracts with brand name producers, or purchase the cheapest possible foods. During one year, Pizza Hut served lunches in 4,500 schools. An article in the "Community Food Security News" states that while

Pizza Hut pizza contains more nutritional value than some other fast foods, two slices use up 40 percent of a child's recommended fat allocation for the entire day and also contain considerable sodium.[15]

When schools contract with fast food chains, they undercut children's present and future health. They implicitly approve eating a regular diet of such food; they imply that such food provides a good choice for nutrition; and they help hook the children on food rich in fat and sodium.[16] The average teenager drinks twice as many soft drinks as glasses of milk. The soft drinks provide sugar and caffeine while milk provides calcium. Bone building mainly occurs before adulthood. The average teenage girl, now consuming 40 percent less calcium than needed, risks broken bones in later years.[17] Breaking a hip when older is not a trivial event. Many victims can never walk without assistance afterwards and complications from the accident can lead to death.

After signing a lucrative contract with the Coca-Cola Co., the Madison, Wisconsin, school district faced community complaints. The input led the district to withdraw the company's right to sponsor a variety of promotional activities including student internships, T-shirts, computer software and teacher recognition events. Several years later, after considerable public debate, Madison became the first city in the country to decide not to renew its lucrative soft drink contract. By 2005, the school district had shifted its position radically and eliminated the sale of soft drinks in elementary and middle schools.[18]

Recent publicity about the health problems of obesity has focused attention on the impact of choices available to students at school. In 2005, regular soda accounted for 45 percent of the sales in schools. But a recent agreement forged by the William J. Clinton Foundation and the American Heart Association with the largest beverage distributors will result in healthy beverage choices for 35 million students in public schools. Only water, unsweetened juice and low-fat milk will be sold in elementary and middle schools. Diet and other low-calorie drinks will be sold in high schools.[19]

Even people who eat healthy foods at home find themselves confronted with unhealthy choices elsewhere. Traveling by car from Wisconsin to Missouri, I found it almost impossible to glean a healthy diet from the food available at the gas stations, convenience stores, and fast food restaurants. If I could find an apple among the chips, I counted myself lucky. The problem exists even when not traveling. I sang in a choir and normally drank orange juice during rehearsal break. One year the nearby vending machine switched from real juice to mixtures of juice laced with corn syrup and water. A similar problem exists for millions of students and workers trying to find healthy snacks or a quick lunch away from home.

Unfortunately, neighborhood programs for children often provide poor nutritional choices. One day I walked by an after-school program at a neighborhood center while eating an orange. When a child asked for a piece, I realized that in three months the only fruit I had seen in the center was that which I had brought for my own snacks. The after-school program served cookies and other treats, partly because they cost less than fruit. After consultation with the food pantry program and the after-school director, fruit was added to the selection.

Hunger

National government decisions largely determine whether the elderly and children in low-income families have enough to eat. Millions of elderly depend upon their Social Security checks to buy groceries. The Earned Income Tax Credit channels money to workers with wages too low to support themselves and their families. In addition to the millions of citizens receiving food stamps, more than 22 million children use the subsidized school lunch and breakfast program.[20] Funding cuts or eligibility changes in these efforts directly affect people's abilities to nourish themselves and their families.

Almost 40 percent of households with incomes below the official poverty line face food insecurity, experiencing actual hunger or the fear of running out of food. A large proportion of such households are headed by working parents receiving low wages. Households with single mothers or elderly or disabled individuals are especially likely to risk hunger.[21]

Changes in government policies indirectly but critically affect neighborhood families. Hmong immigrants to the United States, for example, suffer serious employment handicaps due to language and education barriers. In 1996, those who came to this country as legal immigrants faced the prospect of widespread hunger when Congress eliminated their food stamps. Over a year, the average Hmong family could have lost $435 in benefits. Those with large families would have lost even more. If even as many as 100 families in a neighborhood lost the average amount, this would have reduced neighborhood family income by $40,000 a year. Most neighborhoods cannot easily provide funds to overcome such a drop in their residents' incomes. Many of the neighborhood-based organizations that might help operate on far smaller budgets themselves. Although adult immigrants were ineligible for food stamps, their children remained eligible if born in the United States. However, partly because of confusion about the rules, between 1994 and 1999 some 800,000 eligible children nationally were dropped from the Food Stamp Program rolls despite their families' poverty. Public outrage about this situation, including input from groups with strong neighborhood ties, resulted in Congressional action rescinding the decision for many, but not all, of those who suffered the loss. New regulations increased the numbers of immigrants eligible, but many do not apply, possibly because of confusion about the rules.[22]

Changes in the welfare law resulted in loss of food stamps for millions of others. Partly because of more restrictive rules and partly because of the way states administered the program, the number of participants dropped by three and a half million in one year, 1997, mostly among mostly eligible people. From FY 1994 to FY 1999 participation dropped by over one-third. Individuals often did not realize, and were not told, that they might still be eligible for food stamps once they left welfare.[23]

While the economy was booming in the years following changes in the federal welfare program and many former recipients did receive jobs, requests for emergency food increased. Between 1995 and 1997, requests for emergency food from Catholic Charities USA jumped 14 percent.[24] In the late twentieth century, a number of the federal programs supporting low and moderate income housing also were cut, increasing the number of families who paid 50 to 80 percent of their incomes for rent, leaving less for food. Many elderly cut back on food, often on items crucial for health like fruits and vegetables, in order to pay for medicine. The reduction in affordable housing, combined with reduction in services to the mentally ill and those in drug and alcohol treatment, has pushed many families onto the streets. Homeless families cannot even use food pantries, since food pantries provide groceries that require kitchens for preparation.[25]

Between 25 and 26 million people used food stamps each month in 2006. However, 40 percent of eligible people did not receive them, including many workers.[26] Often workers do not realize that they can participate. Yet in 2007, a couple with two children making $13 an hour, or almost $27,000 a year could be eligible for stamps worth hundreds of dollars a month. A single mother with two children making less than $11 an hour, or slightly over $22,000 a year, could be eligible for benefits worth up to $426 a month.[27]

Many nonprofit organizations provide food pantries or buying clubs. The Allied-Dunn's Marsh Neighborhood Center, in Madison, Wisconsin, for example, housed a food pantry where low-income residents could obtain free groceries, mostly staples and canned goods. It also served as a distribution point for a program open to people of any income that for a set fee, $15.00 a month in 1999, delivered a twenty-five-to-thirty-pound box of groceries to the pick-up point at the neighborhood center. Each person received meat, fruits, vegetables, milk and bread. Such programs are designed to be supplemental rather than basic. A family of four might receive four bags of food from the food pantry, but food pantries often limit use to once a month. Still, food pantries do make a major contribution to alleviating hunger. One year the Hunger Task Force of Milwaukee, Wisconsin, distributed 10,000 bags of food a month through a network of eighty-three food pantries. Some 32,000 people, one third of them children, received food.[28]

Soup kitchens also help, but many do not serve the lowest income neighborhoods. Some church-sponsored kitchens mainly feed only members of their own congregation. Soup kitchens often serve people with some serious mental and abuse problems. Therefore, sponsors must consider safety, both real and perceived, for their volunteer workers, sometimes leading them to select locations outside of the neediest neighborhoods.[29]

Still, millions of Americans depend upon these programs at least occasionally. At the close of the century, before a downturn in the economy, the Hunger Task

Force of Milwaukee estimated that 3 percent of the metropolitan population used the food pantries or soup kitchens at some point each month. Nationally the network of emergency food providers serves about 25 million individuals during the course of a year, almost 40 percent of them children, but this does not always keep hunger at bay. By comparison, the Food Stamp Program serves an average of over 26 million persons each month.[30]

Ironically, people who have higher incomes, who almost always own cars, can save considerable money on their groceries compared to people who must count their pennies. An analysis of twenty-one cities showed that between 20 and 40 percent of those living in the poorest neighborhoods did not own cars.[31] If the neighborhood lacks adequate grocery stores, residents must pay bus or taxi fare out of already strapped food budgets. One study found that a family of three would pay $285 more per year if they bought their groceries at an inner-city supermarket than if they purchased the same groceries at a suburban supermarket.[32] When I lived on Capitol Hill in Washington, D.C., I frequently drove to Virginia to shop, to enjoy cheaper prices, greater variety and fresher vegetables.

The scope of the problem must not be underestimated. Even in Los Angles County, where *everyone* owns a car, computer mapping of supermarket location compared to census data indicated that over one million people unlikely to own cars lived in areas that had no supermarket within one-half mile.[33] Nationally, almost 12 percent of households do not own or have access to a vehicle for personal use.[34] As Hurricane Katrina demonstrated, the availability of cars is even more limited in certain neighborhoods.

Although adequate public transportation theoretically could resolve some of the grocery problem for those without cars, maneuvering heavy grocery bags on and off a bus presents difficulties. Americans who do not own cars tend to be elderly people, who also are likely to be frail, or women with children whose nourishment requires many bags of groceries.

Thus, the biggest protection from hunger for children, the elderly living on fixed incomes, parents working for low wages, and the unemployed rests with various federal food programs. In addition to the 26 million Americans receiving food stamps every month, others benefit from the federally-funded school breakfast and lunch programs, food provided with federal funds to programs for women and infants, child care centers, food pantries, senior citizen centers, and soup kitchens.[35]

Local Community and Neighborhood Contributions

Although major actors affecting families' food security are non-local, neighbors, volunteers, nonprofits and community groups do make significant contributions to alleviating immediate hunger and can take an active role in lobbying for appropriate programs and funding. Neighborhoods can promote healthy eating through partnering with schools and businesses, sponsoring weight reduction workshops, serving healthy food at their programs, and encouraging others to do so. Except in wealthy neighborhoods, the most useful action for a neighborhood to take to eliminate hunger may be educating residents about food stamp eligibility and encouraging participation in the program.

Although only a few neighborhoods have successfully recruited a grocery store, some neighborhood groups have pushed for locating at least convenience shopping nearby. Generally, however, convenience store operations face the same realistic operating costs and problems of grocery stores: how to sell a sufficient volume of products at a high enough price to remain in business. The grocery business operates on a very small profit margin, about 1 percent. When other businesses, such as pharmacies and gas stations, add food products, they concentrate on those with the highest profit margins, often junk snacks, and avoid items likely to spoil, such as fresh fruits and vegetables.

Neighborhoods can publicize the risks and safe ways to prepare, store, and cook food. Neighborhoods also can host food pantries, serve as drop-off sites for cooperative farm programs that provide fresh organic vegetables, host farmers' markets, and sponsor cooking classes that teach easy ways to prepare inexpensive but healthy food. Some groups have worked with school boards and teachers to design school gardens, lunch menus and curriculum that encourage nutritional choices. Others monitor the implementation of programs, and encourage people to sign up for food stamps. Many areas sponsor community gardens that can help booster community cohesion along providing with fresh vegetables. More detailed examples are provided in the section on food in the companion guidebook (see Author's Note, pp. xv-xvi).

Conclusions

This chapter has demonstrated the need to consider the most basic of family tasks, providing adequate nourishing meals, in a broader context. The safety and desirability of what we eat depends indirectly on actions of national actors including the media and federal government. Whether people with inadequate incomes go hungry depends more upon funding for federal food programs than any local or charitable actions. Local and neighborhood efforts are useful supplements to the necessary actions by non-local institutions.

Notes

1. Food Research & Action Center. (2006, November 15). *More than 35 Million of Americans Lived In Food Insecure Households in 2005: Percentage of Households in Worst-Off Category Remains Unchanged.* Washington, DC: Food Research & Action Center. Retrieved January 8, 2007 from http://www.frac.org/Press_Release/11.15.06.html.
2. Food Research and Action Center. (2006, March). *State of the states: 2006. A profile of food and nutrition programs across the nation.* Retrieved 18 December 2006 from http://www.frac.org/pdf/2006_SOS_Report.pdf.
3. Economic Research Service, United States Department of Agriculture. (2002). *Food security in the United States: Conditions and trends.* Retrieved November 17, 2004, from http://www.ers.usda.gov/briefing/FoodSecurity/trends/.

4.   Centers for Disease Control. (2001, December). *Food borne infections.* Retrieved July 27, 2002, from http://www.cdc.gov/ncidod/dbmd/diseaseinfo/foodborneinfections_t.htm.
5.   United States Department of Agriculture, Food Safety and Inspection Service. (2001, April). *Protecting the public from foodborne illness: The food safety and inspection service.* Retrieved April 9, 2001, from http://www.fsis.usda.gov/oa/background/fsisgeneral.htm.
6.   Beck, V. (2006). *Choose wisely. A health guide for eating fish in* Wisconsin. Wisconsin Department of Natural Resources publication number PUB-FH-824 2006. Retrieved March 23, 2007, from http://www.dnr.state.wi.us/fish/pages/consumption/Fish%20Advisory%2006%20web%20lo.pdf.
7.   Food Research and Action Center. (2001, September). *Network reports low-income, working families disconnected from Food Stamp Program.* Retrieved March 26, 2002, from http://www.frac.org/html/news/disconnect.html.
8.   Food Research and Action Center. (2000, November). *Food Stamp Program participation: Five year change.* Retrieved March, 25, 2002, from http://www.frac.org/html/new/fsp/01november5yr.html.
9.   Midwest Research Institute. (2001, March). *Missouri welfare reform outcomes: Food stamps and food deprivation.* Kansas City, MO: Midwest Research Institute.
10. Conversation with Jac Smit, president, Urban Agriculture Network. January 26, 2007.
11. National Center for Health Statistics. (2006, November). *Health, United States, 2006. With chartbook on trends in the health of Americans* (pp.37, 38 and 291). Retrieved December 18, 2006, from http://www.cdc.gov/nchs/data/hus/hus06.pdf.
12. Hayes, V. D. (1998, October 12). An (unhealthy) American dream. *Wisconsin State Journal,* p. 2A.
13. Brownell, K. (1998, July/August). The pressure to eat: Why we're getting fatter (p. 3). *Nutrition Action Healthletter.* Washington, DC: Center for Science in the Public Interest.
14. Jacobson, M. (1998, November). Liquid candy. *Nutrition Action Health Letter,(* p.8). Washington, DC: Center for Science in the Public Interest.
15. Community Food Security Coalition. (1998, Fall). Brand-name fast foods in school cafeterias. *Community Food Security News* (pp. 10-11). Venice, CA: Community Food Security Coalition.
16. Community Food Security Coalition. (1998, Fall). Brand-name fast foods in school cafeterias. *Community Food Security News* (pp. 10-11). Venice, CA: Community Food Security Coalition.
17. Jacobson, M. (1998, November). Sugar: The sweetening of the American diet (pp. 3-6). *Nutrition Action Health Letter.* Washington, DC: Center for Science in the Public Interest.
18. The author followed the newspaper coverage at the time. Conversation with school board staff, December, 2006.
19. Gross, S. (2006, April 5). *Nearly all sodas sales to schools to end.* New York: Associated Press. Retrieved April 5, 2006, from http://news.yahoo.com/s/ap/2006-05-03/ap_on_re_us/soft_drinks_schools.
20. Center on Budget and Policy Priorities. (n.d.). *Food Assistance.* Retrieved November 9, 2006 from http://www.cbpp.org/pubs/fa.htm.
21. Nord, M., Andrews, M., & Carlson, S. (2004, October). Prevalence of food insecurity and food insecurity with hunger—conditions and trends, by selected household characteristics. *Household food security in the Unites States, 2003.* Washington, DC:

United States Department of Agriculture. Retrieved April 6, 2005, from http://www.ers.usda.gov/briefing/foodsecurity/. United States Department of Agriculture (n.d.). *New report shows improvement in hunger, but many challenges remain.* Retrieved April 6, 2001, from http://www.usda.gov/news/releases/2000/09/0301.htm.

22. Food Research and Action Center. (2006, March). *State of the states: 2006. A profile of food and nutrition programs across the nation.* (pp. 6-7). Retrieved December 18, 2006, from http://www.frac.org/pdf/2006_SOS_Report.pdf.

23. Food Research and Action Center. (2006, March). *State of the states: 2006. A profile of food and nutrition programs across the nation.* (pp. 6-7). Retrieved December 18, 2006, from http://www.frac.org/pdf/2006_SOS_Report.pdf.

24. Food Research & Action Center (1998, July 31). *State government responses to the food assistance gap: Second annual report from the Food Research and Action Center and Second Harvest National Food Bank Network.* Washington, DC: Author.

25. Poppendieck, J. (1998). *Sweet charity? Emergency food and the end of entitlement.* New York: Viking.

26. Food Research and Action Center. (2006, March). *State of the states: 2006. A profile of food and nutrition programs across the nation.* (pp. 6-7). Retrieved December 18, 2006, from http://www.frac.org/pdf/2006_SOS_Report.pdf. Food Stamp Program: Average Monthly Participation (Persons). Downloaded 1/9/2008 from www.fns.usda.gov/pd15fsfypart.htm.

27. Food Stamp Program Guidelines: October 1, 2007-September 30, 2008. Downloaded on 1/9/2008 from www.hhs.state.ne.us/fia/guidelines.htm.

28. Leeman, K., food program director of the Hunger Task Force, Milwaukee, WI. (personal communication, November, 1998).

29. Poppendieck, J. (1998). *Sweet charity? Emergency food and the end of entitlement.* New York: Viking.

30. Leeman, K., Food Program Director of The Hunger Task Force, Milwaukee, WI (personal communication, November, 1998). Barrett, A. (2006, September). *Characteristics of food stamp households: fiscal year 2005.* Report No. FSP-06-CHAR. Prepared by Mathematica Policy Research, Inc. for the U.S. Department of Agriculture Food and Nutrition Service. Retrieved January 9, 2007, from http://www.fns.usda.gov/oane/menu/Published/FSP/FILES/Participation/2005Characteristics.pdf. Cohen, R., Kim, M., Ohls, J. (2006, March). *Hunger in America 2006. National report prepared for America's Second Harvest. Final Report.* pp. 1-2. Princeton, NJ: Mathematica Policy Research. Retrieved January 8, 2007 from http://www.hungerinamerica.org/export/sites/hungerinamerica/about_the_study/A2HNationalReport.pdf.

31. Gottlieb, R., Fisher, A., Dohan, M., O'Connor, L., & Parks, V. (1996). *Homeward bound: Food-related transportation strategies in low income and transit dependent communities* (p. 11). Venice, CA: Community Food Security Coalition.

32. Gottlieb, R., Fisher, A., Dohan, M., O'Connor, L., & Parks, V. (1996). *Homeward bound: Food-related transportation strategies in low income and transit dependent communities* (p. 12). Venice, CA: Community Food Security Coalition.

33. Gottlieb, R., Fisher, A., Dohan, M., O'Connor, L., & Parks, V. (1996). *Homeward bound: Food-related transportation strategies in low income and transit dependent communities* (p 8). Venice, CA: Community Food Security Coalition.

34. Aizcorbe, A. M., Kennickell, A. B., Moore, K. B. (2003, January). *Recent changes in U.S. family finances: Evidence from the 1998 and 2001 survey of consumer finances.* Federal Reserve Bulletin, p. 16. Retrieved from www.federalreserve.gov/pubs/bulletin/2003/0103lead.pdf.

35. Food Research and Action Center. (2006, March). *State of the states: 2006. A profile of food and nutrition programs across the nation.* Retrieved December 18, 2006, from http://www.frac.org/pdf/2006_SOS_Report.pdf.

12

Household Maintenance

The Time Crunch

Household maintenance—the preparing of food, obtaining and maintaining clothing, cleaning one's living space—these daily chores fall to family members. Whether these chores can be handled easily or not affects the dynamics of family and community life. Many people find their ability to contribute to neighborhood activities or even to socialize limited by the need to juggle child care, elder care, household tasks and a longer work week. Robert Putnam reports a marked drop in the number of families who eat the evening meal together. Only one-third of families now share this traditional evening ritual.[1]

Despite labor saving devices and convenience foods, the time demands of maintaining a home continue to be high. The need to attend to some chores, such as repairing appliances, has increased. The geography of many communities leaves children dependent upon parental chauffeuring for soccer practice and other after-school activities.

Combining work outside the home with household maintenance can become extremely stressful, especially if the household includes children or an elderly relative. For both men and women, the time available for managing the home front depends upon the rules and structure of the workplace and the time spent in commuting to work. A television community forum on family in Wisconsin elicited more comments and complaints about the difficulties of reconciling demands of work with family responsibilities than comments about family life per se.[2]

A third of all workers report having provided some care for an older relative within the past year.[3] In approximately one-quarter of American households, someone provides care for an older person. Although men contribute to elder care, according to the American Association of Retired Persons the typical caregiver is a married female who provides an average of eighteen hours of elder care a week in addition to holding down a full-time job. On average, this caregiver role lasts eight years.[4] In many cases those providing elder care are also still parenting young children or teenagers.

Juggling home responsibilities and work can result in cutting back on sleep and family time. Lack of time also creates stress, which contributes to a variety of serious health problems. Parental tension hurts children, who often bear the brunt of angry frustration. Thus, one way to support families involves easing the load of everyday chores.

Time, money, neighborhood/housing design, and the division of labor within the household determine the ease of household maintenance. Several adults can split the chores and lessen the burden. The ways that individuals agree to share the jobs, however, remain greatly influenced by society's definition of "men's work" and "women's work." While the proportion of employed men and women is now nearly equal, 40 percent of men still think that a woman's place is in the home. [5]

Although many men have responded positively to the combination of the questions of equality raised by the women's movement and women's massive entrance into the workplace, most women who work outside of the home continue to perform the majority of the household and care-giving tasks. In addition, they generally carry the responsibility for overall coordination and management of the household. [6]

Sociologist Arlie Hochschild calculated that women work the equivalent of an entire extra month a year performing their "second shift" jobs at home. [7] In a detailed study of a hundred couples where both adults worked, she found that the need to squeeze in this extra month's work affected both husbands and wives in a variety of complex and detrimental ways. Those women who performed most of this work slept less than their husbands, suffered illness more often, and eliminated any personal hobbies or interests. Hochschild found that "When Dorothy and Dan described their 'typical days,' their picture of sharing grew even less convincing. Dorothy worked the same nine-hour day at the office as her husband. But she came home to fix dinner and to tend Timmy while Dan fit in a squash game three nights a week from 6:00 to 7:00, a good time for his squash partner. Dan read the newspaper more often and slept longer." [8]

The question of household chores becomes important not only in terms of time pressures on families, but also in terms of the conflicts that can result. Hochschild found that three factors influenced the amount of conflict over roles: differences between the couple in expectations about the proper division of responsibilities, the amount of work actually performed by the husband, and the ways the couple reacted to their different expectations. Overall, Hochschild found a gap between what the men expected, the services traditionally provided by a stay-at-home wife, and what the women desired. Often even when husbands expressed the belief that they should share more equally, they did not. When men did take some of the burden, they generally assumed the more enjoyable and flexible tasks, taking the children on a special outing or handling a non-emergency household repair that could be scheduled conveniently according to their own needs. Women most often performed those daily chores that must be done regardless of mood or inclination: preparing dinner and cleaning up afterwards, supervising the children's baths, and doing the laundry.[9]

The management role—making sure to schedule a child's dental appointment or reminding the babysitter to give John medicine three times a day—remained the woman's responsibility. She coordinated meeting the complicated needs and schedules of the household and all of the services it used. Moreover, she shouldered the unpleasant, and usually unappreciated, task of reminding people of their duties. Nasty dynamics often resulted, with the husband resenting her "nagging," the wife resenting having to ask. This "boss" role can undermine the wife's ability to relax and enjoy her family and home.[10]

Couples struggle not only over conflicting views and expectations, but also over who has the right or power to define legitimate expectations. Is doing the dishes an accepted part of the responsibilities of both or a favor that the man can give on occasion for which he expects gratitude? Hochschild found that, "When couples struggle, it is seldom simply over who does what. Far more often, it is over the giving and receiving of gratitude."[11]

Trying to squeeze in too much work while feeling unsupported leaves women frustrated and angry. Men who assume major chore responsibilities suffer the same time pressures. Those who don't contribute their fair share suffer not only from their spouse's resentment, but also from their own guilt. In the couples she studied, Hochschild found that the marriages were happier when the husbands performed more of the housework and child care regardless of whether either husband or wife held traditional or egalitarian views.[12]

Not only do both partners now generally work, many hold jobs requiring increasingly long hours. By 2002 dual-earner couples with children clocked ninety-one hours of work a week. Employees report working fast and hard with considerable amounts of stress, burn-out, and spillover effect on their moods at home and their energy for family activities. Over seven million individuals work more than one job. [13] Under new regulations issued by President George W. Bush in 2004, some six million workers, including many white collar and service employees, lost their legal right to overtime pay, thus creating an incentive for employers to require longer hours from their workers.[14] In addition, the new technology means that workers can be paged or reached by cellular phones anywhere, interrupting their time off.

Lack of time undermines couples' intimacy and limits their ability to spend Sunday with relatives or chat with neighbors. Sociologist Lillian Rubin, who interviewed blue collar families in the 1970s and again in the 1990s, found that while such activities had been common two decades earlier, "Now almost everyone I speak with complains that it's hard to find time for even these occasional outings. Instead, most off-work hours are spent trying to catch up with the dozens of family and household tasks that were left undone during the regular work week." To juggle child care with two full-time jobs, many couples resort to working different shifts, both to cut child care expenses and to provide the children access to one parent at key times. This, however, hurts their own relationship when, as one woman complained, "you get to see each other maybe six minutes a day."[15]

Even fathers who want to fulfill their parenting and elder care responsibilities and who have stay-at-home wives often find that long hours, out-of-town travel, mandatory overtime, and compulsory moves to other cities limit their ability to follow through on their commitments.

Now 40 percent of employees work nonstandard hours, on weekends, evenings, overnight or on a rotating shift. This includes slightly over one-third of the dual-income couples with children under five years old. A quarter of single mothers work late or rotating shifts and one-third work weekends.[16]

Although some outstanding examples of family-friendly employers exist, the structure and rules of most jobs do not consider family responsibilities. The rules, and especially the unwritten rules for promotion, assume that the worker's first responsibility rests with the company. A national study found that the number of employees who would like to work fewer hours increased rapidly during the 1990s, reaching 63 percent by 1997.[17] Flexible work hours permitting a parent to attend a teacher conference or take a child to the dentist rarely exist. Employers demand overtime, not subject to negotiation without direct or indirect penalties. Indeed, in the late 1990s, one-fifth of American workers found themselves required to work overtime as often as once a week with little or no advance notice.[18] One-third of employees regularly brought work home and one in five took frequent overnight business trips.[19]

The Federal Family and Medical Leave Act requires businesses to grant unpaid leave for persons faced with family emergencies, such as caring for a dying parent. Thirty-five million Americans have taken such leave since passage of the law in 1993.[20] Businesses with fewer than fifty employees, however, are exempt, leaving over 40 percent of the private-sector workforce uncovered unless their states have passed more stringent laws.[21] In addition, many families cannot afford to take unpaid leave. Businesses continue strong resistance to such requirements.

Although some experts recommend part-time jobs as an alternative to juggling a full-time job and family responsibilities, under current workforce arrangements taking a part-time job generally involves a disproportionate cost in lower pay, loss of benefits and promotion opportunities, and often adds the stress of trying to accomplish a full-time job in fewer hours or by working unpaid overtime. In *The Overworked American*, economist Juliet Schor notes that in negotiating her "part-time" contract, one professional employee agreed to base the calculation of her 80 percent job and pay on the basis of a fifty-hour week, acknowledging that to be the standard for professionals in her organization. In addition to the agreed-upon hours on the job, she made business calls while commuting and from home.[22]

Many firms now structure their jobs as part-time positions that do not pay enough for a family to live on. In some families one or both adults hold two, even three, part-time jobs. In addition to the stress of long hours, workers with two jobs suffer stress from double or triple commutes. For example, a woman I know worked at a dry cleaners, part time, for the minimum wage of $5.15 an hour. She worked from 7:00 A.M. to 1:00 P.M. in a grocery store, before driving across town to the dry cleaners to work from 2:00 to 7:00 P.M. She did this six days a week, clocking over sixty hours, in order to survive. But she received no benefits, including health insurance, at either job. She was "making it, but just barely." If she had had a child, the situation would have been untenable. Yet many Americans play out similar scenarios daily.

What Affects Ease of Household Maintenance?

Issues affecting the ease of maintaining a home and family cover almost every aspect of American society. Divorce laws, media messages about gender roles, health insurance regulations, laws and practices regarding overtime and release time from work, and the minimum wage rate all contribute.

All households, but especially those with children, where every adult works outside the home need convenient places to shop, grab a take-out meal on their way home and drop off dry cleaning. As people age they may stop driving a car, making nearby services crucial.

Low-income households suffer more stress from household maintenance than do those with higher incomes. Money enables families to send out for pizza, hire someone to clean the house, and pay the children for performing special chores. Clothes can be washed and dried in a machine adjacent to the kitchen while cooking dinner rather than being hauled in a cart to a laundromat or down three flights of stairs to a coin-operated machine in a dingy basement. People with greater resources can drop clothes off at the dry cleaners on the way to work. Cheaper clothes can be harder to care for and must be repaired and replaced more often. Clipping coupons saves money, but eats time. Older cars require more repairs than newer ones. Access to the right tool makes repair jobs and outside yard work easier. A public housing tenant in a townhouse development in Ohio complained that the management expected her to maintain the yard, but she did not own a decent lawn mover or clippers strong enough to properly trim the tree.[23] Thus, in numerous small and large ways, households with money can handle their daily tasks more easily than those with more limited resources. Having living wages, for example, would enable workers to reduce their hours, hire someone to handle repairs, buy ready-to-eat meals, or at least purchase time-saving household equipment. Thus, helping families and communities flourish depends upon actions of business as well as individuals and neighborhoods.

Health also affects the ease of household maintenance. Single-person households or those without two adults or at least teenage children can suddenly need assistance with basic survival chores during an illness. Increasingly, hospitals release surgery patients the same day or within twenty-four hours, in some cases even after major procedures. Many households are unprepared for such responsibilities.

The design of neighborhoods and the social relationships within them influence the ease of household maintenance. Sharing a household with another family or living in cooperative housing can ease the burden of household chores. This option, however, is often limited by laws and regulation. Thus, the ability of families to easily perform everyday chores rests partly upon the policies and actions of government and the private sector as well as help received from neighborhood organizations, neighbors, and friends.

Notes

1. Putnam, R. D. (2000). *Bowling alone: The collapse and revival of American community* (p. 100). New York: Simon & Schuster.
2. Author's observation.
3. Bond, J. T., Thompson, C., Galinsky, E., & Prottas, D. (2002). *Highlights of The National Study of the Changing Workforce: Executive summary.* Washington, DC: Families and Work Institute. Retrieved April 11, 2005, from http://www.familiesandwork.org/classroom/MPpp_toc.html.
4. Public Policy Institute, AARP, Public Affairs. (2000). *Caregiving and long-term care* (p. 1). Retrieved February 1, 2002, from wysiwyg://14/http://research.aarp.org/health/fs82_caregiving.html.
5. Bond, J. T., Thompson, C., Galinsky, E., & Prottas, D. (2002). *Highlights of The National Study of the Changing Workforce: Executive summary.* Washington, DC: Families and Work Institute. Retrieved April 11, 2005, from http://www.familiesandwork.org/classroom/MPpp_toc.html.
6. Bond, J. T., Thompson, C., Galinsky, E., & Prottas, D. (2002). *Highlights of The National Study of the Changing Workforce: Executive summary.* Washington, DC: Families and Work Institute. Retrieved April 11, 2005, from http://www.familiesandwork.org/classroom/MPpp_toc.html.
7. Hochschild, A., & Machung, A. (1989). *The second shift* (p. 3). New York: Avon Books.
8. Ibid., p. 20
9. Ibid. Rubin, L. B. (1994). *Families on the fault line: America's working class speaks about the family, the economy, race, and ethnicity.* New York: HarperCollins.
10. Hochschild, A., & Machung, A. (1989). *The second shift* (chapters 1-3). New York: Avon Books. Rubin, L. B. (1994). *Families on the fault line: America's working class speaks about the family, the economy, race, and ethnicity* (chapters 4 and 5). New York: HarperCollins.
11. Hochschild, A., & Machung, A. (1989). *The second shift,* p. 18..
12. Ibid., p. 211.
13. U.S. Bureau of Labor Statistics. 2005, May. Women in the Labor Force: A Databook. Report 985. p. 77. Retrieved August 30, 2007 from http://www.bls.gov/cps/wlf-databook-2005.pdf. Bond, J. T., Galinsky, E., & Swanberg, J. E. (1998). *The 1997 National study of the changing workforce: Executive summary* (p. 7). New York: Family and Work Institute. Retrieved April 15, 2003, from http://fwi.igc.org/summary/nscw.pdf. Bond, J. T., Thompson, C., Galinsky, E., & Prottas, D. (2002). *Highlights of The National Study of the Changing Workforce: Executive summary*

(p.2). Washington, D.C.: Families and Work Institute. Retrieved April 11, 2005, from http://www.familiesandwork.org/classroom/MPpp_toc.html

14. Eisenbrey, R. (2004, July 13). *Briefing paper. Longer hours, less pay. Labor Department's new rules could strip overtime protection from millions of workers.* Washington, DC: Economic Policy Institute. Retrieved January 8, 2007, from http://www.epinet.org/newsroom/releases/2004/07/040713overtimeBP.pdf.

15. Rubin, L. B. (1994). *Families on the fault line: America's working class speaks about the family, the economy, race, and ethnicity* (p. 99). New York: HarperCollins.

16. Presser, H. B. (2004, Spring). The economy that never sleeps. *Contexts, 3(2),* 42-49.

17. Bond, J. T., Galinsky, A., & Swanberg, J. E. (1998). *The 1997 National study of the changing workforce: Executive summary* (p. 8). New York: Family and Work Institute. Retrieved April 15, 2003, from http://fwi.igc.org/summary/nscw.pdf.

18. Bond, J. T., Galinsky, A., & Swanberg, J. E. (1998). *The 1997 National study of the changing workforce: Executive summary* (p. 8). New York: Family and Work Institute. Retrieved April 15, 2003, from http://fwi.igc.org/summary/nscw.pdf.

19. Bond, J. T., Galinsky, A., & Swanberg, J. E. (1998). *The 1997 National study of the changing workforce: Executive summary* (p. 8). New York: Family and Work Institute. Retrieved April 15, 2003, from http://fwi.igc.org/summary/nscw.pdf.

20. Pandya, S. M. (2005, April). *Caregiving in the United States.* p. 2. Washington, DC: AARP Public Policy Institute. Retrieved January 9, 2007, from http://assets.aarp.org/rgcenter/il/fs111_caregiving.pdf

21. International Brotherhood of Electrical Workers (2003, January/February). *The Family and Medical Leave Act 10 years later.* IBEW Journal. p 10. Retrieved January 9, 2007, from http://www.ibew.org/articles/03journal/0301/page10.htm.

22. Schor, J. B. (1991). *The overworked American: The unexpected decline of leisure.* New York: HarperCollins.

23. Comment to the author when on consulting contract with the public housing authority.

13

But That's Where the Children Have to Live

American approaches to child rearing reflect our beliefs in individual responsibility, upward mobility for those who study hard, and the ability of volunteers and neighbors to supplement family efforts. Unfortunately, our approach does not fully address the implications of our belief in equality since children are treated very differently depending upon where they live and the income of their parents.

Our family policy, or lack of it, rests largely upon the Norman Rockwell myth described in chapter 2 and the practices of our businesses as well as our aversion to social expenditures. The United States has the lowest rate of social expenditures of sixteen other industrial nations which are members of the Organization of Economic Cooperation and Development. It also has by far the highest child poverty rate, five times that of the countries with the highest social expenditures.[1]

Although communities often consider children at risk as coming from only a few of their families, the facts indicate that many of their children live in households likely to need community support. To the extent their community reflects the national situation, they will be faced with the following realities: one-quarter of their children are currently living in a single parent home, one-half of their children will do so for at least five years during their childhood, one-third will experience poverty, millions have no health insurance and most have mothers in the labor force.[2] Contrary to much popular opinion, these realities are not confined to minorities or to the inner city. In fact, a larger share of the nation's poor children live in rural areas and suburbia than in central cities.[3]

Key Players

The federal government provides much of the funding for meeting the needs of low-income children. It also funds extensive research, technical assistance materials and training for states, local governments, and others on a variety of issues affecting children.

The No Child Left Behind Act created federal standards for schools, tying federal funds to performance. Controversy has arisen about whether the level of funding is sufficient and whether applying a single standard for measuring a school's success is appropriate given the different characteristics of children in different schools and the disparity in funding for schools.

States implement many of the federal programs such as Medicaid. They also establish standards and child-to-adult ratios for child care centers. They control funds for education, set teacher licensing and continuing education requirements, and establish curriculum requirements.

Cities and counties, often with federal or state money, provide programs which tackle underlying causes of child abuse and neglect such as mental illness or alcohol addiction. They provide treatment services and fund community police.

Community police need to be assigned on a long-term basis to provide them the chance to develop trusting relationships with children and their parents. They need encouragement from their supervisors to work with community groups, attend community festivals and organize needed activities. The author recalls an interview with the neighborhood police officer being interrupted not by someone reporting a crime, but by an eight-year old demanding, "Sue, when are we going to start the soccer team?" Sue's network of neighborhood contacts was so extensive that when her office called to tell her about a crime she also heard about the incident from several neighborhood people while walking the several blocks to her office. When a woman had to be busted on drug charges in the middle of the night, Sue was part of the arresting team. She carried a teddy bear for the woman's young child and, turning the child over to her grandmother, sympathized, "Sorry, Ginny, but we had to do this." Ginny later commented that she thought Sue did her job and was fair. Resident respect for law officers and the knowledge that the officers keep confidences and do not spread gossip make it safe for a neighbor to report a crime or a case of suspected child abuse.

Businesses which do not enable parents to check on their children after school by telephone or e-mail, which fail to provide flexible hours, time-off for parent-teacher conferences, have production schedules which leave workers constantly stressed, and avoid paying their fair share of school taxes, hurt parents and their children. In addition to providing decent wages, benefits and flexible work opportunities, local businesses can create a welcoming atmosphere for children and provide them with part-time and summer jobs. Businesses also contribute funds and volunteers for community programs and participate in collaborative partnerships with schools and other community groups.

Nonprofit organizations, churches, mosques and synagogues affect the overall community atmosphere. They can recruit mentors, establish and run programs. They can insist upon appropriate standards for child care providers. They and their board members and volunteers often come from the power structure within a community and can influence business and political decisions. These organizations also conduct research, follow national trends, and monitor conditions and programs.

The media, especially television, plays a major and not always positive role in influencing American children. Although television does include many educational programs, the major purpose of most programming is to sell products. This can have a number of detrimental impacts on children. It teaches them that "he who dies with the most toys wins." It encourages them to want, even crave, things that are not good for them such as cereals laced with sugar. It presents a view of the population which suggests that success and happiness depend upon being young, rich, attractive, Caucasian, and, in many cases, rude or ruthless. Increasingly television emphasizes sex and violence. Recent studies have confirmed what people have suspected for years: watching violent programs increases the chances that a child will behave aggressively and violently both as a child and when an adult.[4] Not only do children watch some 200,000 violent acts while growing up, they also often watch these events without the benefit of talking to their parents about what they see. Much of the time children watch television alone. By 1999 almost 80 percent of sixth graders had televisions in their own rooms.[5]

Adult Supervision

Two-thirds of mothers with preschool children and almost 80 percent of those with children age six to thirteen are in the labor force. Today even the majority of married mothers work outside the home. [6] Very young children need constant adult supervision, not only to prevent them from hurting themselves but also to provide the type of nurturing that creates loving adults and the type of intellectual stimulation that leads to success in school. This means a non-stressed capable parent or a good child care program with a low staff-to-child ratio.

Recent research about brain development documents the importance of certain parental behaviors. A child's ability to see properly, understand language, coordinate muscles, learn, think logically, and control emotions is influenced by how parents or other caretakers treat the child during the early years. If a child misses needed nourishment, love and stimulation during key months, that child will have a more difficult time in developing certain abilities. For example, children who do not receive visual stimulation during the first six months of their lives may suffer impaired visual abilities. The sounds children hear before age three largely determine their adult vocabulary. The ability to think logically and perform math depends upon appropriate stimulation between ages one and four. Children who do not have a consistent loving care giver during their first eighteen months may later lack emotional stability.[7]

Sometimes women can rely upon their own mothers or other family members who live nearby for child care. Relatives care for almost 30 percent of children less than three years old.[8] Although this arrangement has many potential advantages, in some cases the relatives may be unaware of some of the newer findings about childhood development. For example, the tendency to place babies on their stomachs to sleep which greatly increases the risk of death from Sudden Infant Death Syndrome (SIDS) is related both to low income and to the presence of a grandmother in the home.[9]

Many women opt for part-time employment, although some who desire it cannot afford the financial loss or have an employer who will not allow it. Those who do choose part-time work may limit their job choices, hurt their advancement potential, and often lose the opportunity for health care, retirement and other benefits. Given the nation's high divorce rate, young women who choose to remain home with their children risk facing poverty in their old age. PaineWebber investment advisors estimate that a woman taking seven years off during a forty-year employment history will lose one-half of her potential retirement income.[10]

By the age of two almost 30 percent of the children of employed mothers are cared for in child care centers. Basically in child care centers you get what you pay for. A valid case has been made for the fact that the key desirable ingredient in a child care provider is love, which cannot be measured by salary. What can be measured by salary, however, includes education, experience, and length of time working at a particular child care facility. Educational preparation provides child care providers with knowledge of early childhood development, how to create activities that teach cooperation or skills needed for school, how to identify child abuse and what to do about it. Experience provides insight about when the needs of one child may not fit into the morning's planned activity or what to say to an irate parent who will not believe that his child bit another child.

Staff stability provides the children consistency of care by someone who knows both the children and their parents. Because child care wages are low, staff turnover is high. A recent analysis indicates that child care workers will change jobs for as little as five to ten cents more an hour.[11] The annual 30 percent staff turn-over in child care centers suggests that millions of children may be learning that no one understands them, that people who love them will always leave. This may affect their ability to form long term relationships as adults. One study noted that as a career, "childcare is striking for the low returns to investment in education, and the lack of employer-sponsored health insurance."[12]

After the World Trade Center tragedy, many people commented that airport security workers were low wage workers with little training and high rates of turn-over. The public demanded that a more professional staff was needed to watch baggage flow underneath the security machines and passengers walk through the screening equipment. Ironically, similar staffing conditions are deemed adequate to teach children values and nonviolent ways to handle their anger.

Once a child care center has been established, the only places you can cheat, i.e., cut costs significantly, are staff and food. Depending upon the state and local laws you can lower the adult-to-child ratio, hire less qualified teachers or feed the children cookies instead of apples. Feeding children mainly cookies not only deprives them of the vitamins and minerals their bodies need but also teaches them to crave foods laced with fat and sugar, both results detrimental to their long term health. Lowering the adult-to-child ratio can result in children watching television rather than listening to a story, going to a corner for time-out rather than, or in addition to, talking about why they hit Mary and other choices they could have made.

Quality child care has a proven track record of contributing to children's success in school and later life. Such care can have enormously positive impacts on children's growth and development, especially those who come from families with limited education or resources. A number of careful studies have traced the long term effects of well designed child care programs. Successful programs provide not only educational components but also address health and other social service needs and include parent involvement and education. Such programs are not cheap, but they contribute to children's success in later life. They result in greater school success, fewer teenage pregnancies, lower rates of school drop outs, less criminal activity, and greater college attendance. Unfortunately, they are beyond the financial resources of millions of parents without a government subsidy.[13] Yet because of inadequate funding, only one in seven children eligible for such support receives it.[14]

Research has shown that child care programs, such as Head Start, which involve parents and address the range of health and other issues affecting a child's readiness for school, make a difference in children's future success. Yet quality programs reach only a small proportion of the children who most need them. For example, despite a thirty-year track record of success, Head Start has never received enough funding to enroll more than half the children eligible. Early Head Start, the program for children less than three years old, serves less than three percent of eligible children.[15]

Many parents cannot rely upon child care programs because most do not operate during weekends or evenings. As the economy has moved toward a twenty-four-hour, seven-day-a-week schedule, parents need child care which accommodates their schedules, including those who can shift at the last minute for the convenience of the employer. They need arrangements which provide care in unexpected emergencies. Thus, it is not surprising that one-third of the nations' parents must find more than one type of non-parental care for their children.[16] This problem will become worse since jobs requiring night and weekend work and unexpected overtime are likely to increase.

Home-based child care where a woman cares for a small number of children within her home serves almost as many children under age three as formal centers. Some provide excellent, nourishing care. Others provide merely babysitting with limited stimulation and encouragement of either developing minds or appropriate social behavior. Some even violate safety code provisions.[17]

Unfortunately, many child care arrangements in both home-based situations and child care centers not only do not provide the extensive services which may be needed by at risk children, but do not even provide the basic safety, educational and emotional support needed by all children. In fact one study reported that 40 percent of infant care centers and 10 percent of preschool centers provided such poor quality care that the children's development could be harmed.[18]

The same general principles and cost constraints apply to after-school care. The child/staffing ratio is important. The program dynamics changed and the academic and social learning opportunities at the Allied-Dunn's Marsh Neighborhood Center's drop-in after-school program dropped markedly when the number of children increased from fifteen to over twenty-five. Volunteers can help. Any extensive use of volunteers, however, requires funds for screening, including police checks, training, supervision and recognition.

The child "from three to six" refers not to the age of the child but to the period from approximately 3:00 P.M. when young children finish school and the 6:00 P.M. dinner time. This is the time when community space and the availability of adult supervision become crucial.

The teen from 3:00 to 6:00 also needs conscientious community attention since this is the time when most crime occurs and when teens are most likely to get into serious trouble. Since teenagers frequently drop out of formal activities and programs which had appealed to them as younger children, they often return to empty houses. Almost 80 percent of sexual assaults of juveniles occur in a home, often that of the victim or the offender. Most of the offenders are friends, family or acquaintances of their victim.[19] They know when a teen will be alone.

In Wisconsin, the average age of a sexual assault victim in one year was fifteen, that of the offender was twenty-five. Even statutory rapes still can result in physical and emotional harm. Although some assault cases are statutory rape between teenagers who are nearly the same age, they more typically occur between a young girl, average age fourteen, and a man five years older.[20]

Unfortunately, millions of children are left unsupervised after school. The need for supervised activity for older children and teenagers is compelling since most juvenile crime occurs between the time school ends and dinner time, a period when neighborhood adults may still be at their jobs or en route home. Indeed, one study found that while 13 percent of the police chiefs thought that hiring more officers to investigate juvenile crime would help, 69 percent of them listed increased child care and after-school programs as their top priority.[21] Research has shown that good after-school programs reduce delinquency, teenage pregnancy, drinking, smoking and drug use, and increase school performance.[22] Yet child care centers which offer after-school care for young children often will not accept children older than age ten or twelve.

Where the activities need to be located depends upon the situation. Schools often provide the best choice. One small-town school superintendent sponsored extensive programming at his high school, commenting that since the youth were already at school, keeping them there seemed like the most effective approach. He feared that once students left the school grounds, even if headed for a program at another location, they easily could become distracted on the way, stopping to chat with a friend in a gang or meeting a girlfriend and deciding to proceed home with her to an empty house.

Programs at schools, however, do not help children who ride a bus home. Although activities existed at the schools attended by the children in the Allied-Dunn's Marsh neighborhood, most of the children were not allowed to cross the major highway between the school and the neighborhood. Generally parents do not want their children walking home after dark. Crossing guards remain on duty only for a short time after school ends. Some children find a neighborhood activity a few blocks from home more convenient and comfortable than remaining at school, a setting in which many of them are not happy. A neighborhood-based program could accommodate the needs of all the children in a family, including older children who often must return to the neighborhood to care for their younger siblings.

Some now urge providing more programs at churches. Locating programs in churches, however, raises questions about whether they appropriately can serve children of all faiths, or no faith, or will serve only members of their own congregation or those whom they hope to recruit for it.

Role Models

Children need a variety of positive adult role models to provide them exposure to people of different ages, racial, religious, and ethnic backgrounds. They need to understand that people working in "menial occupations" are decent, good citizens performing jobs necessary for a community to function. They also need to be exposed to workers in a variety of professions and businesses.

Children's only knowledge of older persons now often comes from an occasional visit from a grandparent or from television ads which emphasize the ills of aging or, conversely, ignore its problems. Many children lack the opportunity to gain either the compassion they will need as adults to forge decent policy or the understanding needed to prepare themselves for their own aging or that of their parents. Opportunities for such contacts may diminish as retirees move to gated golfing communities with no young families. The question of how to treat older people will become increasingly more relevant as the baby boomers reach retirement, removing their contributions from the economy, and as medical progress increases the number of elderly individuals. On the other hand, the increase in retired people people can be an asset for communities as a source of volunteers.

In addition to their parents and relatives, children can find role models in neighbors, schoolteachers, owners and employees of local businesses, religious leaders, and adults leading after-school programs or activities such as choirs, art classes, or sports. In developing opportunities for children to experience positive adult relationships, communities need to pay special attention to teenagers whose need for adult guidance continues even though they often resist parental or school authority and drop out of activities which had appealed to them at earlier ages. All youth turn to their peers for guidance, but a positive adult relationship can help them steer away from destructive relationships and actions likely to lead to serious or permanent harm. Too often government and other funders focus primarily on programs for younger children.

A savvy school principal in the small town of River Rouge, Michigan, which shares a border with Detroit, commented that teenagers want to belong to a group of kids their own age. The many activities sponsored at that school provided students opportunities to bond with a small group without joining a gang and under the guidance of a "cool" adult. Between 3 and 6 P.M. some 200 of the 900 students stayed for band practice, athletics, and numerous other activities. Wandering the halls, I passed young men and women with shoulders thrown back walking from ROTC and young women in colorful shirts practicing dance routines in the hall. I waited for twenty minutes to talk with the teacher rehearsing a production of Shakespeare's *The Tempest* while he led the fifteen actors in a discussion about how best to handle disagreements among the players. Tough, but fair. Not all adults can continue to relate well to children once they reach middle school, which makes recruiting staff and volunteers difficult. As one teenage girl explained, "It has to be somebody that will hang in there with you, that won't quit even when you're being bad."

Most children manage to grow up to be reasonably happy, self-supporting, law-abiding adults regardless of the failings of their parents or the type of neighborhoods in which they live. Recent research has emphasized what some people call resiliency factors. That is, given a poor home environment, what factors help children thrive anyway? Involvement in such activities as choirs, athletic teams, or music lessons helps. The type of activity does not seem to matter or whether it is sponsored by a school, religious institution or other organization. Having a supportive relationship with an adult matters. This can be a parent, but can also be a teacher, coach, choir director, tutor or mentor.[23]

A number of researchers have explored the factors which appear to help one child survive adverse circumstances while another succumbs to them. An excellent resource is *Investing in Children, Youth, Families and Communities: Strengths-Based Research and Policy*. It summarizes the findings from a wide variety of studies. The authors analyzed factors which increase the likelihood of children having behavior problems and factors which reduced it. For example, for adolescents, having a parent with a mental health problem increases the changes of misbehavior by 128 percent. For teens with no countering strengths, having parent with mental or physical health problems increases the changes that they will misbehave more than twice as much than if they come from a poor, single parent household. This clearly has implications on where to put community resources.[24]

The study also found that positive involvement in school was the most important resiliency factor.[25] This shows the importance of creating mentoring programs and a variety of opportunities for children to feel successful in school, whether through sports, music, and art as well as academics. Unfortunately, both budget constraints and the need to concentrate on the subjects tested by the No Child Left Behind Act have frequently led school districts to cut the funding and time allocated to those very programs which might help children struggling academically with the self-confidence needed for achievement in their more standard academic courses. Involvement in clubs or other outside school activities also reduced problems, but to a lesser extent.[26] Others have stressed the importance of a relationship with at least one caring adult, often a relative but sometimes a teacher or recreational leader.[27]

Child Abuse

Child abuse begets child abuse. Children who have suffered abuse often grow up to become abusers. Abused women often abuse their children. An extraordinarily high percentage of prisoners have histories of physical or sexual abuse. According to some experts child abuse and neglect increase the likelihood of juvenile arrest by more than 50 percent and the chances of arrest when an adult by almost 40 percent. In Rock County, Wisconsin, more than 50 percent of the youth in the juvenile justice system or on probation had been seen in court previously because of abuse and neglect. The rates jumped to 80 percent for Milwaukee youth who had committed murder.[28]

The causes of physical, psychological and sexual child abuse are complex and varied. Children most often are abused by family members or friends of the family. Alcohol and drugs contribute, as does stress, such as that caused by balancing two jobs or home and work responsibilities. Alcohol also contributes to neglect. One visiting nurse in a low-income neighborhood commented that the major neighborhood problem was not the drug users hanging out on the corner, but the women isolated in their homes, quietly drinking and ignoring their toddlers.

Careful studies have shown the effectiveness of nurse home visits. In Elmira, New York, first-time pregnant teens who were unmarried or low income who received home visits from a nurse were less likely to abuse their children. Moreover, four years after the study began, they were 40 percent less likely to have become pregnant again and 84 percent more likely to be holding a job than the teens in the control group who did not receive the nurse's visits. Experts estimate that home visits reduce the rate of future delinquency and crime by 40 percent.[29]

Such assistance can even drastically reduce the rate of child abuse. One physician found that he could predict 80 percent of the future child abuse by new mothers before they left the hospital. With the proper home follow-up visits by trained home visitors, most of the abuse could be prevented.

The potential for child abuse increases when parents must leave their children with understaffed child care facilities with constant staff turn-over and inadequate supervision. I once had a respectable organization offer to establish a badly needed tutoring program at a neighborhood center. When I asked the man offering to help how they screened their volunteers, he responded defensively, "We're all professionals." The center lacked the funds needed for police checks, now more easily available on the Internet, nor could they afford sufficient staff to carefully supervise new volunteers. The offer was turned down. The staff was unwilling to place children in a one-to-one unsupervised relationship with an unknown adult especially since the children tended to trust adults they met in the center. Staff feared that some child might agree to meet his or her new "friend" outside the center.

Education

Children obviously need good schools. Currently Americans are debating almost every aspect of education. Issues include control of schools, class size and teaching methods, bilingual education, testing standards, the role of religion, school-community relations, innovation, racial and ethnic integration, funding, and treatment of those with disabilities. The range of attitudes is illustrated by the gap between those who sue to insure compliance with the Supreme Court decision forbidding school-sponsored prayers to those who advocate federal funding for religious schools or who home school their children to insure their religious training.

Four aspects of schools affect neighborhood children: the quality of the education, the extent to which the schools function as a part of the community, the help the schools provide for children with special learning or behavior problems and for children in trouble, and the school-to-work connections. Considerable debate exists today regarding the best practices. Around the country communities and educators are trying various approaches. Some models have proven track records over time. In her books, *Common Purpose* and *Within Our Reach*, Lisbeth Schorr provides examples of successful models and the ingredients needed for success.[30]

Although many proposals call for major changes in the administration and operation of schools, which may be difficult for a given community, some schools have achieved remarkable success even under very adverse circumstances. The key ingredients seem to be leadership, high expectations for the children, collaboration with other community service providers, and collaboration with parents and the community.

Since the school issues are complex, difficult, and controversial, neighborhoods must carefully consider how to best focus their time and resources. Should the focus be on recruiting volunteers for tutoring programs or tackling system-wide change? Is the crucial problem teenagers flunking math or first graders who need eyeglasses? What do the schools most want from the neighborhood and its parents? What programs have been tried and failed in your school district or nearby districts? Which schools provide successful models? Could your community duplicate them? Does it make sense for the neighborhood organization to be involved in a major way or to serve as a channel for information, letting individuals enlist as they wish?

What kinds of community efforts already exist? How can the neighborhood best partner with them? Does it make more sense to spend limited resources operating a neighborhood after-school program or to focus on insuring that all pregnant mothers receive appropriate prenatal care to improve the chances for healthy children and later educational success? Answering such questions will not only result in more effective action, but also may help avoid splitting the community with acrimonious debates when considering very difficult issues.

A thorough analysis of these issues lies beyond the scope of this book. Several key issues, however, can be mentioned. The quality of a neighborhood's schools affects neighborhood families in multiple ways. First, the reputation of the schools plays a major factor in the marketability of the neighborhood. The author's parents, and millions of others, moved when their eldest daughter reached school age to enroll her in a different school district. A large part of the abandonment of central cities by middle income people of all races and ethnic backgrounds has been flight from financially strapped school districts perceived as inferior.

Money does count. No wealthy school district would advocate improving their schools by cutting their budgets in half. Yet some poorer districts struggle to provide quality education on approximately half the resources of their more fortunate neighbors. One of Milwaukee's wealthier suburbs spends almost $14,000 annually on each of its students compared to the central city's expenditures of slightly less than $9,000.[31] Those numbers include the federal and state funds received by Milwaukee including those provided for the large numbers of Milwaukee children needing special education assistance.

Even greater per pupil discrepancies exist among the states. In one year average instruction expenditure per pupil in eight states, Alabama, Arizona, Louisiana, Mississippi, New Mexico, Oklahoma, Tennessee, and Utah, was less than half of the per pupil expenditure in Connecticut, New Jersey, and New York.[32] Although some differences can be attributed to different costs and the willingness of voters in different areas to pay higher taxes, generally the differences relate to the taxable income base of the school district, the formulas for distribution of state dollars, and to the personal income levels in the community.

Most funding for schools relies upon the local property tax. This not only creates discrepancies between rich areas and poor ones but also makes passing bond issues difficult by pitting retired people against young parents with children.

This is not merely a question of selfish people whose children have already been schooled feeling no obligation as citizens to contribute to the next generation. Most older persons own their homes but many have fixed incomes with limited cash flow. Since housing values have been accelerating in many areas, the retired person pays school taxes not based on their current income but on the value of a non-liquid asset. In some cases, older persons can no longer afford to remain in the homes they have lived in for thirty or forty years. Alternative taxing methods could be devised including basing school financing on a graduated income tax or capping tax payments on homes until the home is sold.

Although the federal influence has increased since passage of the No Child Left Behind Act, financing and control of schools primarily lies with states and local school districts. Local school boards, administrators and teachers control key aspects of school success. When asked for a wish list for improving the success of the nation's schools, one local assistant school district administrator thought, then provided the following: (1) "Skilled teachers who can develop a relationship with their children. That generally means lower class size." By skilled teachers she meant those who were not only prepared professionally in their subject matter and willing to continue learning but also teachers who understood childhood development and could work with parents; (2) All the children in the family in the same age bracket attend the same elementary, middle or high school; (3) The school environment is "safe, secure and a place where it's inviting to be there learning"; and (4) "A diverse place," if not naturally because of diversity in the neighborhood then from arranging boundaries in a manner which matches neighborhoods with different population characteristics.[33]

Paying for these basics, child care, schools, and programs which reduce the likelihood of child abuse, rests with government at local, state and national levels as well as the policies and wage structures of business. There are, however, many aspects of caring for children that are dependent upon what happens at a very local level.

Identifying Neighborhood Assets

Start with parents. Despite the time children spend in school, formal programs, and with peers, the most important asset for creating a nourishing community environment for children remains their parents. The American dream continues to be providing a better life for one's children. While many parents, including those in wealthy suburbs, do not parent well, almost all love their children and care about their futures.

Concern for children will motivate parents, grandparents and other adults to become involved in and support community improvement efforts. One community of 15,000 in the Midwest with a 38 percent poverty rate, one-third of the voters on Social Security, and less than 300 adults with a post high school education passed a multimillion dollar bond issue to build a beautiful high school. Why? One low-wage earner explained, "This is a community that cares about their children."

Parents often will modify their own behavior in order to provide an appropriate role model for their children. A woman recounted how she stopped using drugs after being taken to the hospital in front of her children. Another young mother, who had received permission from her probation officer to leave her house to attend a community meeting, declared that she wanted to learn to read because "they say that you should read to your children."

All communities have adults and teenagers who will pitch in to help with efforts to assist children. While conducting workshops with African American teenagers from a very low-income community, the author handed out a list of skills asking the youth to identify which ones they had and which they would like to learn. They had a number of specific skills: drawing, singing, reading music, working with a group, good body awareness, understanding consequences, being on time, discipline, being articulate, being responsible, and tenacity. Those teens who claimed a skill generally felt they could teach it to someone else.

Every community includes people who are known to be excellent parents. Grandparents, retired teachers, single people who want a relationship with a child—all can help. Businesses can be tapped for funds and volunteers, and can be mobilized to create a community atmosphere in which children feel welcome in local business establishments.

Sometimes people have the skills but little experience or desire to work with large groups of children, especially teenagers. They often, however, could act as mentors or teach short courses to a small group. At least one of the teenagers mentioned above wanted to learn almost everything on a seven-page skills list. The desired activities included fishing, gardening, drawing, learning simple car maintenance, a variety of sports, and skills such as "talking to someone over 60 and having it be fun for both of us." Eight of the fifteen wanted to learn rap music, ten wanted to learn to play the piano, six wanted to learn to sew. Almost any adult skilled in sewing could manage a few lessons for an interested small group of teens.

Although in some cases individual neighborhoods have little influence over many of the players, they can join with others in lobbying for change or voting for politicians who support programs which enhance parents' abilities to provide proper care and education for their children. Some specific ways to accomplish this are included in the *Community Action Guide* (see Author's Note, pp. xv-xvi).

Notes

1. Economic Policy Institute. (2004, June 23) *Economic snapshots. Social expenditures and child poverty—the U.S. is a noticeable outlier.* Retrieved January 6, 2007, from http://www.epinet.org/content.cfm/webfeatures_snapshots_06232004
2. Children's Defense Fund. (2002). *The state of children in America's union: A 2002 action guide to leave no child behind* (p.13).Washington, DC. Retrieved July 8, 2003, from www.childrensdefense.org.

3. Children's Defense Fund. (2001, December). *Facts and FAQs*. Retrieved June 7, 2002, from http//www.childrensdefense.org/cc_facts.htm.
4. Changing the Channels. (n.d.) *Major studies on television violence*. Retrieved January 12, 2007, from http://www.changingchannels.org/effects1b.htm.
5. Robinson, T.N., Wilde, M.L., Navacruz, L.C., Haydel, K.F., & Varady, A. (2001, January). Effects of Reducing Children's Television and Video Game Use on Aggressive Behavior. *Archives of Pediatrics and Adolescent Medicine* 155: 17-23. Putnam, R. D. (2000). *Bowling Alone: The collapse and revival of American community*. (p. 224). New York: Simon & Schuster.
6. Children's Defense Fund. (2005, April). *Child care basics*. Retrieved December 12, 2006, from http://www.childrensdefense.org/site/DocServer/child_care_basics_2005.pdf.
7. Wisconsin Council on Children and Families. (n.d.). *The facts about a baby's brain*. Madison, WI:. Author. Retrieved July 18, 2002, from http://www.wccf. org/projects/babysbrain.html. National Clearinghouse on Child Abuse and Neglect Information. (2001, October). *Understanding the effects of maltreatment on early brain development*. Retrieved May 10, 2002, from http://www.calib. com/nccanch/pubs/focus/earlybrain.cfm. Ratey, J. J. (2001). *A user's guide to the brain: Perception, attention, and the four theaters of the brain*. New York: Random House, Inc.
8. Ehrle, J., Adams, G., & Tout, K. (2001). *Who's caring for our youngest children? Child care patterns of infants and toddlers* (p. viii). [Occasional Paper No. 42]. Washington D.C.: The Urban Institute.
9. Boushey, H. (2003, May 6). *Who cares? The child care choices of working mothers*. Center for Economic Policy and Research, Data Brief No. 1. Retrieved February 16, 2005, from http://www.cepr.net/Data_Brief_Child_Care.htm. National Institute of Child Health and Human Development. (1998, July, 21). *SIDS rate drops as more babies are placed to sleep on their backs or sides*. News release NIH News Alert. Retrieved June 20, 2001, from wysiwyg://100/http://www.nichd.nih.gov/new/releases/Sidsrate.htm.
10. PaineWebber Investment Advisor (personal communication, 2000).
11. First Tuesdays at the Urban Institute. (2000, January 4). *Are there good jobs for low-skilled workers?* p.11. Transcripts of a luncheon roundtable. Washington, DC: The Urban Institute. Retrieved March 1, 2001, from http://www.urban.org/news/tuesdays/1-00/jan00_transcript.html.
12. First Tuesdays at the Urban Institute. (2000, January 4). *Are there good jobs for low-skilled workers?* (p.11). Transcripts of a luncheon roundtable. Washington, DC: The Urban Institute. Retrieved March 1, 2001, from http://www.urban.org/news/tuesdays/1-00/jan00_transcript.html.
13. Newman, S. A., Brazelton, T. B., Zigler, E., Sherman, L. W., Bratton, W., Sanders, J.,& Christeson, W. (2000). *America's child care crisis: A crime prevention tragedy*. Retrieved July 23, 2002, from http://fightcrime.org.
14. Children's Defense Fund. (2005, April). *Child care basics*. Retrieved December 12, 2006, from http://www.childrensdefense.org/site/DocServer/child_care_basics_2005.pdf.
15. Children's Defense Fund. (2005, April). *Child care basics*. Retrieved December 12, 2006, from http://www.childrensdefense.org/site/DocServer/child_care_basics_2005.pdf.
16. Ehrle, J., Adams, G., Tout, K. (2001). *Who's caring for our youngest children? Child care patterns of infants and toddlers* (p.12). Washington, DC: The Urban Institute.

17. Newman, S. A., Brazelton, T. B., Zigler, E., Sherman, L. W., Bratton, W., Sanders, J., & Christeson, W. (2000). *America's child care crisis: A crime prevention tragedy.* Retrieved July 23, 2002, from http://fightcrime.org.
18. Ibid., p. 10.
19. Wisconsin Coalition Against Sexual Assault. (2000). *Teen sexual assault and abuse.* Madison, WI.: Author. Retrieved February 16, 2005, from http://www.wcasa.org/resources/factsheets/teen.pdf
20. Wisconsin Coalition Against Sexual Assault. (2000). *Teen sexual assault and abuse.* Madison, WI: Author. Retrieved February 16, 2005, from http://www.wcasa.org/resources/factsheets/teen.pdf.
21. Newman, S. A., Fox, J. A., Flynn, E., & Christeson, W. (2000). *America's after-school choice: The prime time for juvenile crime, or youth enrichment and achievement.* Retrieved July 23, 2002, from http://fightcrime.org.
22. Turner, S. (1997.). *Building on strengths: Risk and resiliency in the family, school, and community.* In E. Norman. (Ed.). *Drug-Free youth: A compendium for prevention specialists* (pp. 189-201). New York: Garland Publishing, Inc.
23. Turner, S. (1997.). *Building on strengths: Risk and resiliency in the family, school, and community.* In E. Norman. (Ed.). *Drug-Free youth: A compendium for prevention specialists* (pp. 189-201). New York: Garland Publishing, Inc.
24. Sandler, I. N., Ayers, T. S., Suter, J. C., Schultz, A., & Twohey-Jacobs, J. Adversities, strengths, and public policy. In K. I. Maton., C. J. Schellenbach, B. J. Leadbetter, & A. L. Solarz. (Eds.). (2004). *Investing in children, youth, families, and communities: Strengths-based research and policy* (pp. 35-36). Washington, DC: American Psychological Association.
25. Sandler, I. N., Ayers, T. S., Suter, J. C., Schultz, A., & Twohey-Jacobs, J. Adversities, strengths, and public policy. In K. I. Maton., C. J. Schellenbach, B. J. Leadbetter, & A. L. Solarz. (Eds.). (2004). *Investing in children, youth, families, and communities: Strengths-based research and policy* (pp. 35-36). Washington, DC: American Psychological Association.
26. Sandler, I. N., Ayers, T. S., Suter, J. C., Schultz, A., & Twohey-Jacobs, J. Adversities, strengths, and public policy. In K. I. Maton., C. J. Schellenbach, B. J. Leadbetter, & A. L. Solarz. (Eds.). (2004). *Investing in children, youth, families, and communities: Strengths-based research and policy* (p. 36). Washington, DC: American Psychological Association.
27. Turner, S. (1997). *Building on strengths: Risk and resiliency in the family, school, and community.* In E. Norman. (Ed.). *Drug-Free Youth: A compendium for prevention specialist* (especially chapter 5, pp. 189-201). New York: Garland Publishing, Inc. Thornton, T. M., Craft, C. A., Dahlberg, L. L., Lynch, B. S., & Baer, K. (Eds.). (2000, September). *Best practices of youth violence prevention: A sourcebook for community action.* Atlanta, GA: Division of Violence Prevention, National Center for Injury Prevention and Control, & Centers for Disease Control and Prevention.
28. Atkinson. T. (2000, April 24). *Link between child welfare and the juvenile justice system.* Comments presented to the Dane County Democrats, Madison, WI.
29. Kallio, S. (1999, September 28). A case for support: Preventing child abuse is simple expert says--identify at-risk parents and give them a little help. *The Wisconsin State Journal,* pp 2A & 2C.
30. Schorr, L. B. (1997). *Common purpose: Strengthening families and neighborhoods to rebuild America* (chapter 8, Educating America's children, pp. 179-214). New York: Anchor Books. Schorr, L. B., & Schorr, D. (1979). *Within our reach: Breaking the cycle of disadvantage* (chapter 9, Schools, balance wheel of the social machinery, pp. 215-255). New York: Doubleday.

31. Wisconsin Department of Public Instruction. (2001). *Basic facts about Wisconsin's elementary and secondary schools 2000-2001.* Madison, WI: Wisconsin Department of Public Instruction.
32. Hussar, W., & Sonnenberg, W. (1999). *Trends in disparities in school district level expenditures per pupil.* Retrieved June 18, 2002, from http://nces.ed.gov/pubsearch/pubsinfo.asp?pubid=2000020.
33. Gulbrandsen, M., Chief of Staff, Madison Metropolitan School District (personal communication, April 2000).

14

What Can be Done?

Propositions

Recognize reality. If neighborhoods and local communities are to prosper and provide nourishing environments for families, certain issues must be tackled on a national basis. National alignment on four propositions could form the basis for realistic decisions about the commitment, institutional changes, and money needed to thrive. Implementing goals based on these propositions could form the basis for ensuring the American dream for all families.

Chapters 2, 3, and 4 detailed changes in the composition of the family, the community and our institutions which make it increasingly difficult for Americans to enjoy a middle-class life. The second part of the book showed how these changes affect families' ability to fulfill their basic responsibilities: earning an income, providing their members food, housing and health care, maintaining their home and rearing their children. We argue that while local community involvement of volunteers, religious institutions and nonprofit organizations is crucial for family and community well-being, families' ability to fulfill their six basic tasks also rests upon actions by government. Our inability to ensure continued prosperity and well-being for all is hampered by outmoded myths about family, community, and government discussed earlier.

Here I present four propositions which could form the basis for a more realistic approach to establishing a common national vision. I then present scenarios detailing the future if we fail to take action based on the values embodied in the propositions. Since our future depends upon actions of many players, we provide recommendations for actions needed from business, the nonprofit sector, local government, the states, the federal government, and the media, closing with a return to acknowledging the vital role of local community action. The chapters on income, food, housing, health, home maintenance, and children showed the important role of all of these players in supporting family and community life.

The section on the federal government includes desirable actions but also reminds the reader of the various crucial roles that only the federal government can fulfill. By including examples of successful federal actions, we remind the reader that many of the critiques of government currently in the media are based on instances where the government has a role but did not fulfill it well. This book argues that the lack of agreement about the role of government too often focuses our attention on whether the government should do something and detracts from exploring how to make sure it does it effectively and well. The concluding section of this chapter discusses how our lack of agreement on the propositions and the appropriate roles for various players undercuts our ability to implement our basic American values.

Proposition One: All workers deserve to be paid a living wage.

While people can debate the appropriate level for a "living wage," most people would probably agree that a full time worker should be able to support two or three people in reasonable comfort. That is, a worker with a spouse and one child could expect to live in a decent home or apartment with adequate food, medical care, the goods necessary to function in their community such as a telephone and a car, and a few luxuries such as a television set and Christmas presents for their children.

Proposition Two: If certain businesses cannot provide a living wage, the national government should increase the Earned Income Tax Credit sufficiently to provide a living wage to all workers.

There are other possible approaches to the problem of businesses that cannot or will not provide decent salaries, including raising the minimum wage to a living wage level or providing resources through various entitlement programs. A thorough exploration of which approach might be the most appropriate and most politically feasible lies beyond the scope of this book. The first step, however, is for the nation to recognize that in cases where a business provides a product or service without paying a living wage, the underpaid workers and their children are actually subsidizing the consumers' prices and the stockholders' dividends. This is hardly fair.

Proposition Three: Universal health care must be provided, with an emphasis on preventive care and coverage for prescription drugs, mental illness, and drug and alcohol treatment.

Health care is an investment in efficient workers and a fulfilling family life. The current situation saps the energy and resources of families. At present only the very wealthy and those working in a few large organizations can be sure of continued access to health services. Children do not receive dental care or eyeglasses. Teenagers lose their mothers to cancer because the family cannot afford the treatments and drugs. Grandparents cut the pills their doctor prescribed in half to save money. Although many people currently are satisfied with their health care arrangements, increasingly they are being forced to use the doctor or hospital dictated by their insurance plan. Some companies require new workers to pass health examinations to be included in the group plan, and retirees are shocked to discover that their former employers have cut or reduced their promised health care benefits.

Families increasingly will be faced with very painful financial takeoffs. Take the example of a married couple with a teenage daughter. Both parents work. The wife's father, living in another state, is about to be transferred from a hospital to a nursing home. He takes fifty pills a day. His health insurance will not fully cover the costs for his medicine once he leaves the hospital. Will the family pay this cost with the money now being put aside for their daughter's college tuition?

Other industrial countries spend far less on health care, leave health decisions in the hands of the medical profession and provide care for everyone. Their citizens generally report satisfaction with their care and live as long or longer than Americans. The argument against such approaches claims that those systems ration health care. They do. They ration according to seriousness of health condition. They ration resources in favor of prevention rather than expensive interventions in the last months of life. The American system also rations care. The care is rationed according to where you work, where you live, the health providers selected by your boss, and the decisions made by a clerk in the insurance company. In addition, your care depends upon your ability to pay for the basic insurance, the co-payments, and for care not covered such as treatment for mental illness or prescription drugs.

Proposition Four: Affordable quality child care for all workers invests in America's future.

Providing good child care, and especially quality preschool, may be the most cost effective investment society can make. Although the specific arrangements might be determined at the state and local level, a commitment of the entire society and a substantial allocation of resources will be needed. The majority of mothers work outside the home. In order to return to the Norman Rockwell idealized nuclear family with one wage earner, the minimum wage would need to be sixteen dollars an hour even if the couple had only one child. Therefore, most mothers will continue to work. Without their participation in the labor force the economy would collapse. Quality child care which enhances future school success and workforce capability must become not merely an individual family but a national priority.

Other propositions could be added to the list, but clear national acceptance of these four followed by a decision to achieve them would eliminate many of the difficulties families now face in providing for themselves and their loved ones. I called the statements propositions rather than goals deliberately. Goals are something you plan to achieve. A proposition is a statement of something you believe to be true, or, as in this case, a statement of values. If the nation agrees with the propositions, they can then create appropriate goals with milestones and actions. But this will not occur without clear agreement on the basic propositions, an agreement that does not now clearly exist. Most Americans probably actually do agree with the propositions but not at the conscious level that promotes serious national attention and debate about how to create appropriate and achievable goals.

The four propositions selected are crucial for American families and are achievable within a short time period, certainly less than the decade dedicated to putting a man on the moon. Many will cite philosophical or political objections, assuming that economic prosperity will resolve any problems, that the solutions are too expensive, or that the problems only exist because of individuals' moral failings. But the failure to seriously tackle the issues addressed by the four propositions amounts to a tacit agreement to accept the status quo and will lead to the following four scenarios.

Scenarios

Scenario One

The economy increasingly will rely upon workers who cannot support or ever expect to support a family. The gap between rich and poor will increase. The numbers of individuals, including parents, working several jobs will increase. The economy will continue to depend upon a continual stream of new immigrants, including millions of illegal ones.

Scenario Two

The government will not use tax funds to supplement low wages directly or through increased funding for government programs. Individuals lacking food, housing, or health care will need to turn to charity. Many find accepting charity demeaning, an unspoken acknowledgment that neither they nor the work they perform are valuable. This may ultimately affect their morale, self-esteem, and work ethic. They will place the same value on their work as that granted it by their employers and the larger society.

Scenario Three

In 2007, over 47 million Americans lacked health insurance. Those with full time jobs at certain large companies may continue to have excellent health care. Many companies, however, are cutting benefits to workers and those promised to retirees. The employer-based health care system using private insurance companies is failing both in controlling costs and as a means of providing health care for all Americans. Without universal health insurance, many will postpone both preventive care and necessary care.

Scenario Four

Millions of children will raise themselves or be placed in child care and after-school facilities that lack proper staff and safety provisions. Children will arrive at school unprepared to learn. School drop-outs, teenage crime, pregnancy, alcohol and drug abuse rates will rise.

The unwillingness to face the ugly truths represented by these alternative scenarios reflects the tendency of policymaking by myth. Given our faith in individualism and belief in the Horatio Alger myth, the nation has been unwilling to face the realities of the recent structural changes in the economy or family composition.

Facing the Realities

The economy currently depends upon the efforts of millions of workers not being paid a living wage. A large proportion of the job growth for the foreseeable future will be in occupations that do not pay a living wage for even one person, let alone a family. Of the twenty-eight occupations projected to account for 50 percent of the total job growth in the 2006 to 2016 period, the median wage of one-quarter of them will not support a family of four *even* at a poverty level.[1]

Who are these workers? They include the man stocking the shelves at your grocery store, the woman caring for your child at the day care center, the aide feeding your mother in the nursing home, and the woman helping your daughter select a prom dress. None of these individuals should ever expect to live well. Some individuals will manage to move up in their organizations, but few opportunities exist. Most of those opportunities require higher education or specialized training. Moreover, American society cannot function without millions of workers filling the jobs at the "bottom" of the job pyramid.

The weekly median wage paid by a number of types of high-growth jobs is less that the amount nationally needed to rent a two-bedroom apartment. This includes most service jobs and almost anyone working in technical, sales or administrative support jobs except for those in a few specialized areas such as insurance, real estate and high technology. The only occupational categories in which almost all the types of high-growth jobs pay higher wages are those for managers and professional specialists.[2]

Of the twenty-eight growth-producing occupations, the median wage in nineteen of them will not support a family of four at twice the poverty level, a self-sufficiency standard that would provide a very modest standard of living without government subsidies or private charity. Modest means food, housing, child care, transportation to work and for one shopping trip a week but no savings, no entertainment and no meals purchased outside the home.[3]

The options are: raise the minimum wage to a living wage level, provide workers in those industries supplemental income through an Earned Income

Tax Credit, or accept the fact that whoever works in those jobs must anticipate a life of poverty or, at least, constant financial struggle. This applies to workers married to someone doing a similar job.

If we assume that those jobs must be filled, can business afford to pay more? Business used to pay those workers more. Correcting for inflation, the minimum wage was over $7 an hour from 1961 through 1982. At its highest, it reached the equivalent of $9.50 an hour in 1968. For the past ten years it has been $5.15 an hour. Congress has just passed an increase raising the rate in three stages over the next two years. When the entire increase has been reached, a minimum wage worker will earn over two dollars less than a similar worker would have earned forty years ago despite the huge increases in productivity during that time period.[4]

It is not only minimum wage workers who have suffered a loss in wages due to shifts in business practices, the 50 percent decline in unionization since the early 1970s, and the failure of Congress to increase the minimum wage on a regular basis. Between 1947 and 1973 both real family median income and productivity both doubled. From 1973 to 2005 productivity continued to rise, but only one-third of the increased profits were shared with the majority of workers. Instead, the profits from increased productivity flowed to those who owned stock and to increased salaries and benefits for top management. Eighty percent of private sector wage earners work in production or nonsupervisory positions. Between 1973 and 2005 their hourly earnings corrected for inflation increased by exactly thirty-five cents an hour. [5]

In 2006, American workers were the most productive in the world, with $63,885 per year in value added per employee. By comparison, Ireland is the second most productive country. Each Irish worker adds $55,986 per year in value. Part of the difference in productivity results from the fact that Americans work longer hours than European workers. If productivity is measured on an hourly rather than annual basis, the United States falls slightly behind one other country, Norway. Yet U.S. worker productivity measured as value added per hour still amounted to $35.08, seven times the 2006 minimum wage.[6]

The result of raising wages to better compensate workers would be that some prices might rise, stockholders might receive fewer dividends, the price of some stocks would go down, and corporations would have less money to invest in building additional stores overseas or paying high salaries to their executives and board members. If wage increases are unfeasible, then Americans need to make a national decision about whether to subsidize those businesses that cannot pay their workers a living wage or to accept an increasing polarization among the haves and the have-nots and an increase in the numbers of children living in poverty. Is it fair for the woman at the grocery checkout counter to subsidize the ski lodge of the owner of the grocery store chain?

American families, especially women and children, suffer from the lack of universal health care. Because women more traditionally hold the lower paying jobs, work part-time, and change jobs more often, they have health benefits less often and more frequently lose them because of changes in their job situation.

The lack of universal health care not only affects health, it also distorts the job market. Tying the provision of basic health care to the employer encourages firms to locate in states that provide the least oversight of their operations, to subcontract work to firms that provide lower costs through not providing benefits, and to outsource jobs overseas. It discriminates against small businesses, the very businesses most likely to create new jobs. Individual small businesses do not have a large enough pool of employees to cover the risks of an individual with a health problem, nor can they bargain effectively with the insurance companies. One Madison, Wisconsin, small business owner confessed that he solved his problem of obtaining affordable health insurance by getting rid of the employee who was causing the problem. From an economic point of view, a business should only hire young, single workers and fire them when they marry and have children, develop a serious illness, or reach the age of fifty. Business should subcontract or outsource as many jobs as possible so that they will not have to provide health care benefits or contribute to Social Security for their workers.

Many people advocate leaving solutions to individual states. The problem with this, as well as geographically based health maintenance organizations, is that it interferes with Americans' need for mobility. Workers cannot move to another state without the risk of losing coverage, nor can a child move near an aging parent. Moreover, insurance companies can withdraw, or threaten to withdraw, from offering coverage if a state mandates such benefits as coverage for mental illness.

An emphasis on preventive care actually could drastically reduce many costs of health care. More important, it could reduce the family and societal costs of neglecting health care. This is most obvious in terms of prenatal care, immunizations and screening for problems such as lead poisoning among children. It also applies to the provision of mental health care and to alcohol and drug treatment coverage for both teenagers and adults. Millions of dollars now are spent providing prison space for adults who suffered from childhood abuse or neglect in a household with parents who had untreated mental health or alcohol problems. Improper use of alcohol potentially creates problems for society through its role in automobile accidents, the biggest cause of death for those under age 35, and through its contribution to wife and child abuse.

Making quality child care available to all parents means increasing wages and benefits to child care providers on an industry-wide basis, reducing turnover, expanding the numbers of facilities and types of options, and making training, technical assistance and health care benefits available to home-based centers. Costs will be high, but not as high as the prison costs for children who did not learn social skills or whose learning problems escaped notice and treatment.

Several results could occur if the price of services in hospitals, nursing homes and child care centers increased to cover the cost of paying a living wage. Families with higher incomes might have to do without some luxury vacations or buy smaller second homes in order to pay the real costs of caring for their loved ones. Moderate income families would need to budget much more carefully, cutting many consumer purchases. Those services now are being indirectly subsidized by the families of millions of low wage workers who hold the jobs necessary for the nation to operate smoothly. Is this fair?

Whose Entitlements?

The nation could subsidize low wages indirectly through increasing the Earned Income Tax Credit. People question the use of tax funds to provide "entitlements" to low-income workers. The debate about "entitlements" reflects the general suspicion about government spending discussed in chapter 3. It takes on a mythical character. It rests upon the belief that if the government gives a poor person money directly or through programs such as food stamps, this is giving away "our tax money" to an individual. On the other hand, allowing someone to pay less money in taxes through an itemized deduction of the mortgage interest on a vacation home is not considered a tax expenditure. Rather, it is perceived as a well-deserved break from burdensome taxes. The cost to the U.S. Treasury is the same.

The tax code currently provides a number of indirect subsidies to those with higher incomes or wealth gained from inheritance. A working couple with an income of $50,000 a year will pay $8,439 in income taxes on that income. If they didn't work, but instead received all their income from dividends and capital gains, their tax would be only $1,770. If their income was only $20,000, the working couple would pay $2,073 in taxes and the non-working couple would pay $270. (This is cleverly concealed in Form 1040, which is all most people see, with a reference to instructions that refer to a Qualified Dividends worksheet. It finally reveals, after some intricate calculations, how little tax you pay on qualified dividends. It turns out that qualified dividends are all dividends except those from Cuba, North Korea, or Iran.)[7]

Often, however, lower income people do not have the resources to use available tax benefits. The program for Medical Savings Accounts, for example, lets people put money into an account from which they can pay medical bills and deduct the expenses from their taxes. But the program is only available to those less than sixty-five years old who have health insurance. The amount that can be put aside is limited by the amount of their health insurance so that those with the most expensive insurance can obtain the largest tax benefits. Those fortunate enough to use the program might be able to achieve a substantial savings on their medical bills, ultimately paid for by the taxpayers, while a program providing the same amount of money directly for health benefits for low-income workers would be criticized as "creating another entitlement," or even "socialized medicine."

Programs providing funds to states and localities for subsidized child care programs are criticized as "entitlements," but increasing the child care tax deduction for those with higher incomes is heralded as "promoting family values." One is considered "helping families" and the other demeaned as "government spending for entitlements."

Such sleight of hand framing of the discussion adversely affects our willingness to seriously address the issues raised by the four propositions. For example, one in seven households, and almost one-half of those with household incomes less than $23,000, pay more than one-half of their income for housing. Yet in 2005 the 3.2 million taxpayers with incomes of $200,000 and above received $17 billion in tax benefits from buying homes and second homes while the entire budget for the U.S. Department of Housing and Urban Development's programs—including those benefiting over six and a half million lower income family and elderly households–was $31.3 billion. Many of those households paying half their income for housing would qualify for housing vouchers and other assistance but the HUD budget is insufficient to provide the benefits to all who qualify.[8]

For those who want to address the issues raised in this book, what can be done? Work to align the businesses, politicians, opinion-makers, voters, and institutions at every geographic level in voicing support for the values expressed in the propositions. Vote for legislators who will commit to making the needed policy changes and providing the funding needed. Hold the media accountable for accurate and in-depth reporting. Work for congressional, state, and local legislative action. Examine the practices where you work and the organizations to which you belong or support.

Recommendations for Key Players

Business

The chief contribution of business to strengthen American families would be to pay living wages to all employees, including those working part-time. The second contribution would be to structure work in a manner that provides workers predictable schedules but flexibility as needed to accommodate family responsibilities. This includes family leave for caring for sick children, attending parent-teacher conferences, and taking an elderly parent to the doctor. All employees should have the freedom to conduct necessary family contacts, such as checking in with a child after school, without fear of retaliation. A third business contribution would be to support universal health care and, until it is achieved, provide coverage themselves for all employees including those working part-time. The fourth contribution would be to provide on-site child care, referrals to other child care and elder care services, cafeterias and snack areas with healthy food choices, on-site exercise facilities, health education including drug and alcohol counseling, and stress management classes.

These business actions would help families afford adequate food and housing, learn about healthy choices, select nourishing food, exercise on their lunch hour, and care for their children and elderly parents more easily. These contributions are much more significant than business gifts to community projects or encouraging employees to volunteer for such projects.

Many businesses remain excellent community members. They consult with their neighbors, they contribute to community projects, and they encourage their employees to volunteer, in some cases providing paid leave. Responsible businesses pay conscientious attention to negative spillover effects of their operation on families, communities and neighborhoods. They install appropriate environmental equipment to control air and noise pollution from their operations and monitor the results. They follow safety procedures, provide ergonomic computer stations and encourage frequent stretch breaks. Businesses concerned about families consider the effects of the quality, variety and cost of services they offer.

When businesses must make financial decisions that adversely affect their workers, they can be responsible about helping their workers with the emotional and financial consequences. A friend of the author's returned to lunch one day at a high tech firm where she had worked successfully for years. The firm had decided to downsize and eliminate a number of positions, but gave the employees no advance notice. My friend, along with others, found her office locked and was given one-half hour to remove her personal belongings.

When businesses make decisions that may adversely affect a neighborhood, they need to consult with the neighborhood, or at least provide ample notification. Sometimes business decisions rest on inaccurate information about the profit possibilities in the area. Neighborhoods might be able to resolve problems with zoning officials or provide experts on resolving environmental issues. If nothing else, adequate advance notice provides the local residents the opportunity to address the problems that will be created by a vacant store, loss of jobs, or disappearance of the only place to buy food or cash a check.

Nonprofits

Nonprofits can use their credibility and contacts to help focus the nation on the values of honoring all families, all workers, every community and advocating for policies that foster long-term prosperity. They can continue to perform the excellent work they now undertake. National nonprofits have the funds to support research and information dissemination. They provide technical assistance and training to local groups concerned with their issues. With headquarters in Washington, D.C., and often in state capitals as well, they have the access and information to educate legislators about their concerns and to keep their own members informed about legislative or administrative actions. Most maintain up-to-date Web sites. They monitor both government and business. They can provide alternative views and flexible approaches.

Nonprofits also can educate their own members about the realities of American family life, the need for national solutions as well as local actions, the necessity of insuring that resources flow to all families and communities, and the need to eliminate racism. They can use the Internet to increase their understanding about areas that concern them, to bounce ideas off those conducting similar programs, and to locate the most effective models and practices. A number of national groups maintain excellent Web sites on a variety of issues affecting food, housing, jobs, health, and child development. Their data and examples of successful efforts can be used to set goals, eliminate questionable programs, and focus on those actions most likely to be successful.

Many nonprofit organizations and foundations conduct research and lobby on issues affecting neighborhoods and families at both the national and state levels. They also provide this data to the media and media pundits. Neighborhoods need to consider the sponsorship of the research and sources of the data to determine whether the organizations' and foundations' proposals really enhance the ability of families to support themselves and their children. Is the research objective or merely a basis for advocating facile solutions based on the myths discussed in chapters 2, 3, and 4 about the nature of the American family and community today and the operation of major national institutions? For example, some trade organizations exist primarily to serve business. The scientific validity of their research may be questionable since the research is designed to counter efforts by government to control adverse effects of their business operations. Other organizations conduct research designed to promote a particular political stance.

Nonprofits can distinguish between the effort needed to resolve an issue and actions that, while extremely desirable, only relieve immediate suffering, often for a few individuals or a selected group. They can consider whether the subtle, often unconscious, distinctions between "the deserving poor" and "the undeserving poor" remain valid in today's economy. Those families who lost income because of September 11 were treated as "deserving." A man who lost his job in the economic downturn that followed is "undeserving" because "there are lots of jobs out there." A woman who is homeless because she cannot find an apartment she can afford with the income from her minimum-wage job in a nursing home is "undeserving" because she should have gotten a better job. Making such, often unconscious, distinctions between "deserving" and "undeserving" poor contributes to the impression that the correction for low wages and lack of appropriate services is charity, and ignores the extensive changes in structural conditions needed to eliminate the widespread poverty totally unrelated to the quality of individuals' work, spending habits, or character.

Nonprofits could take leadership in changing the national dialogue and in pressing for effective national policies by government and business that acknowledge the contribution of all American workers. Those who believe that the problem of poverty would be solved if people would just get a job and work hard should read Barbara Ehrenreich's *Nickel and Dimed: On (Not) Getting By in America*, which describes her experiences working as a waitress, hotel maid, house cleaner, and Wal-Mart salesperson.[9] Her more recent book, *Bait and Switch: The (Futile) Pursuit of the American Dream*, points out that even those with college degrees, marketable skills, and work experience are now vulnerable to being laid off and can find themselves unable to obtain another well-paid job.[10]

Local Government

Local government actions remain crucial for every aspect of community and neighborhood life affecting families. County and municipal economic development efforts create jobs. Zoning boards affect opportunities for home-based business, environmental protection for neighborhoods, the cost of land for development and hence housing, the location of group homes and apartments. Local government officials inspect the safety of restaurants and send public health nurses to neighborhood community centers. Local governments in this country control the resources available to schools and a variety of social programs. The list could continue for pages.

How much local governments can support their families depends upon the tax base of individual governmental entities, the extent to which inequalities of the tax base are alleviated through state or federal subsidies or program funds, and the relationships between local governments and neighboring communities. It also depends upon (a) the extent of cooperation and optimism within the community; (b) the amount of racial or ethnic tension or other group animosities; c) the extent to which community leaders choose to address neighborhood concerns and support neighborhood-based efforts; (d) the extent to which the community can create shared visions; (e) the extent to which leaders can mobilize resources, individuals and organizations to implement those visions; and (f) the extent to which the community has effective procedures and practices for settling differences.

The relationships among local government entities affect families in direct and indirect ways. Many of the measures needed to create decent settings for family life require regional cooperation and, in most cases, regional funding. Watersheds cross political boundaries; good public transportation requires a regional approach. Residents and nonresidents use parks.

The indirect connections among various geographic localities are more subtle. Many Americans have negative opinions of cities, often based on inaccurate media presentations. This makes them less willing to enter into regional approaches for addressing problems and less supportive of regional, state, or national government funding for city programs. In the long run, however, these attitudes become counterproductive. People fleeing unattractive cities produce suburban sprawl, often creating the very traffic jams and lack of open space they fled to avoid. Social problems in cities may receive more publicity and be more concentrated than those elsewhere, but are not unique and cannot be contained. Drug dealers and gangs move from their central cities bases into nearby small towns. The warning signs about the increasing gun violence by teenagers were apparent well before several white students made national news when they shot classmates at Columbine High School in suburban Littleton, Colorado. But the problem of teenagers shooting each other had received little national attention as long as it seemed confined to minorities in central cities.

Suburban areas cannot thrive with unhealthy city cores. Vibrant cities provide more than places for the occasional museum experience. The economic prosperity of suburban areas is tied to that of the adjacent cities. In some cases suburbs have recognized their interest in cities and are forging creative partnerships.

Despite the recommendations of planners and academics in favor of regional planning, the parochial interests of political leaders counter such approaches, especially metropolitan governments. Some areas, including Portland, Oregon, and Atlanta, Georgia, have been successful in addressing concerns on an area wide basis. Any regional approach, however, needs to be structured in a manner that does not disenfranchise specific racial or ethnic groups or inner-city residents.

States

What can states do? States regulate, tax, operate a wide variety of programs, fund studies and services, and create visions. Cities, counties, towns and townships exist only under guidelines established by states. States determine under what conditions these entities can expand their boundaries, tax their residents and deliver their services. States administer the justice system, controlling certain aspects directly, and others indirectly through such actions as establishing standards for admission of lawyers to the bar. States determine location and maintenance of major highways and large parks. They operate universities. They license and set continuing education requirements for numerous occupations from barbers to school teachers. They implement and allocate the funds for many of the federal programs.

Through the tax system, states determine who pays for state services: businesses, workers, people who inherit money, people whose income comes primarily from investments, employed individuals, property owners, or people who buy consumer goods. States allocate funds to local governments directly and through program funds. The distribution formulas and the structure and operation of the programs determine who benefits and who pays. States can play a major role in redistributing income. They can establish state minimum wages, adopt a state Earned Income Credit Tax program, and provide statewide health care programs for those who lack insurance. They can insure that all children in the state have access to food, shelter and decent schools. They can lobby the national government for needed changes in program funding or operation. They can encourage or impede regional approaches. Governors can use the bully pulpit to counter racism and promote living wages.

The Federal Government

The national government remains the bastion of the principle of one America. The U.S. Supreme Court decides questions of equal rights to justice, to education, to voting privileges and determines many of the rules governing business operation. Control of the issues of most concern to American families rests with Congress. Congress passes laws shifting funds from one locality to another, from one purpose to another. Will tax dollars go to build more highways or for mass transportation? Will oil companies receive large subsidies? Will the elderly receive Medicare coverage for prescription drugs? Will the minimum wage provide a living wage for all employed persons? Will people who cannot afford housing on the private market have decent alternatives? Will the needy receive food stamps to close the gap between their income and money necessary for food?

Although the issue may appear to be money, the key lacking ingredient is political will. The lack of political will results partly from the myths discussed in earlier chapters. If government programs are labeled bad and the private market is labeled good, it becomes politically difficult to purchase collective goods or to provide basic necessities to people whose incomes are too low to afford them. Thus, a government attempt to provide health care for all Americans is considered by many to be an interference with the private market despite the fact that the private market will not provide affordable coverage for everyone. Indeed, to protect their profit margins, companies often refuse coverage to individuals likely to need extensive treatment and refuse coverage for certain medical problems. This may increase the dividends to insurance company stock holders, but does not resolve the national health care problem.

America is the only major industrial nation that does not feed its children. The United States trails other industrial nations in providing universal health care, parental leave and attention to the welfare of young mothers and their children. Its infant mortality rate ranks among those of much poorer nations. Many European nations automatically provide home visits by nurses or other experts to assist new parents, a service that drastically reduces child abuse. Some continue visits for several years to insure that mothers are knowledgeable about basic health and nutrition care, to answer new mothers' questions, to provide them moral support, and to spot potential problems, such as an alcoholic parent or a child's learning disabilities.

In the interest of insuring that all American families enjoy at least a modest standard of living, the federal government could redistribute income from areas with wealthy residents or tax bases to those less fortunate. It could clarify the real cost of tax write-offs, which often shift the burden to those least able to pay.

To counter the anti-government sentiments calling for a limited government role in public affairs, the federal government needs to claim credit for its successes. The decline in deaths from smoking and Sudden Infant Death Syndrome both resulted from action by federal government agencies. Government research created the technology that made the Internet possible. Social Security reduced the poverty level of older persons by one-half. The national parks and the Smithsonian represent investments by the federal government. Hundreds of small towns enjoy live theater and traveling art exhibits because of federal funding. The list could continue, but rarely do people think about the benefits they enjoy from government investments.

Federal funding for social goals matters. The funding prevents millions of retirees and working families from falling into poverty or experiencing hunger. Federal funding often has provided the catalyst for innovative local efforts. Funding provided to national nonprofits enables them to collect and disseminate information about positive successful programs and provide training and technical assistance to their members. Millions of dollars, grassroots creativity, and volunteer effort have already been spent devising successful programs and approaches that can be tailored to other communities. Reinventing the wheel takes time and energy that might better be devoted to implementing proven successful programs.

The federal government also should claim credit for the major role it plays in establishing and maintaining the framework in which businesses and individuals can make fortunes. It manages monetary and fiscal policy and maintains the legal system that supports predictable operations. Modern businesses cannot thrive in countries lacking such supports. Although it often is said that the market controls the economy, governments establish the rules which enable the market to function. Without government, corporations could not be founded nor could contracts be enforced.

Unless we recognize the positive benefits of government programs and its important role in balancing the needs of the public with the needs of the private sector, the role of the government in supporting families and communities may not be fully recognized or supported. The decline in wages for millions of Americans over the last thirty years has at least partly been a result of changes in the laws governing labor unions and the monitoring of business/labor relationships. It also has been influenced by the changes in immigration laws increasing the supply of low-wage workers as well as trade agreements increasing the influx of goods produced by countries with low wages and lower standards of safety and environment control. Congress could change the laws governing the minimum wage to adjust automatically for inflation, or expand the Earned

Income Tax Credit program. The government could hold business responsible for contributing back by operating in a manner that supports all Americans, not merely a privileged few.

Attitudes also affect how the government plays one of its major roles, monitoring business, state and local government activities. Monitors rarely win popularity contests, yet the role is crucial. Over the last decades the trend has been to deregulate business, lessen protections for labor unions and permit greater consolidation of business. A shift occurred at the end of the twentieth century transferring more responsibility and funds from the federal level to the states. While there are certain advantages to this approach, it increases the ability of special interests to influence laws and regulations.

This shift of power to state and local levels is reflected by the extent of money flowing into states from national firms and organizations to influence state judicial elections. In Wisconsin, for example, advocates of school choice who mostly lived in other states provided last-minute funds to Jon Wilcox who was running for reelection to the Wisconsin Supreme Court. The court was expected to rule on the legality of providing vouchers to private religious schools. Judge Wilcox, who had been behind in the polls, was reelected, and later voted in favor of using millions of Wisconsin taxpayers' dollars for religious schools. In addition to involving out-of-state residents in determining policies for Wisconsin's schools, the fund-raising effort actually violated Wisconsin's laws regarding campaign donation limits. The Elections Board later levied the largest fine in its history against the campaign and the fund-raising organizers, $60,000. Judge Wilcox paid $10,000 on behalf of his campaign, but he did not recuse himself from deciding such issues.[11]

In the second half of 2002, the United States Chamber of Commerce spent $11.3 million on lobbying and related activities that included endorsing hundreds of candidates, placing one million telephone calls and posting two million pieces of mail. The Chamber's Institute for Legal Reform spent $17.3 million. Seventeen of the 18 candidates they supported for state supreme court justices or attorney generals won.[12]

The philosophy of state judges matters to all Americans. Candidates actively supported by the U.S. Chamber of Commerce are likely to reflect business interests even when they come into conflict with other public interests. Businesses generally have fought environmental laws, objected to workers' safety regulations, minimum wages and requirements for large businesses to grant unpaid leave for those caring for a newborn or a dying parent. They seek to avoid legal responsibility for defective products that harm Americans.

Although many businesses do operate with both profit and the public interest in mind, others routinely take actions to maximize profits despite potential damage to people or the community. For example, most television commercials aimed at young children encourage them to eat and drink products which ultimately will harm their health. If the companies did not believe that they were influencing the children, they would not spend millions of dollars on the ads.

Only action by the federal government resulted in reducing the content of lead in gasoline and paint. Lead poisoning leads to severe mental, physical and emotional health problems, and is especially harmful to the proper development of young children. In fact, one study traced a marked reduction in crime during the 1990s to the fact that the children who reached the ages most likely to commit crime had grown up after the most prevalent sources of exposure to lead had been eliminated. [13] Currently, however, businesses are importing toys for young children from China which in some cases have exceeded American standards for lead safety.

Letting the private sector operate without government oversight can have detrimental results on families. The lack of government oversight can be due to inadequate legal authority or insufficient staff. The nation must decide to what extent it can depend upon industry self-regulation and voluntary action for insuring product and food safety.

The recent problems in the mortgage market have indirectly hurt many people who were not irresponsible but now find that they cannot sell or refinance their homes or that banks will no longer provide mortgages in their entire neighborhood. The problem began with difficulties in the subprime mortgage market, a sector of the private financial market not regulated by the government. Banks must follow certain guidelines when lending, but the unregulated market could encourage people to take out loans even if they would not be able to meet their payments when the predictable rise in their adjustable rates occurred along with a downturn in housing prices. The resulting foreclosures cost many of those buyers their homes and quickly spread to other parts of the mortgage and financial markets. Many innocent Americans will be adversely affected.

The view that limited government is best also reduces our ability to carefully consider threats to our security that are unrelated to foreign terrorists. Lack of investment in our physical infrastructure led to deaths from flooding in New Orleans and a bridge collapsing in Minnesota. Lack of investment in alcohol and drug treatment creates spouse and child abuse in our homes and deaths on our highway. Between 9/11 and the end of 2006, in Wisconsin alone alcohol-related accidents killed 1,695 people, or over half as many as died on 9/11.

Considerable discussion has occurred about the potential terrorist threat from foreigners entering the country. But little attention has been given to the fact that 650,000 prisoners are released from state prisons each year. Most of them will not have had job training, educational opportunities or treatment needed for drug, alcohol, or mental illness problems. Generally they will not receive help through re-entry programs, and a third will not even be under supervision of parole officers. Prisoners also return to our communities from federal prisons, and nine million people are released from jails each year. With limited education and job opportunities, these individuals represent a vast pool of individuals potentially disaffected from American society and available for recruitment into drug and other illegal activities. [14] The increase in mandatory sentences for drug offenses along with a decrease in rehabilitation programs resulted from federal and state legislative decisions. The results represent a situation in which our attitudes may have detracted from making the best cost/ benefit decisions for society.

The Media

The ability of the public to make good decisions rests partly upon the ability to obtain accurate information. Since radio and television operate over airwaves owned by the public, the government sets the rules for their operation. In recent years, the government has permitted greater consolidation of the media, with a few large private companies owning television networks, radio channels, and newspapers. Since most Americans obtain their information about events which influence their lives from television, the accuracy and extent of coverage matter.

Debate has been occurring about the quality of news coverage. Critics complain that the need to make profits for stockholders leads to programming, including news reports, aimed at entertaining rather than informing. The resources devoted to investigative journalism have been reduced along with those devoted to covering local community issues. If the trend continues, Americans may find that the only news that is available is that provided by one or two corporations to reflect their business interests and enhance value to their stockholders. The news from local television and radio stations and newspapers may be produced nationally and fail to discuss local community issues at all or report them only from the viewpoint of benefit to the national corporation. Only an informed electorate can make sensible decisions, yet an independent media is one of the bulwarks of a democratic society and especially important in encouraging local community action.

What can a responsible media do? First, it can acknowledge that it plays a role in setting societal trends, that what it portrays affects attitudes and actions. Increasingly the news reporting consists of novel events designed to entertain but ignores in-depth information Americans need to make informed decisions about their lives, especially about political and policy choices. Second, the media can provide more in-depth coverage through investigative reporting, ask more informed and harder questions and demand accountability during interviews. When politicians, business leaders or others distort their records, the media itself could correct the record.

The media could check the facts behind the statements of politicians, explain the meaning of the terms used and the implications of the details of the policies. For example, in January 2007, during the debate about the increase of the minimum wage and the proposal to couple that increase with tax breaks to small businesses, I listened in vain for an explanation of the definition of small business. In most federal programs it refers to businesses with up to 500 employees, hardly the mom and pop store conveyed by the discussion. In addition, a quick reading of the proposed legislation showed that the definition of "at risk youth" for which tax credits would be granted would be changed to include all new hires between ages eighteen and forty. While interpreting the exact implications of proposed legislation may require both time and expertise not available to many in the media, some facts extremely readily available were not reported nor were incorrect or misleading statements by politicians or commentators challenged. To take another example, minimum wage jobs were frequently referred to as entry level positions useful to provide job training to teenagers, implying that the jobs would help prepare them to move up the employment ladder. In fact, as discussed in chapter 8, most minimum wage jobs are held by adults, and their possibilities for advancement are extremely limited.

The media could also be careful when reporting and interpreting statistics. For example, the rate at which African Americans use illicit drugs is slightly higher than the rate for whites. But because whites are a higher proportion of the population, the number of whites using illicit drugs, *including crack*, is greater. As discussed in chapter 6 and recently noted by Supreme Court, the greater number of blacks in prison for drugs has more to do with the way the criminal justice system works than with the extent of drug use by blacks.

Listening to the media, one would hardly have realized that both teenage pregnancy and crime declined during the 1990s and continued to do so in the twenty-first century although the crime rate began to rise in 2005.[15] Depending upon the media reports, one would believe that all Americans are heavily invested in the stock market, that most travel frequently by airplane and all would benefit from tax cuts designed to provide most of the benefits to the wealthy. In his book, *Democracy and the News*, Herbert Gans points out that reporting on economic news generally is confined to analysis of the stock market or current scandals. It ignores the underlying issues regarding the structural changes in the workforce and work place concerns such as safety conditions and the declining wages for large sectors of employees.[16] The media focus on soccer moms and single, young professionals ignores the realities of life faced by most families. The majority of them do not enjoy high-paying jobs or an upper-middle-class lifestyle. The factual information is readily available, but rarely added to the media reports.

The media could focus on long term problems and issues with widespread consequences rather than repeating endless details about this week's "hot story" or "flavor of the week." An airplane crash killing 200 people merits extensive coverage followed by weeks of analysis of the causes. But even frequent flyers face far more risk of death during their regular automobile travel. The fact that three or four women a day die from domestic abuse will not merit coverage since the incidents are scattered across the country and considered a part of normal life.[17]

The media can stop ignoring issues perceived to affect only minorities and inner cities. The anniversaries of Columbine see a rehash of the events, yet ignore the deaths of far more children shot during the previous year in their own homes and neighborhoods by relatives, friends, and acquaintances. On most days eight American children die from gun violence, either murder or suicide.[18] What would be the effect on the nation if the evening news each night reported how many children had been shot to death that day?

The media could shift from facile analysis of problems to in-depth discussions, acknowledgment of positive actions and results, consideration of the cost-benefit analyses of programs and societal costs of ignoring important problems. Although some television does provide more adequate coverage, too frequently the media coverage consists of reporting on political opponents or pundits exchanging critiques and blame.

Many newspapers do carry reports of research on matters that concern families, although usually buried on inside pages. For example, a small item on an inside page of the author's local paper noted a study claiming that one in three teenagers believe it is safe to try methamphetamine and one-quarter of them believe it provides benefits.[19] The problems connected with methamphetamine have not received major media emphasis even though by 2005 treatment for medical problems caused by the drug accounted for an increasing number of emergency room visits, in some hospitals as high as 20 percent of their patients.[20]

Sometimes even when the story is accurate, the headline conveys a distorted interpretation. Photographs often reinforce negative stereotypes.

Local newspapers and radio stations can be more responsible about coverage. They can report positive news about the community. They can avoid using code words, like Welfare Mom or Deadbeat Dad, adding gratuitous negative innuendos or misleading headlines. For example, a story in a Madison newspaper stated that a robbery had occurred in the Nakoma Plaza shopping center, "near the troubled neighborhood of Allied Drive." In fact, the robbery had not occurred in the neighborhood, the robber did not live in the neighborhood, and Allied Drive referred to only one street within a larger area with many attractive homes often referred to as the Allied-Dunn's Marsh Neighborhood.

The rise of large media corporations has increased these problems. Control of the airways and cable networks, the relationship between reporting and commentary, the extent of independent investigative reporting all affect the ability of the nation to obtain the information it needs to make realistic decisions. A conference on media reform noted that the public outcry against further media consolidation resulted partly from people's concern about losing local coverage of community events. To make informed decisions about their lives and especially about political and policy choices, Americans need more than sound bites.

Yet the media can play a positive role in promoting change. The facts about the increasing obesity of both adults and children and the serious health implications have been known for at least ten years but until recently were largely ignored by schools, food companies and restaurants. Now, widespread media publicity is resulting in some changes.

An article describing the positive effects of a Seattle effort to reduce unnecessary hospital deaths by improving emergency service cited Atlanta as a negative example. Atlanta officials took action. Four years later, Atlanta had improved its emergency response and service system fivefold. Among a number of other actions, Mayor Shirley Franklin ordered all 8,000 city employees to be trained in CPR. Similar concentrated efforts in our major cities might save as many as 1,000 lives a year. [21]

The Internet will play an increasingly important role in information dissemination; note the increase of blogs and their contribution to the national dialogue. Access to the Internet provides individuals and organizations an opportunity to present their views and data to a wide audience. Whether this situation continues depends upon federal and state lawmakers and how access is provided and financed.

Local Communities and Neighborhoods

For each of the six tasks that individuals and families must accomplish–earning an income, providing food, housing, and health care for their members, maintaining the home and rearing their children—local efforts matter. If communities and local organizations function well, their families can flourish more easily.

To a much larger extent than most people realize, neighborhoods can and do create themselves. The way neighbors treat each other, their own property, and their area's streets affects the immediate atmosphere and the long term prospects for the area. The relations they establish with police, other service providers and local business matter.

Neighborhoods can re-create themselves. Many neighborhoods and communities have decided to solve problems, create a better atmosphere for their children, and improve the upkeep of their area. Often they succeed. Numerous examples will be found in the *Community Action Guide* (see Author's Note, pp. xv-xvi).

To recapitulate: communities need to provide a safe and attractive physical space, a nourishing social environment for a range of different types of relationships, a variety of stores and institutions, economic strength and political clout. Local organizational strength and positive neighborhood relationships can be developed through actions as simple as sponsoring an annual Fourth of July parade or as sophisticated as operating a complex multi-million dollar Community Development Corporation. Neighborhoods can sponsor community centers, parks, or other places where people can gather informally. They can promote individual actions, organize programs, lobby for desired policies and programs, and monitor actions of the institutions and governments affecting their area. Although not sufficient to address the issues raised by this book, local efforts remain absolutely crucial.

Honoring American Values, Families, and Community

In terms of valuing American families and communities, who owes what to whom? Our answers can be distorted by the myths about the realities of family structure, the economy and our institutions discussed in earlier chapters. Currently our approach seems to be "winner take all." That is, those who have managed to achieve high incomes whether through their own efforts or inheriting money are entitled to spend their wealth as they wish. Taxes are discussed in terms of taking away "your money." Many European countries consider high taxes to be the cost of living in a society where children do not suffer hunger and everyone has preventive health care. The attitude that businesses and those with higher incomes should not be required to pay higher taxes ignores the reality that in most cases they could not have achieved those high incomes or their business profitability without the support of government-financed infrastructure. It also assumes that their success owes nothing to the daily toil of the less well-paid workers in their own industry or the businesses that supply it goods and services. The developers of suburbs relied upon the federally financed highways, the pharmaceutical industry relies upon having an educated workforce and basic research conducted by the universities, the entrepreneur relies upon the federal government to protect the patent for his invention and the courts to uphold it. The basic research necessary for the Internet was financed by the federal government. Hospitals cannot function without nurses' aides.

This leads us back to the discussion of "the deserving poor" and "the undeserving poor." As long as our myths allow us to believe that if people are financially stressed it is their own fault, we cannot take steps to address issues that actually threaten our families and the American dream.

The analysis of the twenty-eight high-growth jobs in chapter 8 was undertaken partly to point out the nature of the lowly paid jobs of the future and give people a realistic picture of who the disadvantaged may be. Unfortunately, the picture drawn in that chapter was too optimistic. Between 2006 and 2016, 174 occupations were projected to either be static or declining. Many of these are currently low-wage occupatipns, but twenty-four ofthe 174, representing about 120,000 (6.7 percent) of the 1.77 million lost jobs, have a median wage that would support four or more people at a self-sufficiency standard, assumed to be twice the poverty level. These 200,000 jobs may be lost, and many of the newer jobs will not pay equivalent wages. Of the 570 growing occupations expected to employ slightly over 20 million people, some 60 percent, providing jobs for 12 million workers, have median wages below that necessary to support a four-person family at a self-sufficiency standard. That standard would provide a modest standard of living with no savings and no meals purchased outside the home. The income calculation, however, assume that the worker can work a forty hour week with no lay offs.

Unfortunately, many jobs now provide either inadequate hours or short-term unemployment due to seasonal layoffs or dips in the economy.

Thus, the financial problems faced by millions are not due to their own inability or unwillingness to work hard. Millions of people who follow the rules of society still end up with serious financial difficulties through no fault of their own. Many more find they must turn to government programs than is generally realized. Indeed, Mark Rank calculates that by age sixty-five some 40 percent of Americans will have used a cash welfare program, and over two-thirds will have used one of the major in-kind programs such as food stamps, Medicaid, or housing assistance. Most people do not use the programs for long periods, but rely upon them for a short-term crisis caused by such circumstances as economic downfall with its resulting job losses, changes in family circumstances due to death or divorce, or health problems. [22]

Despite the fact that millions of hard-working Americans use these programs, politicians regularly complain about "entitlements," implying that the programs to help people cope with misfortune encourage irresponsibility. Perhaps because of the programs' negative connotations, none have ever been funded sufficiently to serve the entire population that would be legitimately eligible to receive the benefits.

We do not, however, consider tax benefits to be "entitlements." Thus, those who are better off can receive tax refunds for buying a house, putting money into a special account to finance their health care or a grandchild's college education, or buying a ticket to an expensive gala event raising money for the opera. All are costs to the taxpayer. None is considered an "entitlement." The problem with this approach is not only that it violates the concept of equality, but also that it prevents the nation from making a realistic assessment about long-term investments in our future. Our business executives make decisions based on quarterly stock market prices and our legislators on the basis of the next election. Oddly enough, those who have most investment in making realistic long-term national decisions may be the much maligned civil servants. The tenure of a politically appointee serving in a high position in the federal bureaucracy is probably two to four years. Thus, he has no personal advantage for any action that will not pay off in clear accomplishment or prestige within that time frame. But the career civil servant often has not only a dedication to his career but also an institutional memory about which programs worked and which failed.

What would the difference be if we took a long-term view? How many lives would have been saved and what would America look like today if we had invested in mass transit lines running to the areas that were to be developed as suburbs? Finland did just that. What would be the condition of our highways and the annual motor vehicle fatality statistics if we had invested in more efficient railway service? Japan did. If we believe that families should be completely self-reliant, we will not spend money even on programs that have a proven track record of success or those that offer a large potential return on investment.

I know how to significantly cut the school drop-out rate, teenage pregnancies, and youth crime. It would take approximately ten to fifteen years. Investing in high-quality preschool programs has an extremely high rate of return both for the individuals and the society. Participation in high-quality child care programs significantly increases a child's changes for success in school and reduces the likelihood of dysfunctional behavior. The cost for several years of high-quality preschool for an "at risk" child will be considerably less than the cost of prison for that same child ten to fifteen years later. [23]

One analysis projected that a targeted voluntary high quality preschool program only for the three and four year olds in the bottom one-quarter of the income distribution would require an initial investment but by the sixth year of operation would pay for itself in savings to the government. By year 2050 the savings due to reduced government costs, increased earnings of the individuals and decreased crime would be $315 billion annually. A program covering all three and four year olds would begin paying for itself by year nine and be saving the nation $779 billion annually by year 2050.[24]

Child care is only one of the programs that would provide a long-term investment pay off. Doing a cost-benefit analysis for specific programs is beyond the scope of this book, but the data is readily available. Every dollar spent on WIC (the federal program for the care of women, infants, and children) saves three dollars in hospital costs within the first year of the child's life. The lifetime medical costs of a severely underweight or premature infant are $500,000. Yet WIC is not fully funded. It would cost $28 billion to remove the lead from children's homes. How much more will it cost to educate the children suffering from a variety of mental health problems and learning difficulties due to lead poisoning? Some 600,000 babies will be born this year with elevated levels of mercury, again leading to a variety of expensive health and learning problems. None of this is new information. Nor does it absolve individuals or parents of responsibility for their own well being or that of their children. But it does raise the question of why our national attention does not focus more realistically on a cost-benefit analysis of our policies and the results both of expenditures of our direct tax money and of the indirect tax subsidies given through the tax code.

The question of deserving and undeserving also raises the issue of charity and religious involvement. The commitment and efforts of religious groups and their members have been crucial in every community-based effort I have been involved in. Their crucial contributions, however, can obscure the necessity for national efforts. What may be needed is not charity, but justice—not a better soup kitchen but entitlement to a fair wage or, barring that, to income provided through the Earned Income Tax Credit or via food stamps or housing subsidies.

Our separation of the deserving and undeserving obscures the vital fact that the private market has neither the inclination, mission, or in many cases the skills or knowledge to provide many services that are deemed crucial to a vital society. The private sector provides bookstores, not libraries. During the Reagan administration, the federal government largely withdrew from its role of providing funds for the building of low-income housing. The private market has not stepped in to fill the gap. Almost all of the affordable housing for the past thirty years has been built by nonprofits, much of it financed by tax write-offs for the well-to-do. Habitat for Humanity has provided many individual houses, but the efforts of its dedicated volunteers, while they help build community networks and help individual families, cannot possibly match the need.

While fulfilling the nation's dream of equality and pursuit of happiness does require the collective efforts of individuals, families, volunteers, religious and community organizations, we conclude that local efforts are necessary, but not sufficient. If the nation effectively met the challenges raised by the four propositions presented at the beginning of this chapter, the lives of millions of American families would change radically. Families themselves could more easily handle many of the issues considered in the chapters on family tasks. Successfully addressing the four propositions would not eliminate all need for additional neighborhood effort and community programs or for federal safety net programs, but it would reduce the extent of assistance needed. If, for example, working parents had higher incomes, they could more readily afford housing on the private market and pay child care providers a living wage. If people could afford the services on the private market or obtain them through easily accessible public programs, many of the heroic efforts of community-based organizations would be unnecessary. Rather than delivering groceries to food pantries, the community-based organizations could turn their creative abilities to enhancing community life and solving problems that cannot completely be solved by increased funds alone, such as teenage smoking, racism or community conflicts. They could spend their energies creating gardens, community festivals and celebrations.

A vision for the twenty-first century could be an expansion of the American dream. Traditional American values have included a belief in individualism, hard work, honoring family, respect for private property, the use of government resources to further the common good, equality, generosity, fairness, grassroots and volunteer participation in community affairs, and a respect for the inherent value of each individual. The dream has included the belief that the future would be better for one's children.

Americans still hold these values. Our future, however, is being undermined by the way we are interpreting some of these values and by clinging to outdated myths about our families, communities, institutions, government, the economy and what individuals owe to the community and common good.

If we value hard work, is it acceptable for a full time worker to earn so little that he cannot afford to have a child?

If we value children, is it acceptable to have the highest rate of infant mortality of any industrialized country, 200,000 children sleeping on our streets every night, and eight a day killed by gunfire?[25]

If we value young people, can we ignore the fact that an average of eighty-one commit suicide each week?[26]

If we value the individual, is it acceptable to deny health care to millions or to have 800,000 people homeless each night? Is it acceptable that three to four women every day die as a result of domestic violence?[27]

If we value marriage, should we not address more seriously the circumstances that put stress on marriage including financial difficulties due to low wages, the inability to telephone a child after school from work, inadequate child care or lack of support when caring for an aging parent?

How can the nation meet these challenges? While flying to Austin, Texas, the author was discussing the book with a stranger in the adjacent plane seat. The man expressed one conservative view after another. Finally, rather than continuing to try to clarify my arguments, I said, "Why don't you read this?" and handed him this chapter. Much to my amazement, after reading it he said, "I agree with everything you said. Now how will you pay for it?"

At first I was concerned, started mentally calculating the amount of money spent recently by the federal government in tax cuts mostly to benefit those already well-off. Then I realized that the answer to the question of how to pay for it lies beyond this book. This is the strongest and wealthiest nation in the world. If people agree with this book's arguments, collectively the nation can figure out how to pay for it.

Notes

1. Kuriansky, J., & Brooks, J. eds. (2003). *Setting the standard for American working families. A report on the impact of the Family Economic Self-Sufficiency Project nationwide*. p. 2. Washington DC: Wider Opportunities for Women. Retrieved January 24, 2007, from http://www.aecf.org/upload/publicationfiles/working%20hard.pdf.

Methodology

The US Department of Labor Bureau of Labor Statistics develops occupational projections every two years. The most recent version covers the period 2006-2016, and the base data was released December 4, 2007.[a] Along with summary reports, the data is available in various formats online.

For our analysis, we used *Occupational employment projections to 2016: Appendix: Employment by occupation, 2006 and projected 2016* in an Excel spreadsheet format[b] and *Occupational Employment, Training, and Earnings: Occupation Report* as a database query generating an HTML table.[c]

For the most part, this data uses individual occupation codes. The notable exceptions, where the Bureau of Labor statistics grouped the codes, are as follows: 25-1000 – Postsecondary teachers; 29-1060 – Physicians and surgeons; 45-1000 – Supervisors, farming, fishing, and forestry workers; and 53-4010 – Locomotive engineers and operators.

Distinct occupations were separated from occupation summary lines by the following logic: [occupational code last digit not zero] or [occupation is last in a group] → [distinct occupation]. From this, we obtained 790 distinct occupations.

To obtain rank in growth, distinct occupations were then sorted in descending order based on number of additional jobs (Numeric change, column F). The occupation with the greatest number of additional jobs was 29-1111 - Registered nurses, with 587,349 additional jobs. The occupation with the least number of additional jobs was 43-5081 - Stock clerks and order fillers, with 130,722 lost jobs.

Percentage of total was then calculated by dividing the additional jobs value for each occupation by the additional jobs value for 00-0000 - Total, all occupations.

To obtain rank in median income, 2006 median annual earnings data[c] was merged by occupation title, and the resultant table was sorted in ascending order by median annual earnings values. The lowest paying occupation was 35-3031 – Waiters and waitresses ($14,850) and the highest – Airline pilots, copilots, and flight engineers ($141,090). Median earnings data was not available for 37 distinct occupations, but this did not hamper our analysis.

To obtain persons supported by median at poverty level or persons supported by median at 2 times the poverty level, the median income value was compared with poverty level tables generated from the 2006 poverty level values. In 2006, the poverty level in the continental United States was $9,800 for the first person, and $3,400 for each additional person in a family.[d]

    a. Bureau of Labor Statistics. (2007, December 4). *Employment Projections: 2006-16.* Press release. Washington DC: author. Retrieved January 30, 2008 from http://www.bls.gov/news.release/pdf/ecopro.pdf.

    b. Shniper, L.; Dohm, A., *Occupational employment projections to 2016: Appendix: Employment by occupation, 2006 and projected 2016.* Monthly Labor Review, November 2007. Retrieved January 30, 2008, from ftp://ftp.bls.gov/pub/special.requests/ep/ind-occ.matrix/mlrappendix.zip.

    c. Bureau of Labor Statistics. (2007). Occupational Employment, Training, and Earnings: Occupation Report. Retrieved from http://data.bls.gov/oep/servlet/oep.noeted.servlet.ActionServlet?Action=emprprt&Occ=XXXXXXXXXXX&Number=All&Sort=earn&Base=2006&Proj=2016&EdLevel=&Search=List&Type=Occupation&Phrase=&StartItem=0.

    d. Leavitt, M.O. (2006, January 18). *Annual Update of the HHS Poverty Guidelines.* Federal Register 71(15): 3848-9. Retrieved January 30, 2008, from http://aspe.hhs.gov/poverty/06fedreg.pdf. In 2006, the poverty level in the continental United States was $9,800 for the first person, and $3,400 for each additional person in a family.

2. U.S. Bureau of the Census. (n.d.). *Household Data Annual Averages. Table 39. Median usual weekly earnings of full-time wage and salary workers by detailed occupation.* Retrieved November 12, 2003, from ftp://ftp.bls.gov/pub/special.requests/lf/aat39.txt.

3. See note 1.

4. Values calculated using the CPI Inflation Calculator of the U.S. Department of Labor. http://146.142.4.24/cgi-bin/cpicalc.pl.

5. Mishel, L., Bernstein, J. & Allegretto, S. (2006). *The state of working America 2006/2007.* p. 45-46 and Table 3.3. *Hourly and weekly earnings of production and nonsupervisory workers, 1947-2005.* Washington, DC: The Economic Policy Institute. Retrieved December 12, 2007, from http://stateofworkingamerica.org/swa06-01-family_income.pdf and http://stateofworkingamerica.org/tabfig/03/SWA06_03_Wages.pdf.

6. International Labour Organization. (2007, September 2). New ILO report says US leads the world in labour productivity, some regions are catching up, most lag behind. Geneva: International Labour Organization. Retrieved September 3, 2007 from http://www.ilo.org/global/About_the_ILO/Media_and_public_information/Press_releases/lang--en/WCMS_083976/index.htm.

7. I am indebted to Alan Dobry for this calculation.

8. Joint Committee on Taxation. U.S. Congress. (2006, April). *Estimates of federal tax expenditures for fiscal years 2006-2010 (JCS-2-06). Table 1. Tax expenditure estimates by budget function, fiscal years 2006-2010.* p. 33. Retrieved January 20, 2007, from http://www.house.gov/jct/s-2-06.pdf. Joint Committee on Taxation. U.S. Congress. (2006, April). *Estimates of federal tax expenditures for fiscal years 2006-2010 (JCS-2-06). Table 3. Distribution by income class of selected individual tax expenditure items at 2005 rates and 2005 income levels.* p. 49. Retrieved January 20, 2007, from http://www.house.gov/jct/s-2-06.pdf. U.S. Department of Housing and Urban Development. (2004, February 3). *Fiscal year 2005 budget summary.* Retrieved January 20, 2007, from http://www.hud.gov/about/budget/fy05/budgetsummary.pdf.

9. Ehrenreich, B. (2001). *Nickel and dimed: On (not) getting by in America.* New York: Henry Holt and Company, LLC.

10. Ehrenreich, B. (2005). *Bait and Switch: The (Futile) Pursuit of the American Dream.* New York: Metropolitan Books.

11. Segall, C. (2001, March 6). Wilcox accepts burden in campaign money case: Supreme court justice to pay fine for committee. *Wisconsin State Journal*, pp. A1 and A7.

12. U.S. Chamber of Commerce. (2003). *2002 accomplishments: Advancing true legal reform.* Retrieved May 28, 2003, from http://www.uschamber.com/government/accomplishments/legalreform.htm. U.S. Chamber of Commerce. (2003). *U.S. Chamber 6-month lobbying costs top $28 million.* Retrieved February 22, 2003, from http://www.uschamber.com/press/releases/2003/february/03-22.htm.

13. Nevin, R. (2000, December 13). Research Links Childhood Lead Exposure to Changes in Violent Crime Rates Throughout the 20th Century. Washington, DC: Office of Juvenile Justice and Delinquency Prevention National Conference. Retrieved September 25, 2007, from http://www.icfi.com/Markets/Community_Development/doc_files/LeadExposureStudy.pdf.

14. McLean, R.L., & Thompson, M.D. (2007).Repaying Debts. A publication about how policymakers can increase accountability among people who commit crimes, improve rates of child support collection and victim restitution, and make people's transition from prisons and jails to the community safe and successful. p. 1. New York: Council of State Governments Justice Center. Retrieved December 12, 2007, from http://www.reentrypolicy.org/publications/repaying_debts_full_report;file.

15. The Alan Guttmacher Institute. (2004, February 19). *U.S. teenage pregnancy statistics with comparative statistics for women aged 20-24.* Retrieved March 2, 2004, from http://www.guttmacher.org/pubs/teen_stats.html. March of Dimes. *Quick references and fact sheets: Teenage pregnancy.* Retrieved June 22, 2007 from www.marchofdimes.com/professionals/14332_1159.asp. Travis, J. and Waul, M. (August, 2002). *Reflections on the crime decline. Lessons for the future?* Washington, DC: Urban Institute.

16. Gans, H. J. (2003). *Democracy and the news.* New York: Oxford University Press, Inc.

17. Neil Websdale. (2003, November). Reviewing Domestic Violence Deaths. *NIJ Journal* (National Institute of Justice), 250, 26-31. Retrieved May 29, 2007 from http://www.ncjrs.gov/pdffiles1/jr000250g.pdf.Committee Against Domestic Abuse. (2004, March 2). *What is battering? What is equality?* Retrieved March 2, 2004, from http://www.inspire-hope.org/home.html.

18. Children's Defense Fund. (2007, January 25). *Protect Children, Not Guns 2007.* Washington DC: Author. Retrieved March 26, 2007 from http://www.childrensdefense.org/site/DocServer/Protect_Chidren_Not_Guns_2007.pdf?docID=3221.

19. Anon. (2007, September 19). Teens Say Getting Meth Would Be Easy. *Wisconsin State Journal.*

20. Zernike, Kate ((2006, January 18). Hospitals Say Meth Cases Are Rising, and Hurt. *The New York Times*. Retrived September 27, 2007, from http://www.nytimes. com/2006/01/18/national/18drug.html?r=2&adxnnlx=11381364.

21. Anon. (2007, August 24). Opinion: A Template for Saving Lives. *USA Today*. Retrieved September 25, 2007, from http://blogs.usatoday.com/oped/2007/08/ a-template-for-.html.

22. Rank, M. R. (2004). *One nation, underprivileged: Why American poverty affects us all*. (p. 102-103). New York: Oxford University Press.

23. Newman, S. *et al*. (2000, January). *America's Child Care Crisis:A Crime Prevention Tragedy*. p. 6. Washington, DC: Fight Crime: Invest in Kids. Retrieved September 26, 2007, from http://www.fightcrime.org/reports/childcarereport.pdf.

24. Lynch, R. G. (2007, May). *Enriching Children, Enriching the Nation: Public Investment in High-Quality Prekindergarten*. Washington, DC: Economic Policy Institute. Excerpts retrieved September 26, 2007, from http://www.epi.org/content. cfm/book_enriching.

25. Burt. M. R. (2001, September). *What Will It Take To End Homelessness?* Washington DC: The Urban Institute. Retrieved March 26, 2007, from http://www. urban.org/uploadedPDF/end_homelessness.pdf. Children's Defense Fund. (2007, January 25). *Protect Children, Not Guns 2007*. Washington, DC: Author. Retrieved March 26, 2007 from http://www.childrensdefense.org/site/DocServer/Protect_Chi- dren_Not_Guns_2007.pdf?docID=3221.

26. Centers for Disease Control. n.d. The State of the CDC. Protecting Health for Life. p. 3 Retrieved August 30, 2007, from http://www.cdc.gov/about/stateofcdc/cdrom/ SOCDC/SOCDC2004.pdf.

27. Burt. M. R. (2001, September). *What Will It Take To End Homelessness?* Washington DC: The Urban Institute. Retrieved March 26, 2007, from http://www.urban.org/up- loadedPDF/end_homelessness.pdf. Neil Websdale. (2003, November). Reviewing Domestic Violence Deaths. *NIJ Journal* (National Institute of Justice), 250, 26-31. Retrieved May 29, 2007 from http://www.ncjrs.gov/pdffiles1/jr000250g.pdf.

Bibliography

Addams, Jane. (1910). *Twenty years at Hull House*. New York: Macmillan.

Alinsky, Saul A. (1946). *Reveille for radicals*. Chicago: University of Chicago Press.

Altman, Irwin. (1975). *The environment and social behavior*. Monterey, CA: Brooks-Cole Publishing Company.

Altman, Irwin. (1977). *"Privacy as an interpersonal boundary process."* Address presented to the American Psychological Association, San Francisco, CA.

———. (1977). *"Privacy regulation: Culturally universal or culturally specific?"* Salt Lake City: University of Utah.

Anderson, Elijah. (1990). *Street wise: Race, class and change in an urban community*. Chicago: The University of Chicago Press.

Andress, Shelby; Roehlkepartain, Eugene C., eds. (n.d.). *Working together for youth: a practical guide for individuals and groups*.

Arnstein, Sherry R. (July, 1969). "A ladder of citizen participation." *Journal of American Institute of Planners*, 35:216-224

Auletta, Ken. (1983). *The underclass*. New York: Vintage Books.

Baggett, Jerome P. (2001). *Habitat for humanity: Building private homes, building public religion*. Philadelphia: Temple University Press.

Banks, C. Kenneth, & Mangan, J. Marshall. (1999). *The company of neighbours: Revitalizing community through action-research*. Toronto: University of Toronto Press.

Baum, Howell S. (1997). *The organization of hope: Communities planning themselves*. New York: State University of New York Press.

Beach, Mark, & Beach, Oralee S. (1978). *Interracial neighborhoods in the urban community*. Unpublished manuscript. Rochester, NY.

Beamer, Glenn. (1999). *Creative politics: taxes and public goods in a federal system*. Ann Arbor: University of Michigan Press.

Becker, Fred W., & Dluhy, Milan J., vol. eds. *Solving urban problems in urban areas characterized by fragmentation and divisiveness*. Vol. 7

Bender, Thomas. (1978). *Community and social change in America*. New Brunswick, NJ: Rutgers University Press.

Bendick, M., Jr., Jackson, C.W., & Reinoso, V.A. (1994). Measuring employment discrimination. In Skolnick, J.H. & Currie, E. (Eds.). *Crisis in American institutions*. (10th ed.). New York: Addison-Wesley Educational Publishers, Inc.

Biddle, W. W. (1968). *The community development process: The rediscovery of local initiative*. New York: Holt, Rinehart and Winston.

Blank, Rebecca M. (1997). *It takes a nation: A new agenda for fighting poverty.* Princeton, NJ: Princeton University Press.

Borkman, Thomasina Jo. (1999). *Understanding self-help/mutual aid: Experiential learning in the commons.* New Brunswick, NJ: Rutgers University Press.

Bott, Elizabeth. (1971). *Family and social network.* 2nd ed. London: Tavistock.

Botvin, Gilbert J., Schinke, Steven, & Orlandi, Mario A., eds. (1995). *Drug abuse prevention with multiethnic youth.* Thousand Oaks, CA: Sage Publications.

Bray, Robert M., and Marsden, Mary Ellen, eds. (1999). *Drug use in metropolitan America.* Thousand Oaks, CA: Sage Publications.

Burby, Raymond J. III; & Weiss, Shirley F., with Donnelly, Thomas G.; Kaiser, Edward J.; Zehner, Robert B.; Lewis, David F.; Loewenthal, Norman H.; McCalla, Mary Ellen; Rodgers, Barbara G.; & Smooklet, Helene V. (1976). *New communities U.S.A.* Lexington, MA: Lexington Books, D.C. Heath and Company.

Burkhart, Lynne Connolly. (1981). *Old values in a new town: The politics of race and class in Columbia, Maryland.* New York: Praeger.

Cahill, Spencer E., & Lofland, Lyn H. eds. (1994). *Community of the streets,* vol. 1. Greenwich, CT: JAI Press, Inc.

Cahnman, Werner J. (1973). *Ferdinand Tönnies: A new evaluation.* Leiden: E.J. Brill.

Cahnman, Werner J., & Rudolf Heberle, eds. (1971). *Ferdinand Tönnies: On sociology: Pure, applied and empirical.* Chicago: University of Chicago Press.

Cary, Lee J., ed. (1970). *Community development as a process.* Columbia: University of Missouri Press.

Chekki, Dan A., ed. (1998). *American community issues and patterns of development,* vol. 8. Stamford, CT: JAI Press, Inc.

Chekki, Dan A., ed. (1999). *Varieties of community sociology,* vol. 9. Stamford, CT: JAI Press, Inc.

Coontz, Stephanie. (1992). *The way we never were: American families and the nostalgia trap.* New York: Basic Books.

Coontz, Stephanie. (1997). *The way we really are: Coming to terms with America's changing families.* New York: Basic Books.

Craven, P., & Wellman, B. (1974). "The network city." In *The Community: Approaches and Applications.* Edited by Marcia Pelly Effrat. New York: Free Press.

Dahrendorf, Ralf. (1968). *Essays in the theory of society.* Stanford, CA: Stanford University Press.

de Tocqueville, Alexis. (1969). *Democracy in America.* Ed. J. P. Mayer, trans. George Lawrence. Garden City, NY: Doubleday.

Denton, Frank T., Fretz, Deborah, & Spencer, Byron G. eds. (2000). *Independence and economic security in old age.* Vancouver: UBC Press.

Ehrenreich, Barbara. (2001). *Nickel and dimed: On (not) getting by in America.* New York: Henry Holt and Company, LLC.

Ehrenreich, Barbara. (2005). *Bait and switch: The (futile) pursit of the American* dream. New York. Metropolitan Books. Bibliography. p. 246.

Ewalt, Patricia L., Freeman, Edith M., Poole, & Dennis L. eds. (1998). *Community building renewal, well-being, and shared responsibility.* Washington, DC: National Association of Social Workers Press.

Feagin, Joe R. (2001). *Racist America: Roots, current realities, & future reparations.* New York: Routledge Press.

Ferguson, Ronald F., & Dickens, William T., eds. (1999). *Urban problems and community development.* Washington, DC: Brooking Institute Press.

Fischer, Claude S. (1976). *The urban experience.* New York: Harcourt Brace Jovanovich.

Fischer, Claude S.; Jackson, Robert Max; Stueve, C. Ann; Gerson, Kathleen; and Jones, Lynne McCallister; with Baldassare, Mark. (1977). *Networks and places: Social relations in the urban setting.* New York: Free Press.

Fischer, Claude S.; & Phillips, Susan L. (October, 1979). *"Who is alone? Social characteristics of people with small networks."* Working Paper 310. Berkeley: Institute of Urban and Regional Development, University of California.

Fischer, Claude S., with Stacey Oliver. (March, 1980). *"Friendship, sex, and the life cycle"* Berkeley: Institute of Urban and Regional Development, University of California.

Galbraith, John K. (1978). *The affluent society*, 3rd rev. ed. New York: New American Library.

Gans, Herbert J. (1962). *The urban villagers: Group and class in the life of Italian-Americans.* New York: Free Press.

Gans, Herbert J. (1968). *People and plans.* New York: Basic Books.

Gans, Herbert J. (1995). *The underclass and antipoverty policy: The war against the poor.* New York: Basic Books.

Gans, Herbert J. (2003). *Democracy and the News.* New York: Oxford University Press, Inc.

Gardner, Stephen E., Green, Patricia F., & Marcus, Carol, eds. (1994). *Signs of effectiveness II. Preventing alcohol, tobacco and other drug use: A risk factor/resiliency-based approach.* Rockville, MD: U.S. Department of Health and human Services, Public Health Service, Substance Abuse and Mental Health Services Administration, Center for Substance Abuse Prevention.

Granovetter, Mark. (1973). "The strength of weak ties." *American Journal of Sociology*, 78:1360-1380.

Greenberg, Michael R. & Schneider, Dona. (1996). *Environmentally devastated neighborhoods: Perceptions, policies, and realities.* New Brunswick, NJ: Rutgers University Press.

Hallman, Howard W. (n.d.) "Neighborhood-Based Organizations: Reflections on Fifteen Years' Experience." Unpublished manuscript.

Hamid, Ansley. (1998). *Drugs in America: sociology, economics, and politics.* Boston: Jones and Bartlett Publishers.

Hesselbein, Frances; Goldsmith, Marshall; Beckhard, Richard; & Schubert, Richard F., eds. (1998). *The community of the future.* San Francisco, CA: Jossey-Bass Publishers.

Hillery, George A. (1955). "Definitions of community: Areas of agreement." *Rural Sociology*: 111-23.

———. (1968). *Communal organizations: A study of local societies.* Chicago: University of Chicago Press.

Hochschild, Arlie, with Machung, Anne. (1989). *The second shift.* New York: Avon Books.

Keating, W. Dennis, Krumholz, Norman, & Star, Philip eds. (1996). *Revitalizing urban neighborhoods.* Lawrence: University Press of Kansas.

Keller, Suzanne. (1968). *The urban neighborhood: A sociological perspective.* New York: Random House.

Lanker, Brian. (1999). *I dream a world: Portraits of black women who changed America*, rev. ed. New York: Stewart, Tabori & Chang.

Livezey, Lowell W., ed. (2000). *Public religion and urban transformation: Faith in the city.* New York: New York University Press.

Litwak, Eugene. (1960). "Geographic mobility and extended family cohesion." *American Sociological Review* 25:385-394.

Litwak, Eugene. (1965). "Extended kin relations in an industrial democratic society." In *Social Structures and the Family Generational Relations.* Edited by E. Shanas and G. Streib. Englewood Cliffs, NJ: Prentice-Hall.

Litwak, Eugene, & Szelenyi, Ivan. (1969). "Primary group structures and their functions: Kin, neighbors and friends." *American Sociological Review* 34:465-481.

Marris, Peter, & Rein, Martin. (1967). *Dilemmas of social reform: Poverty and community Action in the United States.* New York: Atherton Press.

Massey, Douglas S., Durand, Jorge, & Malone, Nolan J. (2003). *Beyond smoke and mirrors: Mexican immigration in an era of economic integration.* New York: Russell Sage Foundation.

Maton, Kenneth I., Schellenbach, Cynthia J., Leadbeater, Bonnie J., & Solarz, Andrea L. (Eds.). (2004). *Investing in children, youth, families, and communities: Strengths-based research and policy.* Washington, DC: American Psychological Association.

Mayer, Neil S., with Black, Jennifer L. (1981). *Keys to the growth of neighborhood development organizations.* Washington, DC: Urban Institute Press.

Mazel, Ella (Ed.). (1998). *A treasury of quotes on the past, present, and future of the color line in America. "And don't call me a racist!"* Lexington, MA: Argonaut Press.

McCubbin, Hamilton I. (1995). *Resiliency in ethnic families under stress: Theory, reality, and research.* Minority Scholars Lecture Series: Inaugural Lecture. University of Wisconsin-Madison.

McCubbin, Hamilton I., Thompson, Elizabeth A., Thompson, Anne I., & Futrell, Jo A. (1995). *Resiliency in ethnic minority families: African American families. Vol. 2.* The University of Wisconsin System: Center for Excellence in Family Studies.

McMahon, Anthony. (1999). *Taking care of men: Sexual politics in the public mind.* Cambridge: Cambridge University Press.

Michelson, William; Levine, Saul V.; & Spina, Anna Rose. (1979). *The child in the city: Changes and challenges.* Toronto: University of Toronto Press.

Moore, Robin, & Young, Donald. (1978). "Childhood outdoors: Toward a social ecology of the landscape." In *Children and the Environment,* edited by Irwin Altman and Joachim F. Wohlwil. New York: Plenum.

Myers, Jr., & Samuel L. eds. (1997). *Civil rights and race relations in the post Reagan-Bush era.* Westport, CT: Praeger.

Naparstek, Arthur J.; Biegel, David; & Spiro, Herzl R. (1982). *Neighborhood networks for humane mental health care.* New York: Plenum Press.

Newman, Oscar. (1976). *Design guidelines for creating defensible space.* Washington, DC: National Institute of Law Enforcement and Criminal Justice.

Norman, Elaine, ed. (1997). *Drug free youth: A compendium for prevention specialists.* New York: Garland Publishing, Inc.

O'Brien, Jodi, & Howard, Judith A. (1998). *Everyday inequalities: Critical inquiries.* Oxford: Blackwell Publishers.

Oldenburg, Ray. (1989). *The great good place: Cafes, coffees shops, community centers, beauty parlors, general stores, bars, hangouts and how they get you through the day.* New York: Paragon House.

Perry, Clarence Arthur. (1929). *Neighborhood and community planning. New York: Regional plan of New York and its environs.* New York: Regional Plan of New York.

Pollin, Robert, & Luce, Stephanie. (1998). *Living wage: Building a fair economy.* New York: New Press.

Poppendieck, Janet. (1999). *Sweet charity: Emergency food and the end of entitlement.* New York: Penguin.

Putnam, Robert D. (2000). *Bowling alone: The collapse and revival of American community.* New York: Simon & Schuster.

Rank, Mark Robert. (1994). *Living on the edge: The realities of welfare in America.* New York: Columbia University Press.

Rank, Mark Robert. (2004). *One nation, underprivileged: Why American poverty affects us all.* Oxford: Oxford University Press.

Ratey, John J., M.D. (2001). *A user's guide to the brain: Perception, attention and the four theaters of the brain.* New York: Vintage Books.

Rich, Richard C. (March, 1980). "The dynamics of leadership in neighborhood organizations." *Social Science Quarterly,* 60:570-587.

Rich, Richard C. (November, 1980). "A political economy approach to the study of neighborhood organizations." *American Journal of Political Science,* 24:559-593.

——. (May, 1981). "Interaction of the voluntary and governmental sectors: Toward an understanding of the co-production of municipal services." *Administration and Society,* 13:59-76.

——. (1982). "The political economy of public services." In *Urban Policy under Capitalism,* edited by Norman I. Fainstein & Susan S. Fainstein. Beverly Hills, CA: Sage.

Rich, Richard C., ed. (1982). *The politics of urban public services.* Lexington, MA: Lexington Books, D.C. Heath and Company.

Rich, Richard C., & Rosenbaum, Walter A., eds. (1981). "Citizen participation in public policy." *Journal of Applied Behavioral Science*, 17.

Rosenblum, Nancy L. (2000). *Membership and morals: The personal uses of pluralism in America*. Princeton, NJ: Princeton University Press.

Ross, Heather L., & Sawhill, Isabel V. (1975). *Time of transition: The growth of families headed by women*. Washington, DC: Urban Institute.

Ross, Murray. (1955). *Community organization: Theory and principles*. New York: Harper and Row.

Rubin, Lillian B. (1994). *Families on the fault line: America's working class speaks about the family, the economy, race, and ethnicity*. New York: HarperCollins.

Rusk, David. (1999). *Inside game outside game: Winning strategies for saving urban America*. Washington, DC: Brookings Institution Press.

Sandler, Martin, & Hudson, Deborah A., with Weiss, Carol, & de Guzman, Neil. (1998). *Beyond the bottom line: How to do more with less in non-profit and public organizations*. New York: Oxford University Press.

Schoenberg, Sandra Perlman, & Rosenbaum, Patricia. (1980). *Neighborhoods that work: Sources for viability in the inner city*. New Brunswick, NJ: Rutgers University Press.

Schorr, Lisbeth B. (1997). *Common purpose: Strengthening families and neighborhoods to rebuild America*. New York: Anchor Books.

Schorr, Lisbeth B., & Schorr, Daniel. (1979). *Within our reach: Breaking the cycle of disadvantage*. New York: Doubleday.

Sharpley-Whiting, T. Deneen. (2007). *Pimps up, ho's down: Hip hop's hold on young black women*. New York: New York University Press.

Shulman, Beth. (2003). *The betrayal of work: How low-wage jobs fail 300 million Americans and their families*. New York: The New Press.

Skolnick, Jerome H., & Currie, Elliott. (1997). *Crisis in American institutions*. (10th ed.) New York: Longman Press.

Smookler, Helene V. (1975). "Deconcentration of the poor: Class integration in new communities." Ph.D. dissertation, University of California.

Steckel, Richard, & Lehman, Jennifer. (1997). *In search of America's best nonprofits*. San Francisco, CA: Jossey-Bass Publishers.

Stein, Maurice R. (1972). *The eclipse of community: An interpretation of American studies*. Princeton, NJ: Princeton University Press.

Suttles, Gerald D. (1972). *The social construction of communities*. Chicago: University of Chicago Press.

Tan, Amy. (1989). *The joy luck club*. New York: Ivy Books.

Toffler, Alvin. (1970). *Future shock*. New York: Random House.

Tönnies, Ferdinand. (1963). *Community and society, gemeinschaft und gesellschaft*. Edited by Charles P. Loomis. New York: Harper and Row.

Traeder, Tamara, and Bennett, Julienne. (1998). *Aunties: Our older, cooler, wiser friends*. Berkeley, CA: Wildcat Canyon Press.

Warren, Donald I. (1977). *"Social bonds in the metropolitan community: A conceptual overview."* Rochester, MI: Oakland University.

Warren, Donald I. (1982). *Helping networks: How people cope with problems in the urban community*. Notre Dame, IN: University of Notre Dame Press.

Warren, Roland L. (1978). *The community in America*. 3rd ed. Chicago: Rand McNally.

Warren, Roland L., ed. (1973). *Perspectives on the American community: A book of readings*. 2nd ed. Chicago: Rand McNally.

Webber, Melvin M. (1970). "Order in diversity, community without propinquity." In *Neighborhood, City and Metropolis*, edited by Robert Gutman and David Popenoe. New York: Random House.

Wellman, Barry. (1979). "The community question: The intimate networks of East Yorkers." *American Journal of Sociology*, 84:1201-1231.

Wellman, Barr, & Haythornthwaite, Caroline. (2002). *The internet in everyday life*. Oxford: Blackwell Publishing.

Williams, Lena. (2000). *It's the little things: The everyday interactions that get under the skin of blacks and whites*. New York: Harcourt, Inc.

Wilson, William Julius. (1997). *When work disappears*: *The world of the new urban* poor. New York: Vintage Books.

Wireman, Peggy. (1977). "Building good advisory committees: Some important considerations." In Patricia Marshall, ed.., *Citizen Participation Certification for Community Development: A Reader on the Citizen Participation Process*. Washington, DC: National Association of Housing and Redevelopment Officials.

Wireman, Peggy. (1997). *Partnerships for prosperity: Museums and economic development*. Washington, DC: The American Association of Museums.

Wireman, Peggy. (1984). *Urban neighborhoods, networks, and families: New forms for old values*. Lexington, MA: Lexington Books, D.C. Heath and Company.

Wireman, Peggy, & Sebastian, Antoinette. (1986). "Important considerations for environmental assessments of housing sites for the elderly." In *Housing an Aging Society*. Edited by Thomas O. Byerts, M. Powell Lawton, & Robert J. Newcomer. New York: Van Nostrand Reinhold Co.

Wirth, Louis. (1938). "Urbanism as a way of life." *American Journal of Sociology*, 44:1-24.

Wolf, Peter. (1999). Hot towns: The future of the fastest growing communities in America. New Brunswick, NJ:, Rutgers University Press.

Wolfe, Alan. (1998). *One nation, after all: What middle-class Americans really think about: God, country, family, racism, welfare, immigration, homosexuality, work, the right, the left and each other*. New York: Penguin Books.

Young, Michael, & Wilmott, Peter. (1957). *Family and kinship in East London*. London: Routledge and Kegan Paul.

Index

For Product Safety Concerns and Information please contact our EU
representative GPSR@taylorandfrancis.com Taylor & Francis Verlag GmbH,
Kaufingerstraße 24, 80331 München, Germany

Batch number: 08153776

Printed by Printforce, the Netherlands